NAPOLEON AT ST. HELENA

HENRI-GRATIEN BERTRAND

Napoleon at St. Helena

THE JOURNALS OF GENERAL BERTRAND FROM

JANUARY TO MAY OF 1821, DECIPHERED AND

ANNOTATED BY PAUL FLEURIOT DE LANGLE

TRANSLATED FROM THE FRENCH BY FRANCES HUME

DOUBLEDAY & COMPANY, INC., 1952

GARDEN CITY, NEW YORK

CONTENTS

Translator's note, page 7
Introduction, page 9

CHAPTER ONE: JANUARY 1821—PAGE 29
CHAPTER TWO: FEBRUARY 1821—PAGE 66
CHAPTER THREE: MARCH 1821—PAGE 104
CHAPTER FOUR: APRIL 1821—PAGE 128
CHAPTER FIVE: MAY 1821—PAGE 210

Notes to Chapter One—January 1821—Page 245
Notes to Chapter Two—February 1821—Page 269
Notes to Chapter Three—March 1821—Page 284
Notes to Chapter Four—April 1821—Page 295
Notes to Chapter Five—May 1821—Page 309
Appendix I—The Transcription of Bertrand's Diary—Page 312
Appendix II—The Emperor's Death Mask—Page 314

5

TRANSLATOR'S NOTE

"Written in the style of an inventory," is how M. Fleuriot de Langle has described General Bertrand's writing, for it can hardly be considered as having a literary style. Yet however enthralling an inventory may be to a person intimately familiar with every detail or subject to which it refers, the same can hardly be said for the casual or average reader. This, therefore, was the main obstacle that had to be overcome in translation: how to follow the text as accurately and closely as the French would permit, and yet make it interesting and easy reading for the general as opposed to the scholarly reader.

The difficulties of smoothing out the General's notes, at times almost telegraphic in their terseness, have by no means been completely overcome. This has been due to two reasons. First and foremost, there was the peril of filling in gaps in the text itself. Bertrand, of course, was well aware of what he was referring to, but—in common with many people of higher intellectual attainment than he—he failed to make his meaning clear through the omission of some essential detail. For instance, on page 33 he stated after speaking of Queen Caroline: "The King conferred the Ribbon of the St. Esprit." Here Bertrand was obviously referring to the King of France, but he failed to say on whom the ribbon was conferred.

Throughout the original text there are literally hundreds of such omissions. Some of them could be filled in or supplemented from the editor's notes, or from internal evidence. There remain nevertheless many passages which are rather rough and obscure. In certain cases the notes themselves are not sufficiently explicit; those, for instance, concerning the two Mesdames Dillon.

The second difficulty in presenting Bertrand's Mémoires sprang from his love of the impersonal and of the third person singular. He referred to himself throughout in the third person, except in moments of great emotional stress, as during the illness of Mme. Bertrand and when the Emperor was dying. Moreover, in some long passages Bertrand did not make clear whether he was still referring to the Emperor, or was referring to himself. In one passage he used the third-person plural to refer to General and Mme. de Montholon and, without indicating the change of subject, to refer to "the English" as well. Many such cases of doubt I have clarified by restating the subject. In others, I have taken the liberty of amplifying a reference for the benefit of the English reader.

INTRODUCTION

"Of all the people who surrounded the Emperor at St. Helena, one stands out above the others. This is Grand Maréchal Bertrand. He did not wager his devotion but fulfilled all his duties with a fine serenity. He remained aloof from intrigues whose sole aim were expectations that had assumed the aspect of a Fata Morgana."

These lines were written in 1912 by the authoritative pen of Frédéric Masson. This historian, who had just published *Napoléon et sa famille*, had spent years patiently weaving together, thread by thread, the pattern of the painful existence that his hero had dragged out on the Promethean rock. The Emperor's captivity had become so familiar to Masson that he could flatter himself that he knew, almost from day to day, every episode. That is why the tribute which he pays here to the memory of the Grand Maréchal is important; and in our eyes this praise retains an undeniable weight and value.

Is it possible to forget, moreover, that as early as 1908 Frédéric Masson had admitted before an audience at the Société des Conférences that no one could claim to tell the story of the six years of the Captivity "so long as the memoirs of Grand Maréchal Bertrand and those of the manservant Marchand should remain unpublished"? A gap—a yawning abyss—existed in the French accounts of St. Helena, and one that should be filled. Frédéric

9

Masson did his best to accomplish this, which is to say that he worked at it unremittingly.

He very soon had the joy of chalking up to himself a choice prize. This was the *Mémoires de Marchand*. Through his friendship with Count Desmazières, a grandson of Marchand, he obtained the loan of the manuscript in question and had the beautifully written copy made that today is in the possession of the Bibliothèque Thiers.

Having, to the great advantage of his St. Helena studies, "wangled" the *souvenirs* of the Emperor's manservant, Masson cherished the ambition of adding to them the memoirs of another of Napoleon's servants, those of Louis-Etienne Saint-Denis, better known in the chronicles of the Captivity under the name of the "Mameluke Ali."

But here Masson encountered the sign: no poaching. At most he was able to obtain permission to glance rapidly through pages which he would certainly much have liked to peruse at leisure. Hasty as his examination had been, he nevertheless came to the conclusion, printed at the beginning of his book *Napoléon à Sainte-Hélène*, that after General Gourgaud both Marchand and Saint-Denis were the only diarists able to contribute "information on the final period of the Emperor's life, to be found nowhere else". In this manner he covered up the slight discomfiture to which he had been subjected by the heirs of Mameluke Ali. The *Souvenirs d'Ali* were only published in 1927, thanks to the efforts of M. Gustave Michaut, professor at the Sorbonne.

There remained the Mémoires of the Grand Maréchal.

All attempts made by Frédéric Masson to bring these to light having remained futile, it seemed humiliating to the eager, and veteran historian to have to admit that he had met with a refusal, had drawn a blank. He thought to get out of the situation by means of a subterfuge.

With a truly Norman subtlety, and a peasant-like craftiness worthy of an old poacher of the Normandy Bocage, he disguised his deception with a phrase of skillful implication rather than precise assertion, saying that "what I have been able to learn of the Bertrand memoirs would seem to show that they were written very belatedly, and that they contain obvious errors of memory."

The biographer of Napoleon at St. Helena, never having held in his hands the original manuscript of the memoirs and forced to content himself with baseless rumors, nevertheless dared to make a definite pronouncement, rather than to defer or reserve his judgment.

Possibly one may accept the hypothesis that, by a classic stroke, Masson in his reference to the memoirs of the Grand Maréchal may have asserted what was wrong in an effort to learn the truth. Perhaps he hoped that a sally of this kind would force the heirs of the Grand Maréchal out of their reserve and provoke them to make reply. That would be his only excuse. But let us examine the result of such an attitude among his followers and emulators.

Every error that is repeated gains credit through its very repetition and increases in seriousness.

That this is only too true may be seen from the fact that, following in the footsteps of Frédéric Masson, the late Octave Aubry, pilgrim to St. Helena, unfortunately fell even more heavily into the same error as his predecessor.

"Two diarists," he wrote in 1935, "still await publication, which it is hoped will not be long delayed. These are Bertrand and Marchand. Despite several attempts, I was unable to gain access to the first manuscript, which is jealously guarded, but its general shape and tenor are known. It was written long after the return to France of a disillusioned and embittered man, who in it above all gives free rein to his personal spite. This manuscript would therefore appear to be of secondary importance."

The person primarily responsible for so erroneous a judgment is, of course, Masson himself. Twenty-three years separate Masson's book from that of Aubry. In what concerns not only the memoirs but also the memory of the Grand Maréchal there has been a noticeable progress in error.

But how is it possible to admit that a manuscript "jealously" hidden could be known in its essential, its outline, and its general tenor? To accuse the Grand Maréchal of having expressed "resentments" in his memoirs amounted to making a deliberate mockery of the character and moral value of a man whom everyone had joined in recognizing as a model of devotion and of dignity. A man who was of a most rare and exemplary kind of fidelity. That the good, honest, placid, and virtuous Bertrand should suddenly have become transformed into a vindictive, embittered, and spiteful individual, spilling over everything and everyone—and why not over Napoleon himself?—the acrimony of his feelings, is something that appears to be highly improbable; above all in the present text wherein the man and the diarist merge into one, where the qualities, the very faults of the one, become the qualities and faults of the other. Indeed, according to the testimony of everyone, who had always proved himself to be a more devoted servant of his master? Among the Emperor's companions only three, the Grand Maréchal, Marchand, and Ali, had followed him to both Elba and St. Helena. No one of them had played his part more zealously or carried out his duty more punctiliously than had Bertrand. He had sacrificed his comfort and peace of mind to serving the Emperor. He had carried the cult of the Emperor to the verge of adoration. It had even been one of the mainstays of his personal religion. Add to this a love of truth and you have the double key to this noble character.

It would have been extraordinary—however many-sided human nature may be—for such a man to have made a sudden *volte-face*, to have denied his ideals, to have categorically refuted his reputation and a lifetime of honor, and given credit in his journal to the echoes of the internecine quarrels that poisoned the air of Longwood.

It was essential to cut short such suspicions, not to say defamations of this kind. Let it be stated once and for all that it was wrong to say that Bertrand wrote his memoirs "belatedly." He wrote them from 1816 onwards day by day: or at the very least within a period closely contemporaneous with the events he described. During five years he wrote his diary *on the scene* at St. Helena and not, as has been gratuitously stated, *after his return to France.* The physical description of his manuscript, to be given later, furnishes proofs capable, so I hope, of convincing even the most skeptical.

Before beginning this demonstration, which is indispensable though of necessity somewhat dry, the reader may be interested to learn how we came to have the good fortune of having in our hands the unpublished memoirs of the Grand Maréchal.

During the summer of 1919 we heard the memoirs referred to in definite fashion. With the late Edouard Driault, founder of the *Revue des Etudes Napoléoniennes*, and an Italian friend, Count J.-B. Spalletti, a descendant of Murat through the Rasponi, we were being conducted through the Invalides by the Deputy Governor, Colonel Paul Payard (tragically killed shortly afterwards when he was knocked down by a tram in the Place Vauban). We were standing together in front of the marble shaft and the sarcophagus of porphyry in which the Emperor lies *ab aeternum* in all his glory, with the sun streaming down through the gilded windows.

While the entrance to the chapel was bathed in the blinding June sunlight, Colonel Payard spoke to us of St. Helena and among other things deplored the fact that of all the Emperor's companions, especially those of the last group, the voice of the Grand Maréchal should be the only one to remain silent.

"It is all the more inconceivable," he mumbled into his mustache, "in that the manuscript of Bertrand's memoirs, inherited by his daughter Hortense, who later became Madame Thayer, was bequeathed by her to M. Ernest Razy, Councilor to the Audit Office, with instructions to have it published twenty-five years after her death. As Madame Thayer died on December 25, 1889, it isn't difficult to calculate that in 1914 these memoirs should have been published!"

I made a note at the time of the Councilor's name; then we separated at the gate of the Invalides, opposite the dome whose spire blazed against the iridescent sheen of the sky above Ile de France.

The day at last dawned that was to satisfy the impatience of this seeker; but it was not before the autumn of 1946. When the strongbox containing the Grand Maréchal's papers was opened, out from its interior spilled piles of documents relating to the Captivity. Among these papers of every possible shape and size— letters of the Grand Maréchal, holographs, copies or translations— were large copy books bearing authentic watermarks. These were the pages of the famous diary, covered in closely written and microscopic handwriting. To sort out the piles of paper and collect all the scattered elements of the principal manuscript was the exciting and pleasurable work of two afternoons.

But after the first thrill of emotion, what a formidable surprise! A quick glance through the scribbling books of the Grand Maréchal revealed that the writer had taken stringent precautions against the curiosity of paleographers! The hunter and seeker are one and the same, runs the old adage. Here it appeared that the undergrowth was devilishly heavy, the thickets terribly prickly. Whosoever would hunt the game must run the risk of lacerating himself. What matter to the seeker, provided he attained his goal?

But would he attain it, was what he soon came to ask himself in some anguish. Had he not engaged in an adventure that would take him months or years of effort and patience? He no longer had any doubt that if he were to win, he would need to combine the application of a Chartist confronted with an unknown script with the shrewdness of a decoder who unravels the mysteries of secret cyphers. Recalling Champollion and the Rosetta Stone, and the Amourabi obelisk discovered in Persia by Jacques de Morgan, he wondered why he had not been initiated under the guidance of such a master into the science of Egyptology and dedicated to the profession of epigraphist! Then the hieroglyphs of the Grand Maréchal would have seemed less obscure.

More modestly he compared himself not with Champollion and the Pères Scheill but with the crossword-puzzle lovers and their problems. But at least the ingenious enigmas to be solved by these enthusiasts covered only a small surface, whereas here they continued for page after page in a spate of words reduced to their shortest possible form. At times words *as well as proper names* were reduced to nothing more than an initial or a hieroglyph. The editor's perplexity increased as the parts of speech approached the point of vanishing altogether. When he had succeeded in deciphering this cryptographic text, he found that the absence of any punctuation presented him with further problems of interpretation.

To translate French—into French! A strange sport and an odd way of passing one's time! If it be a science, where is it taught? If it be a sport, in which stadium, in which arena, can one be trained?

Should this seeker moan over the slowness and dryness of his task, kind friends would rush to comfort him with well-tried platitudes: "Habit becomes second nature . . ." "With determination and patience . . ." Your servant! Therefore, permit him to set before you a random selection of the scrawls over which he labored for three years, with a magnifying glass in his hand and a tear in his eye.

"N. so. le mat. encal: il. déj. bi. se. trv. un peu fat; le so. il est f. g. Le Gm. me. ar. à l'E. Il di. av. l. jo. av. l. fa. pend. uneh.; l'E. ét. so. le mat. en cal. et av. déj. de bo. ap; si cela cont. il ser. gue. en 15 j. il. dig. bi. ceq. ma; il. di. au D. q. se. p. m. q. f. ces. l. q. . . ."[1]

Or do you like this other passage better? "Il. f. mauv. te. L'E. ne. so. p. N. a. f. ét. d. sa. sal. de bil une Ba; il. dde au Gm. sil sa. ce. q. c'e. C' une ma. de G. il d. dab. q. cest un bal. p. ses enf. Est ce p. ser. à desc. sur un remp; peu d'esp. p. un ing. sa. f . . ."[2]

The solution of these two little problems is to be found under the dates January 20 and 21, 1821, of the translation. To make it easier for the reader to understand the difficulties of the transcription, the editors have kindly consented to reproduce the entire page from which these passages have been taken. They have even gone so far as to reproduce an enlarged facsimile of a few lines that have obstinately resisted all efforts to decipher them. If, at the sight of this last passage, some willing auxiliary is able to find in his fertile or ingenious mind the solution of the problem, no false pride will prevent us from taking advantage of his ability; on the contrary, he will be commended for having rendered us a personal service.

However clear a facsimile may be, it in no way dispenses us from giving a physical description of the manuscript. This is a somewhat austere duty, for which we crave the indulgence of the reader, but

[1] 20 janvier—"Napoléon sort le matin en calèche. Il déjeune bien, se trouve un peu fatigué; le soir, il est fort gai. Le Grand Maréchal mène Arthur à l'Empereur; il dîne avec lui, joue avec lui familièrement pendant une heure. L'Empereur était sorti le matin en calèche et avait déjeuné de bon appétit. Si cela continue, il sera guéri en quinze jours. Il digère bien ce qu'il mange; il dit au docteur qu'il se porte mieux, qu'il faut cesser le quinquina."

[2] 21 janvier—"Il fait mauvais temps. L'Empereur ne sort pas; Napoléon a fait établir dans sa salle de billard une bascule. Il demande au Grand Maréchal s'il sait ce que c'est. 'C'est une machine de guerre. Est-ce pour servir à descendre sur un rempart?' Peu d'esprit pour un ingénieur, sacré f . . ."

one which no paleontologist would shirk. The description is especially warranted in this case, where doubts have been cast on the authenticity of the Bertrand memoirs; or rather, I should say, where the diarist has been suspected of writing them *long after the events* according to Frédéric Masson, and *well after his return to France* according to Octave Aubry.

The time has come to give some explanations on this score. An examination of the watermarks is in itself sufficient to refute completely all such allegations.

The Grand Maréchal wrote his Mémoires on a strong laid paper of English make, of ledger size usually 33 or 33½ centimeters long and 22 or 22½ centimeters wide.

During 1816 and 1817 Bertrand regularly devoted one copy book to the notes for each month. From 1818 to 1820 his enthusiasm waned; however, beginning with the second semester of 1818 he kept a calendar of events; chronology has been assured or correctly established with the help of this succinct memorandum, which duplicates the diary.

The first three copy books of 1816, from April 14 to the end of July, as well as those for October and November, bear the watermark *D.&.C.* 1813; those of August and September: *C. Wilmott, 1813*; and the December book: *J. Ansell, 1812*.

In 1817 this last paper-maker provided the material for the months of January, March, and May. *J. Whatman & W. Balston 1814*, that for February, April, and August. *J. Bates 1814 or 1815*, that for June–July; and *J. Jellyman 1814*, that for September and November; while the *D.&.C. 1813* reappeared in the month of October.

At the beginning of the year 1818 the Grand Maréchal used a supply of paper from this last maker and towards the end of the year some from *Golding & Snelgrave 1815*, which lasted him for all of January and February, 1819. Then he jumped about a bit: in April of the same year he would sometimes scratch away on a wove paper watermarked *Ipping 1813*, sometimes on a *T. Edmonds 1816* for the months of August and September; resuming occasionally the *D.&.C., 1813* or the *Golding 1815*.

In 1820 the *Edmonds 1816* shared the favors of the Grand Maréchal with a *Stacey Wise, 1818*. Throughout this entire period three makes of paper were used whose trade-marks serve as tail-pieces to certain chapters of the manuscript of the present volume and are visible through the paper mould opposite the name of the makers. This mark, in an oval surmounted by a royal crown, is sometimes the figure of a woman holding a lance and a shield, symbolizing Britannia; at others a crowned lion holding a spear and a bunch of thunderbolts; at others a heart surmounted by the number four and in the center of which, placed in lozanges, are the initials V.E.L.C.

From 1821 the Grand Maréchal, who had recovered his former punctuality and who knew, alas, that his diary would not continue for long, permitted himself the luxury of a handmade paper measuring 31 by 22 centimeters, from the stationers J. Whatman, Balston & Co., or S. C. Wise, bearing the dates 1818 or 1819. The Whatman 1819 is the paper on which the Emperor wrote his will.

Here the dates assume considerable importance: with a displacement that is only normal in such cases, they progress in order as the diary progresses. If, therefore, it were admitted that Bertrand wrote his diary "belatedly," it would be necessary to grant him the soul of a very subtle forger; or to assume that he had acquired a supply of paper at St. Helena, first taking the precaution of examining the watermarks and of aligning the dates found on them: an absurd hypothesis. Such a deception would be unthinkable coming from such a man, especially at the beginning of the nineteenth century, when the art of falsification and of forgers had not yet attained the degree of perfection to which it has been brought today.

Octave Aubry was quite right to have rejected on his own responsibility a similar hypothesis with regard to Montholon. Montholon had been accused of having belatedly made up (possibly while he was imprisoned in the Fortress of Ham after the abortive coup d'état at Boulogne) those Conseils de Napoléon à son fils, the dictated copy of which bears the date April 17, 1821. However, the penciled draft of this superb piece is among the papers left by Frédéric Masson, and it was written on a sheet of paper bearing the watermark S. C. Wise 1818, which was also used for the Report on the Autopsy, May 7 and 8, 1821.

"To pretend that Montholon wrote this document around

1840," remarked Aubry, "it would be necessary to assume not only that he had preserved the draft of the note, but that for twenty years he had kept an unused double sheet of paper identical in size and watermark, and that he had used this to give an air of authenticity to his fabrication. This, of course, is not impossible, but we incline towards a much more simple explanation: that of the genuineness of the document."

Well spoken, well reasoned! Accordingly, why refuse to the Grand Maréchal—whose document covered five years and an imposing number of sheets of paper—what has been accorded to Montholon? A single sheet is much easier to falsify than a whole sheaf.

It is also difficult to conceive how the Grand Maréchal after returning to France could have retained in his memory the thousands of facts that he recounts without the help of any notes. For none have been found among his papers, other than those of the *Diario.* Pico della Mirandola himself would have quailed before such an achievement.

Moreover, deductions made from the content assure us that Bertrand's diary—the least "styled" of all journals—is in fact one of those authentic documents written in the margin of events as and when they took place, and into which has entered no kind of literary fraud. The appearance of the manuscript is sufficient guarantee of this. It is a typical disorderly jumble in which a writer devoid of vanity confided his thoughts, rather in the manner of someone piling worn linen and unassorted articles of wearing apparel helter-skelter into a bag. There is no room in such luggage for those rhetorical artifices which enable a writer to "wash and brush up."

Furthermore, it may be observed that for the month of December, 1816, the Grand Maréchal had written in capital letters at the beginning of a notebook of his diary: "Dates and notes which may be used as a continuation of the diary of Las Cases and which date from December 25, day on which M. de Las Cases was arrested. The Diary of M. de Las Cases should begin at the going on board of the French frigates at Rochefort."

Unless one assumes this title to have been added afterwards—whereas actually it is written in the same faded ink and the same handwriting as the rest of the page on which it appears—only one conclusion can be reached. Bertrand wrote it at a time when the little colony at Longwood was still upset by the deportation of Las Cases.

Does this mean that the Grand Maréchal claimed to fill the place left vacant by the *exeat* of the editor in chief of the *St. Helena Gazette?* Or to have believed himself capable of inheriting the pen of Las Cases and of signing the editorials?

That such was not the case is obvious from the text of the diary itself. Its tone is modest, almost humble, and would seem to profer itself as an excuse. Add to this the fact that the Grand Maréchal had not waited for the departure of Las Cases to start his journal but had begun it seven months earlier, upon the arrival of Governor Hudson Lowe—a well-defined date of whose historic importance Bertrand would seem to have had some foreboding.

The Testimony of Bertrand—What does history not owe to Bertrand, the chronicler of Longwood! Some idea of this debt may be gained from a perusal of the pages which follow, even though they are no more than a fragment of the whole diary. Thanks to them, everyone can better realize just how much would have been lacking in the annals of St. Helena, all the intimate knowledge of the drama played out at Longwood we should have missed if, once having finished the task of the imperial dictations, Bertrand had let the ink dry on his pen, and after returning home to Hutt's Gate or his little cottage with the uneven stairs, he had through laziness, apathy, or weariness put away his writing desk and refused to set down in black and white some of those minute details for which our curiosity is always eager; inasmuch as they bring us closer to Him whose aspect posterity is never tired of scrutinizing while striving to penetrate all His secrets.

Bertrand and his notebooks will help above all to dissipate that "atmosphere of lies" of which Lord Rosebery has spoken in *The Last Phase,* one of the most intelligent books to have been inspired by St. Helena. Deliberately thickened by all the "literary" writers who swarmed at Longwood, an aura of imposture and legend too often enveloped the accursed island in a haze as close and difficult to dissipate as a London fog. This indeed has frequently misled the footsteps of the historical writer and rendered his path as hazardous as though he were walking along the edge of a precipice as abrupt as the chasm of the Devil's Punch Bowl.

In this respect the presence of a mentor such as Bertrand has a calming effect. One feels that he is devoid of all literary pretensions, so unaware is he of the pleasures of writing. So much so, that to apply the term editing to his memoirs seems inadequate and almost pointless. Bertrand's prose affects the thankless dryness of Tironian notes. He is discreet to the point of referring to himself as rarely as possible and then always in the third person. He seldom takes part in the discussion. He effaces and forgets himself as much as any eyewitness possibly can. If there was anyone at Longwood who knew how to refrain from the use of the word *I*, and who disdained to take part in the gossip and tittle-tattle of Longwood, who forgot his own sensitiveness and a *fortiori* kept quiet about his personal resentments, it was he.

Is this to say that Bertrand's journal solves all problems and clears away the cloud of enigma that has hung over the rock of St. Helena? Such a state of affairs would be too good to be true. Despite Bertrand's assistance, one must, to follow the advice of the wise, remember to be suspicious, and to be cautious. The *Mystère en pleine lumière*, to recapture a title dear to the heart of Maurice Barrès, is an invention of the novelist. In reality, things always reveal themselves in a complex aspect; as in nature, with an interplay of light and shade, of sunlight and mist.

In the deepest shadows, however, from now on there is for us a lighthouse, rather a burning lamp. However meager its beam, it sheds its light through the windows of the cottage in which the Grand Maréchal sits busily adding to his mounting pile of scribbling books. And it is already an immense thing to know that this observer, conscientious and faithful, is there, keeping watch in the night.

The value of Bertrand's account, frank, sincere, and impersonal as it is, can nowhere be better assessed than during the psychological period of decline, when the hero who has straddled his century is about to take leave of life.

Here Napoleon forgets bit by bit, in the misfortunes to which he has abandoned himself, that he once had the power to dominate and to govern Europe. He becomes just an ordinary man—and what is worse—unfortunate man. But this gradual metamorphosis, which Bertrand's journal enables us to follow day by day, hour by hour, and minute by minute, becomes all the more moving when it is broken here and there by some imperious accent.

Confined more and more to the retreat of his sickroom, the Emperor suffers and complains, moans and sighs. The doctors around him alternately torment him with their untimely or useless remedies, or with an almost breath-taking indifference grease the slope down which their patient edges little by little towards the abyss. They exercise their profession.

As with the doctors, so with the priests. Buonavita, the dyspeptic, and Abbé Vignali, a kind of Corsican shepherd dressed in a cassock, carry out their duties with moderate zeal, tempered by the feeling that they are only there for the onlookers and purely as a matter of form. The Emperor calls for their help only in extremis and then with so many precautions that obviously their presence worries him. He makes a sacrifice to ritual; but he has no profound faith. On this subject Bertrand's testimony should be retained by anyone wishing to create for himself a religion out of the religious beliefs of the Emperor.

The servants, Marchand, Noverraz, Pierron, Ali, transformed into nurses, take turns in caring for the bedridden Emperor, who moves painfully from one of his little camp beds to the other, in search of a less uncomfortable position. Their frequent clumsy efforts to help, wrest from him cries of rage or pitiful moans.

Reduced to the rôle of mere scribes and soon of nurses, the two generals Montholon and Bertrand spell each other at the bedside of the Emperor, who does less and less work and inflicts upon them more rarely the fatigue of taking down dictations in longhand. This is the time of increasing indifference, the approach of the "long vacation." Now the desks remain padlocked, the scratching of goose quills becomes less frequent. Gradually the ink dries at the bottom of the china inkwells. As fast as the worktable is cleared and the piles of books and records lessen, medicine bottles, syringes, bottles of licorice, anis water, and orange-flower water— all the battery of a sickroom in fact—swarm over the tables in the prisoner's bedroom.

The shaded lamp and the night light fight a losing battle with the darkness into which every day sinks increasingly, vegetatingly, the life of one who formerly had ruled the world. Yet, in the midst of all this mediocrity, the nimbus of past glories, the gilded reflection of his conquering Eagles, form a halo around the smooth face being slowly molded by death, diffusing an unreal clarity in which he becomes transfigured.

"What day is it, Bertrand?"

April 22, 1821, in the evening. Is this the end? Not yet. . . . Suddenly, in the half-light a voice resounds, the voice of command, saying: "Write!" This is like the old days of Bourrienne, Fain, and Méneval, when the imperial order had bent the secretary over his desk and left him asleep there.

The Grand Maréchal is at his post. Booted, spurred, tight-laced, resigned, and ready. How right to have remained on the *qui vive!*

"I have made three wills," announces the Emperor. "The first is not to be opened until it reaches Paris. It must be said that it was taken to Europe by Buonavita, so as to prevent the English from laying hands upon it. The second is a codicil to be opened here and shown to the English; in it I dispose of everything I own here, so that they cannot take possession of anything. The third is for the Empress. Marchand has been intrusted with delivering these wills at the time and in the manner that I have indicated to him. . . ."

The hands of the clock surmounted by a rose, and those of the alarm clock captured at Potsdam, must revolve twice upon themselves before the voice will stop. Posedly, methodically, with emphasis, retrogressions, and repetitions that shape, mold, engrave, and etch, the voice lists article by article the final recommendations.

Religion—place of burial—*hoc erat in votis*—instructions to the Family in general and to each member in particular—tactics to be followed for their establishment in America or in Europe—manuscripts to be disowned—final diatribe against the English ruling classes, against the enemy of yesterday, of today or of tomorrow— provision for the future of the testamentary executors—program for the education of his son—bequests to his son—bequests of money to his servants—the use they should make of them—use to be made of the six million one hundred thousand francs left on deposit with Laffitte—the percentage of interest this banker should pay the heirs—sums to be recovered from Prince Eugène and from the settlement of the Empress—employment of funds from the private estate—rules of conduct governing the marriage of his nieces and nephews—arrangements to be made in favor of his illegitimate children—instructions for the personal guidance of the Grand Maréchal—the souvenir for Lady Holland—reproaches for this or that—criticisms of Lafayette, Carnot, Bernadotte, Fouché, Augereau, or Marmont . . . Every paragraph of this relentless memorandum drops like the beads of a rosary, rolls forth like the monotonous verses of a litany. Nothing or no one is forgotten. Everyone must receive his due either of praise or blame, and his final recommendation. This is a dying man who, before slipping into the shades, draws up and checks his balance sheet, revises his accounts, and checks his additions—"I am searching my conscience, as I wish to pay all my debts, including those of my youth"—who invokes the future and retraces the past of which he denies nothing: not even the affair of the unhappy Duke. . . .

The occasion is feverish yet calm. Here is Napoleon in his entirety, with his greatnesses and his weaknesses, his contrasts, his eager imagination allied to an icy realism, his love of order carried to minuteness, his generosity and his meannesses, the charm of his smile to the humble, and the severity of his contempt flung at the cowardice of the great. It is forever he with his middle-class care for detail, his rather fussy exactness of an administrator, his need to repeat, to hammer, his Corsican obstinacy, his prodigiously meticulous memory, "his mental outlook of the leader of a principality" (as Madame Mère used to say) which caused him to distribute bequests as though they were thrones. His determination to strip off "the tyrant's hide"; and at the same time there is his ungovernable need to lead, to impose his will, to dictate his law upon men and things, on nature, on illness, and on death itself, since even as a dying victim, with one foot in the grave, he refuses to admit that he has been vanquished.

That is what Bertrand, and only Bertrand is able to make us feel. He has done this only by means of making an exact copy, one from which all phantasy has been banished. If he is moved, his emotions remain so repressed that never once does the hand recording the final imperial dictations tremble, and no quaver alters the firmness of the outline. The Grand Maréchal is the Clerk of History. Had he done no more than render to posterity the signal service of writing down the *Conversations de l'Empereur* on April 22, 24, and 26, 1821, every lover of Napoleon would owe him an eternal debt of gratitude.

It is now more than a hundred years—May 5, 1847—since the Grand Maréchal was laid to sleep beside his august master under the dome of the Invalides. We would have liked the date of publication of this journal, so long delayed, to have coincided with the centenary of his interment in the Temple of Fame. What a magnificent and appropriate opportunity it would have been to have laid on his marble tomb, symbolically intertwined, the palm of bronze and the pen of steel which, in the words of Alfred de Vigny, is not devoid of beauty. But it is not a little the fault of General Bertrand himself and of his mistrust of posterity that it was not possible for us to have paid him this homage in time.

With all due respect to the fainthearted, the hour when Truth issues forth mirror in hand from her hypogeum should never be delayed. This allegorical figure is worthy to embellish a tomb, and would not have disgraced that of the Grand Maréchal himself.

Devoted even in death to the cause of the Hero guarded by his victories, an honest spectator of good faith, here Bertrand the diarist from the depths of the crypt of the Invalides claims your attention. He demands it all the more imperiously in that he has remained silent for so long.

Listen then, undismayed by its ruggedness, to this *Voix de Sainte-Hélène*, which, silent for 128 years, finally brings forth its message from the other side of the world.

It brings the reader not only the last words of the prisoner of Longwood but also echoes of the murmurs which rose around the bedside of the Emperor, inside those deplorable huts in which was consummated one of the most tragic agonies of history. And if the details of these semi-Shakespearean scenes, of which the Old House was then the stage, surprise the reader with their mixture of realism and the sublime, remind yourself that in this case literature and the abominations of rhetoric have played no parts.

Humble or ordinary realism springs from an unvarnished account of the facts themselves. As for the impression of pathos and grandeur, it arises from the text like the diffused light that fills the sky before a storm—a sky whose ashen color is suddenly rent by a diagonal stroke of flame that throws people and things into an unforgettable relief.

This purple and golden ray is the light of Fame, torch of the living, sun of the dead.

NAPOLEON AT ST. HELENA

CHAPTER ONE

January 1821

In *the morning* the Grand Maréchal went to see Napoleon. When he went again in the afternoon Mme. Bertrand accompanied him and General Montholon was there as well. The possible departure of Mme. Bertrand and her children from St. Helena was discussed and everyone present expressed surprise at the idea. The atmosphere became somewhat tense, and it was said that such a thing would not go unnoticed in France. Mme. Bertrand would certainly not be happy and would miss the affectionate care and attention of her husband. Also, she would need money and would not have any. Her husband, of course, would be quite content to administer her property, but this would not satisfy her. That evening the Emperor told Dr. Antommarchi the whole story, though it could not be said that he did so maliciously.

The following morning he sent for Antommarchi and went over the incident once more. On the whole, Antommarchi behaved extremely badly. He went to see the Grand Maréchal and asked him what on earth Mme. Bertrand had been thinking of to have created such a scene. The Grand Maréchal replied that his wife had accompanied him with the intention of being agreeable to the Emperor, but that Napoleon himself had gone out of his way to provoke her. And, in any case, he added, much of what the

Emperor had said was so exaggerated that singularly little of the actual truth remained.

Antommarchi then became offensive and called Bertrand names. When the Grand Maréchal asked for an explanation, he refused to say anything further, and merely whistled.

Napoleon was much depressed when the Grand Maréchal again went to see him. He had sent for Antommarchi and had eaten a fairly good dinner. This had made him feel somewhat better, and the incident of the previous afternoon had been forgotten. He began to tell the Grand Maréchal of the situation in which Saliceti found himself at Marseilles. Saliceti had always been strongly pro-Napoleon, so much so indeed, that upon seeing him Napoleon used to say, in the words of faithful old Paoli, "He, at least, is one of us."

The Emperor was First Consul when at Tarare, on his way to Lyons, he met a woman and asked her just what she thought had been gained by recent events in France, commenting: "After all, they have only replaced one master by another."

"Oh no, it's quite different," she had replied. "You see, the other was king of the nobility, whereas this one is the people's king." "A profoundly significant remark," the Emperor noted.

Napoleon had finished reading *The Siege of Danzig*, by Labaume, and later discussed it with Bertrand, as he was in the habit of doing.

"It's quite good," he said, "though nothing out of the ordinary. Rapp was an honest man who knew his job, but he was incapable of defending such an important fortified position or of carrying out all the necessary preparations. He had 33,000 men under him. Yet he fails to mention the enemy strength, which must have been considerable. At the beginning of the siege, the opposing forces mainly consisted of recruits, but towards the end of the siege the enemy must have had some 50,000 men. The book contains the very false premise that in defending fortified towns the position is improved if the surrounding country is held; in other words, is spread out. That is not the point of a fortified town.

"It may be assumed that an attacking force is, generally speaking, stronger and superior in numbers to the besieged. Should the besieged expose themselves, they run the risk of being swept away from their base, and of having to fight a series of costly battles. They are only able to fight to advantage within the shelter of their own fortifications. In the case of Danzig, for instance, where the besieged were stronger than the attackers, it would have been advisable to have concentrated within the fort and then, one morning, leaving the gunners, engineers, and sappers to defend the fortress, to have made a sortie onto the river Nehrung with 15–16,000 men, and to have captured everything that came to hand; possibly some 5–6,000 men, besides livestock, etc.: then two or three days later to have captured the equipment, and pushed on to Pitzkendorf with three or four columns, mopping up everything that could be found—men, guns, munitions, and baggage trains. Another time Rapp could have pushed on as far as Oliva. He would then have had control of the surrounding country, and he could have raised the blockade or, possibly, have prevented the enemy from reaching the Oder. He might even have prevented Prussia from declaring war.

"One cannot say as much for the situation at Alexandria. It was a mistake to have put all our strength into the field in the Rosetta extension, because afterwards it was impossible to disengage. Whereas there would have been no objection to having withdrawn troops from ramparts that were sufficiently well covered by guns to be, in consequence, free from the danger of attack. In this way General Menou was unable to fend off the attack on the tongue of land towards Fort des Arabes. However, the case of Alexandria remains open to further discussion, because Alexandria was not a fortified town and the Rosetta position amounted to very little."

Another time, after he had been reading Prince Charles's book on the Italian campaigns, Napoleon said:

"It's a good book, but not so good as the first one was, because the Archduke did not play an active part in the campaign and because he was not in command in Italy. His aim is to praise Moreau at the expense of General Kray. I was unaware that the Austrian forces in Italy were present in such considerable strength. In Germany, the Austrians had 37,000 cavalrymen, at a time when we had only 17,000. With such an overwhelming superiority of cavalry, the French forces should never have been allowed to cross the Rhine. If I had been in command of that cavalry, no sooner would the French have put their first vehicle across the Rhine, than I would have had them cut off.

"The Austrians have absolutely no idea of how to use cavalry. They have always possessed superiority in this arm, but they have never known how to use it. Their principle has been to keep it in reserve and to use it sparingly because it costs them a great deal. That's not true. Cavalry is not expensive. A man and a horse cost no more than two men, possibly less, especially in the poorer countries. In France, even in Corsica, a conscript costs 3,000 francs while a horse costs only fifteen or twenty louis.[1] What a tremendous advantage I possessed when I had superiority in cavalry, as I proved during the 1815 campaign. If Murat had been there when Grouchy was in command, in all probability the Prussians would have been defeated."

The Emperor thought that he had no cavalry in Italy, and now finds that he had fully as much as the Army of the Rhine. At Marengo, the Austrians didn't know how to use their cavalry; though, to be sure, it enabled them to cover their retreat. It may even have been thanks to their cavalry that they were spared any major disaster and were able to make good their retreat.

"In war," said Napoleon, "the difficult thing is to assess the enemy's strength. That is something that comes only with the instinct for war. There is no such thing as intellect in war, especially not at the speed with which we make war today. That was well enough in the days when a position was held for about two months. Prince Charles took a week to do what I carried out in a quarter of an hour.

"At Ligny there were as many opinions about the strength of the enemy as there were persons present. Good little Guyot said there were only 10,000 men. If I wanted to know the strength of the opposing cavalry I would ask Bessières:

" 'How many do you think there are over there?'

" 'About 6,000, Sire, six squadrons of cavalry at the most. The enemy is pulling out.'

" 'Bessières only sees the front line,' Guyot would remark, 'but don't forget that there's a second line in the wood.'

[1]One louis equaled a twenty-franc gold piece. Translator's note.

"And so each of them judged things according to his own ability and character."

The Emperor examined the field of battle at Bautzen, through his glasses. The next day, the enemy having withdrawn 30,000 men, there was some uncertainty as to whether the opposing forces were weaker. Some thought that the position looked less strongly held, whereas others saw the same number of camp fires. On the whole, nothing definite could be made out. That is the kind of thing that makes a general's job so difficult. And there lies the difference between war on land and war at sea. At sea at least one knows what one is up against. But on land one can never be sure. [. . .]

"Without doubt," the Emperor said, "the books of Jomini and other such writers are quite good. Just as the remarks I have made are good. But all that doesn't make a great general. Personally I wouldn't recommend a single volume. War is a business that is governed by the actual moment.

"Rivoli took place right on the dot. An hour more and I would have been lost. Had I waited until all the enemy columns were in motion before I attacked, I would have been surrounded and attacked by forces three times my strength. Then I would indeed have been lost. It would have been wiser to have retired on to Castelnuovo. If I had been beaten, everyone would have said that it was through ignorance. That it was obvious that my flank had been turned and that I was lost. This goes to show that all arguments about past events are useless. Nevertheless, criticisms have their use, though they won't make a general."

January 7—The schooner that sailed from England on October 7 arrived today. It brought newspapers of October 4 and 5. The main items were Mr. Brougham's defense of Queen Caroline, and that the King of France had conferred the Ribbon of the St. Esprit.

When the Emperor had finished with the first volume of Labaume's *History of the Fall of the Empire*, he handed it to the Grand Maréchal to read.

"There's nothing to it," he said. "The writer is unfamiliar with political events. He believes that the King of Prussia had issued instructions to General York, and was in agreement with him.

In this he is wrong. The King of Prussia acted in all good faith. He did not want to break with France. He believed in my star, in my personal genius, and in French resources. He told the French Ambassador:

" 'It is not generally realized what France is like. She will recover, and it won't be long before she will reinvade Germany with an army of 300,000 men. My great-uncle Frederick had neither the genius of the Emperor nor the resources of France at his disposal, and yet he still managed to extricate himself from even more difficult situations, and, when all seemed lost, he recovered and reappeared more brilliant than before.'

"The King of Prussia had a poor opinion of the Russians. M. de Hardenberg had only the interests of Prussia at heart, and he considered them best served in helping France. If I had been willing to reunite Prussia, to return the fortified towns, and the Grand Duchy of Warsaw, to make Prussia independent, and to arrange for a marriage to take place between one of the King's sons and a princess of the royal family—or possibly an adopted one—, Prussia would have remained an ally of France. 'If you want an alliance against Russia,' M. de Hardenberg would say, 'Surely we are the natural line of defense. Therefore give us back our former independence.'

"On the whole, that would have been the safest thing for them. France had already occupied their country. With the Russians, they had to risk the possibility of a war that might not turn out to their advantage."

The Grand Maréchal has been reading a book about Hannibal's crossing of the Alps. He agreed with the author that Hannibal must have crossed by the Petit-St.-Bernard Pass. But the Emperor was of the opinion that he went by Mont Genèvre. First, because it is natural to take the shortest route. Second, because Hannibal captured Turin before pushing on to Milan, at that time the capital of his allies and his principal objective upon entering Italy. Since he took Turin, it must have been because it was on his way. What was the point of going out of his way to take Turin, instead of marching directly upon Milan? If Polybius's text is consulted, which is very short, it gives no information beyond saying that Hannibal lost 20,000 men while crossing the Alps, which is a lie.

He lost nothing, not even a wagon. Polybius says that Hannibal blew up boulders with vinegar—what old wives' nonsense.

M. Cole has written to the Grand Maréchal to ask him for the money that he owed him.

January 10—The Governor, Sir Hudson Lowe, sent over some books from his own library. These consisted of the *Mémoires* of Bernadotte; a volume on education attributed to the Emperor, which had been found at St. Cloud and, rather surprisingly, bore the date of July 1812, when the Emperor was in Russia. Then there was a volume of improper stories about the Westphalian Court, which didn't even possess the merit of being amusing.

Whoever wrote the wretched thing on education made an attempt to imitate the Emperor, and to plagiarize some of his ideas by saying that it was the soul and not the mind which made the man, because the Emperor often remarked: "He that is without soul must have some feeling."

Bernadotte's work was written with a certain moderation in regard to the Emperor. He had suppressed the nonsense which figured in his reports. There was much boasting about the battles he had fought. On the whole, he has accomplished little. Bernadotte tries to prove that he owed nothing to the Emperor, that his rise in the world had nothing to do with Napoleon; but he doesn't succeed. The Emperor made several penciled notes in the margins of the book.

The truth is that the Emperor did everything for Bernadotte because he had married Désirée Clary, who had been the Emperor's first love. Napoleon was to have married her when he was at Marseilles and when she was already his sister-in-law.

One day, when she was very young, she hid under Napoleon's bed. Formerly, when telling me this story, Bonaparte said that he warned her mother about it. But nowadays, he says that it was because he had taken her c—— and the maidenhead of her c—— that he created Bernadotte a marshal, prince and king.

Sweden had made the first overtures to the Emperor at Donau-wörth, before the battle of Wagram, in 1809. The Emperor had just arrived from Paris. The Prince of Neufchâtel had lost his head. The Emperor was worried about the Army—didn't in fact know where the Army was. He said to M. de Wrede, the Swedish envoy:

"For the moment I have other things to think of. I must see to the Army."

"Oh," replied De Wrede, "the Austrians are of no importance: their business will soon be settled. Therefore, do attend to ours."

The Swedish Ambassador had wanted Prince Eugène, the Viceroy of Italy, as a candidate for the Swedish throne, but the matter of religion was a major obstacle. The Emperor disliked the Viceroy intensely, and the Princess [Augusta-Amelia] was a daughter of the King of Bavaria; her entire family was extremely Catholic, and she would have thought herself in Hell had she found herself married to a Huguenot. It was partly this question of religion that prevented the Queen from remaining in Sweden. Bernadotte merely said that he was a Protestant, and no further questions were asked. He failed to mention the fact that his son was called Oscar because he was the Emperor's godchild, and that Napoleon had given him the name while he was in Egypt.

For four days the Emperor has been taking pills to tone him up. He stopped taking them today.

M. Buonavita came to see the Grand Maréchal at the suggestion of his doctor, who had told him to apply to the Grand Maréchal about returning to Europe on account of his bad health. The Emperor had told Antommarchi to tell M. Buonavita that he would see to it that he had a good post at Rome, which pleased M. Buonavita very much indeed.

The Grand Maréchal mentioned M. Buonavita's request to the Emperor, who thought it advisable that he should approach the Governor. "Let him be allowed to leave at once," he said, "he is of no use to me here."

On the whole Napoleon was not at all grateful to Buonavita or to Vignali for having accompanied him to St. Helena. Buonavita was too old to be of much use, and Vignali had been wrong to have allowed the papers to publish the fact that he was a doctor. In this way he had gained an importance to which he wasn't entitled. He was not a doctor, but a medical tyro. The severe diarrhea with which the Emperor has been troubled, he attributes to some pills that were prescribed by Abbé Vignali. The diarrhea stops of an evening.

The Emperor has been reading Hume on Cromwell. He made the following comments on the subject to the Grand Maréchal:

"Cromwell only ruled for four years. He was not a great soldier. He won only two battles: one against Charles I, the other against the Scotch at Dumbarton. The English Revolution can in no way be compared to ours, just as Cromwell and I have nothing in common. Cromwell accomplished everything through the use of force. Whereas I acted in an orderly manner and according to the law. Charles I, nevertheless, behaved better than Louis XVI, for he didn't try to defend himself at his trial."

"The only point of resemblance is when you ousted the Deputies at St. Cloud with armed force," Bertrand remarked.

"But that was an entirely different matter. In the first place, I possessed the authority conferred on me by decision of the Conseil des Anciens, in accordance with an article of the Constitution which had transferred the Conseil to St. Cloud. It was a civil, and not a military revolution. In reality it was Sieyès and the civilians who were acting. I was little more than their agent. Of course, the incident didn't turn out quite as they had expected. I reaped the benefits, though at the time I was not the principal figure. Sieyès and the civilians had merely looked upon me as their instrument. Sieyès had wanted me to place the sixty seditious deputies under arrest the previous evening, then all would have been over. But I objected to that because I wanted to do everything in a proper manner.

" 'You will regret it,' Sieyès told me, and he was right. He knew the Assemblies and the lay of the land. If I had done what he suggested, all the fuss would have been avoided. It would have been quite sufficient to have prevented the Deputies from reaching St. Cloud.

"I have been held responsible for the Constitution of the Year VIII. That is a mistake. I had nothing to do with it. It was entirely Sieyès work, and I didn't interfere.

"As a man, Sieyès was greatly esteemed. A very high opinion was held of his personal ability. It was thought that, for some time, he had had a new constitution in his pocket, already drawn up. It came as a great surprise not to find it ready. Such a one as he did present was hailed as admirable; as 'a triumph of human intelligence.' So many disadvantages had been experienced from the people having the vote that some form of control over them was felt to be desirable.

"The Senate possessed the power of nomination. This two-part election was a bad thing, for the deputies merely became the servants of the Senate . . . That was one of Sieyès ideas. It was thought that a silent Legislative Body, could be simultaneously Parliament, Grand Council, Court of Justice, and *Tournelle*. The Council of State and the Tribunate pleaded before this Areopagus, which listened to them in silence. As I remarked to Sieyès at the time:

" 'You have mistaken the shadow for the substance, and you have set up a puppet monarchy instead of a real one. You should have moved with the times. People are tired of assemblies.' "

Napoleon had read Cromwell by Villemain, and as he told the Grand Maréchal, he was quite pleased with it.

"It's a sound book, but on the whole, one that tells very little. Just what is he trying to prove? That everything ends by a monarchy? The French Revolution, to be sure, ended like that. Wasn't I a king? I was a lawful king, a legitimate king, so legitimate in fact, that even today I could govern France without any difficulty.

"I want everything that the French want. They don't want an aristocracy. No more do I. They don't want party politics, no more do I. They want the good of the nation, and so do I. They want a stable financial situation and no more plundering of the exchequer. No one wants that more than I do. War? They will want that before I will, because they feel the urge for action, and above all, the need for a good army.

"All Frenchmen would be willing to go to war for the sake of acquiring Belgium or the Rhineland. They would also be willing to make war so as to ensure the independence of Italy, because that would redound to their personal credit. They would be willing to go to war for the sake of regaining their ascendancy over Germany, etc."

The Grand Maréchal had mentioned Labaume's book to the Emperor, who returned to the subject of Prussia.

He said that he really could have prevented the Prussians from making an alliance with Russia. As a matter of fact, at the time, they asked for nothing better. M. de Narbonne had returned with favorable assurances. The Prussians were hurt by the conduct of the Duke of York. At Dresden or at Prague, the Emperor could have made certain of the neutrality of Austria by sacrificing Venice, in addition to the Illyrian provinces: in other words, if he had been willing to return to the treaties of Campo-Formio and of Lunéville. That would have been Austria's real political rôle.

But at the time, the Emperor had felt that he was not in a position to make such a sacrifice. He had not yet come to that. The war still held many chances of success, as later events were to prove. A peace negotiated after the battle of Leipzig with the loss of Italy and the natural frontiers was more honorable than the surrender of Venice would have been at that time. As things turned out, events were to prove that the campaign could be successful. The battle of Dresden brought Austria to her knees. If St. Cyr had marched, the Vandamme episode would never have taken place. It would all have been over. Metternich had already dispatched an envoy charged with negotiating peace. The Mac-Donald episode was also quite unexpected. It is possible that Fouché had already begun to betray him, but the Emperor was unaware of it.

"I could have pushed on successfully after the first day of the battle of Leipzig. The author of this book reproaches me with having failed to agree to proposals made by the Legislative Body that I, the Emperor, should declare acceptance of the natural frontiers, which, would have shown to the French nation a genuine desire to make peace, and would have rallied public opinion.

"In the conversation I had with the deputies, however, I succeeded in convincing them that this would be a mistake. Of necessity I would have to accept their conditions, and in consequence, I could start negotiations along such lines, but I told them that if this were made public, it would provoke the immediate desertion of all the troops in the Rhineland Confederation, those of Holland who were occupying the fortified towns, and those of the entire Italian Army. It would be necessary to evacuate Italy immediately and to sacrifice an army of 60,000 men. The deputies were convinced. I also wanted the Chamber of Deputies and the Senate to say that no negotiations were to be carried out while enemy troops remained in the territory. This might have prevented the crossing of the Rhine.

"Although the deputies were convinced, people like Senator Lambrechts and others of equally bad faith were not and, as matters stood, were never likely to be. I have no wish to attack Lafayette now; after all, he is a member of Parliament; posterity will judge him. I think that I personally should have had Fouché, Lanjuinais and Lafayette hanged."

The Battle of Vittoria was a most unfortunate incident. As usual, the Austrian Emperor hesitated to take action. He was afraid of the Army of Spain, because he thought that the Emperor held very strong forces in reserve there. At any moment things might be settled in Spain, and then Napoleon would be in a position to call upon that army. However, news of the Battle of Vittoria came at the critical moment and made up his mind for him. The English Army invaded France, whereupon it suddenly became quite impossible to extricate the army from Spain.

The only Ambassador who knew the Austrian Emperor was M. de Narbonne. It appeared that the former French Ambassador —Otto, Count de Morlay—had been an honest man, quite capable of repeating whatever Metternich told him to say, but not at all likely to understand or to know what he was driving at. M. de Narbonne found this out at once. He went to see Mme. Bagration whose salon was the source of most of the political intrigues. He called there one morning in informal dress, put his feet comfortably up on the fire irons, and chatted with the women. It happened to be a day on which most of the party in opposition to Metternich were present. The conversation was general, and M. de Narbonne had no fear of annoying the Austrian Emperor. In the course of conversation he stung him into coming out into the open. The Emperor gave himself away and was exceedingly put out about it afterwards. It was no easy thing to have made Emperor Franz angry, and to have tricked him into dropping his mask.

The Grand Maréchal took his son Arthur Bertrand, in full dress, to see the Emperor.

In his book Labaume tells what the Emperor told him to say to the viceroy when they reached the Elbe:

"Should the enemy bring four guns into position, turn sixteen guns against them."

And yet, he fails to understand the meaning of this, although it is based on a sound military principle worth developing . . .

When an enemy is in full retreat, generally speaking he has little in the way of artillery. He is forced to keep on the move and has to evacuate his guns and equipment at the same time. Whereas pursuing troops have no need for such measures; they have as many guns as they require, which is one of the great advantages of being in a position to advance. In the beginning, the retreating force is able to hold a position with some thirty guns, which is about all they will have at their disposal. They can then unmask their artillery and bring it into place against the first column to make contact with them. This column, however, is forced to wait for its infantry and artillery to catch up with it. This gives the retreating force the advantage of an hour or two. But this initial gain is soon lost, and thereafter the retreating force can only fight to disadvantage, and must ultimately be overwhelmed by the superior strength of the advancing troops.

What the Emperor told Labaume, and what he failed to grasp, the Emperor actually carried out at the time, as Labaume himself tells us. General Drouot ordered eighty guns to be brought up. He smashed the enemy artillery, and forced it to retire.

"I never received any co-operation from my family," the Emperor said. "If I had not tried to obtain it, I would have been successful much more easily."

Prince Joseph was a mild-mannered man of many qualities, but he was quite incapable of carrying out any undertaking and he could do nothing methodically. He much preferred the company of women, not entirely for sexual pleasure and satisfaction, but simply because he enjoyed their society. This was precisely what Cardinal Ruffo told the Emperor. The Neapolitans had a much higher opinion of Murat than they had of Joseph.

"It's quite true, of course, that Prince Joseph resembles you," he said. "He speaks Italian like a Tuscan and he is very pleasant. But he attends to nothing. He's forever shut up with some woman reading Torquato Tasso and Aretino. Murat, who is less of a natural intelligence, suited us much better. In the first place, he had built up an army, and he had a military manner and appearance that were most attractive. Also, he looked after your interests. He knew how to get around people, and, like Bernadotte, he had his own way of flattering and of being successful. On the whole he was a more capable man than Joseph.

"If you had left Murat in Spain," the Cardinal continued, "The Spanish business would have been settled."

"I believe," the Emperor said to Bertrand, "that if I had been prepared to sacrifice Joseph, I would have succeeded. It's true that Joseph never looked after anything. What is more, he thought himself a great soldier. He recognized a certain superiority in me, but that was about all. He thought himself much better than Suchet, Masséna, or Lannes.

"What a curious idea," I would say to him, "why you are not even so good as the captain of light infantry posted at your door. If you found yourself at the head of thirty or a hundred men in front of the enemy, in spite of your courage, you would not know what to do. And you would probably flee like a coward. Whereas that brave but mediocre man at your door—who, however, knows his job—would hold up the enemy, take cover behind a hedge or a wall, and hold up an attack by superior forces. You are very different from the Emperor Alexander, who, when Marshal Lannes fell asleep in his coach, kept the flies off him for fear they should wake him. He looked upon Lannes as a hero. He realized his value and respected it, whereas you aren't even aware of it."

"Joseph should have flattered Suchet," the Emperor went on, "because he had need of him, and because Suchet was his superior in military ability. Talent likes to be flattered. When Jerome reached Pultusk, he wanted to take over command of the cavalry from Murat. 'But you're mad,' I said. 'What! Do you think that you are capable of leading a squadron of cavalry into battle. What astounding conceit!' "

The Emperor feels better than on the previous day, though is still somewhat weak. He consents to take some quinine, which is much simpler than the pills he has just been taking that contain valerian, iron, and quina. The doctor said that the iron had disagreed with him. Hortense took her brother Arthur to see the

Emperor who, for the past week, has been in the habit of coming down to the salon every afternoon at about four.

In his book Labaume says that the Emperor committed serious blunders.

"Then let them do better, the great fatheads," the Emperor said, when he read this. "If I ever do take to writing, I will make mince-meat of them all in one duodecimo volume.

"I could write up all my campaigns," he continued. "As a matter of fact I have held out the hope that I may do so, but in that case I would have to be in good health, or else to have left this place.

"No doubt I did make mistakes; some were my fault while others were not.

"When Marmont and Sebastiani told me that the entire enemy army was on its way to Saint-Dizier, that in fact they had seen it, I was forced to believe them and to go there. Otherwise I would have reached Paris much sooner. No doubt on the first day of the Battle of Leipzig I could have had Marshal Marmont with me, had I been aware that General Blücher was two or three days march away. But Marmont had told me that he was only two leagues [eight kilometers] distant.

"When General Meerfeldt was taken prisoner at Leipzig, he was astonished to see Murat. He expressed his amazement and let fall a few words which hinted that Murat had been in touch with Austria. As a matter of fact," the Emperor went on, "Murat had already begun to betray me. He did not come to Dresden at the request of the Emperor, as the writer assumes, but in common with the rest of Europe, out of surprise at the outcome of the Battles of Bautzen and Dresden. He thought that I was on the verge of recapturing my ascendancy, and he regretted the negotia-tions that he had already begun with Austria. He came to Dresden to see if there were still time in which to grasp a fortune. Although he had already begun to betray me, he fought bravely, just as it is said that Prince Eugène of Savoy fought courageously at the battle of Chiari under Villeroi, at a time when he was already negotiating with Austria and the enemies of Louis XIV."

Two ships have just arrived from India. The Emperor continues to feel very weak. He doesn't want to take any more quinine. "There are many different kinds of weakness," he says, "and just because the iron and valerian pills happen to suit M. Buonavita or Mme. Bertrand, there is no reason to assume that they will suit me. Medicine isn't quite so simple as that, it would be too easy if it were."

He is in need of a change, but he doesn't know just what Castlereagh would permit. It would do him good to sweat.

The Grand Maréchal told the Emperor that he really should write up his Russian and Dresden campaigns, as well as the campaign of 1814.

"Oh no, that one is not necessary," the Emperor replied. "Everybody agrees that it was very fine. While we were at Elba, Wellington told me that he was studying it carefully, but that he had not yet understood it."

"What about the Russian campaign?"

"That's well known, too," the Emperor replied. "It is common knowledge that what caused it to fail was that in one night I lost 30,000 horses. And the burning of Moscow was such a fabulous thing. The campaigns of Lützen and of Bautzen are also very well known."

"Yes," said Bertrand, "but between the Battle of Dresden and that of Leipzig, there were a series of difficulties that no one has explained and that need to be understood. You had planned to retake the Elbe and to march on Berlin. Then why did you leave 25,000 men at Dresden when you learned of the desertion of Bavaria?"

"Quite so—but the circumstances need to be understood. As a matter of fact, I went to considerable trouble over the campaigns of Prince Charles, and we now have information that alters everything. One should have access to the papers of the Prince de Neufchâtel. All the information is there, reports, marching orders, etc. An arrangement should be made with his widow or with his children. It could be pointed out to them that it is a question of prestige, their own as well as that of their father. Oh! If only I were in Europe, I could accomplish an immense amount in the course of a year."

One day the Emperor talked to Bertrand about General Berwick.

"Berwick was a good second-rate general. It is difficult to decide about the siege of Lille. Would it have been a good thing to have attacked the lines? If Vendôme had been in charge, I think that he would have decided to attack and that he would have been successful."

"When they had been unmasked," Bertrand said. "Vendôme himself would have said that they were unassailable."

The Emperor continued: "Those tactics were well enough on that day. But say, instead, that the attack had been made on the first day? That a courier had been sent and a conference called. Wars aren't fought like that. Vendôme was asked whether he was prepared to guarantee success. Who the devil would be willing to give such a guarantee? The whole success of an attack may depend on the lives of one or two couriers, or some such stupidity. Louis XIV wanted them to attack. Vendôme wanted to attack. In this he was quite right, but he wasn't in command. The Duke of Burgundy was there. This was one of the worst systems that Louis XIV had adopted. Of course, the country was pleased to see the heir to the throne at the front, and that was obviously worth taking into consideration. But for the successful prosecution of the war, it was most inconvenient."

At Leipzig the Emperor saved all his cavalry, because that same night Murat had ordered it to cross the Partha and these instructions were carried out. In this way, the Emperor still had a strong cavalry after the Battle of Leipzig. The Guards were also across the river with their artillery. That was the Emperor's great advantage at the Battle of Hanau. There the lost, routed mass of men were almost worthless until they saw the Guards; after that they did well in the van and attacked courageously. The troops that Wrede had detached and sent to Frankfort weakened them, it is true, and yet may have saved them, because, as the Emperor had no troops to send to Frankfort, he was forced to go there himself. Otherwise he would have pursued Wrede and, in view of his superior strength in cavalry, would probably have destroyed that army.

"The truth is that at Prague I never wanted peace at the price of having to sacrifice Venice. I was not in a position to make such a concession. Had I wanted to do so, Austria would never have declared war.

"The fact is that at Châtillon I didn't want peace, because of the former frontiers. I thought it not only shameful for France, but for me as well. I would have saved the country if Marmont had not been a traitor, if Augereau had not been a traitor; and if Paris had not been in touch with the enemy, I would have saved France.

"Augereau had 24,000 men, all seasoned troops drawn up before Lyons. To oppose him, the enemy had only the Prince of Hesse-Homburg with some Rhineland contingents and a small corps of Austrians. He had, in other words, only a rabble to overthrow, while back of him was the town of Lyons, which could have usefully provided some sharpshooters. Perhaps Suchet could have done better. When Marmont betrayed me, I had nothing with which to reproach him. Who could have expected such a thing? In my ultimatum to Caulaincourt I said that I would agree to anything, provided that the port of Antwerp and the town of Mainz were not surrendered, because I would quite definitely have nothing to do with such conditions. It was only a question of gaining time, which should have been easy with those bases. Caulaincourt lacked ability.

"After Leipzig I should have marched on Hamburg, even if it had already been occupied by the enemy. With the numerous artillery I had at my disposal, I could have forced the town to capitulate . . ."

January 20—Napoleon went out for a drive in the morning. He lunched well and then felt somewhat tired. In the evening he was very cheerful. The Grand Maréchal took his son Arthur to see the Emperor. He dined with him and then played with him in a friendly fashion for an hour. The Emperor had been out for a drive in the morning and had a good appetite for lunch. If this keeps up, he will be quite recovered in a fortnight. He digests his food well. He told the doctor that he feels much better and that the quinine should be stopped.

January 21—The weather is bad. The Emperor didn't go out. He has had a seesaw installed in the billiard room, and he asked the Grand Maréchal if he had any idea what it was.

"Some kind of war machine, I suppose," Bertrand said. "Is it possible to use it for getting down onto a rampart?"

"Well, that's not very bright for an engineer—God's teeth!"

At first the Emperor said that it was a swing to amuse the children, then he finally admitted that it was for himself. It seems that it will be good exercise for him, if he can use it for half an hour every day, and that it will make him sweat.

Mme. Bertrand laughed at seeing the Emperor seated on a seesaw and said that someone really ought to make a cartoon showing the Emperor on one end, and all the crowned heads at the other end unable to raise him off the ground, and the caption should be: a cure for liver. The truth is that the Emperor is very heavy; he weighs more than Noverraz, who is over six feet.

January 22—Arthur Bertrand went to see the Emperor, who showed him the seesaw and told him that it was a gun. Afterwards he and the Grand Maréchal got up on it to amuse the child. Napoleon had been on it for a quarter of an hour in the morning and didn't feel any the better for it. He got off because he had just had dinner and was afraid that it might upset him.

The Grand Maréchal had read Bernadotte's book, and he discussed it with Napoleon, who said:

"It's very badly put together. It is difficult to make out just what he is aiming at. I am amazed, not at the fact that Bernadotte couldn't do any better, but that there wasn't someone in his entourage who could have done better. There is a lack of skill, not only in the choice of what has been told, but in what has been omitted. It is too absurd that he should pretend to owe nothing to me and hides the fact that Oscar is my godson."

The Emperor maintained that Bernadotte owed his entire career to Désirée [. . .]

Bernadotte made a mess of the Abo affair. At the time he should have arranged for his son to marry a Russian princess. In that way he could have got everything he wanted, because he was then of some importance and it was the interview at Abo that saved the Russian monarchy by releasing the Finnish Army, which then went into action against the Emperor Napoleon's right flank. If the meeting at Abo hadn't taken place, the Emperor really would have been victorious.

Bernadotte will not be firmly established on his throne until he has married his son to a Prussian or to a Russian princess. Until then, he will not be settled. It's really extraordinary that his son, who is twenty-two and an heir apparent, should be unable to get married. This is the truth of the matter. The son of Gustave IV, who is a nephew of Emperor Alexander, has aroused interest. He is not responsible for the sins of his father. Sweden was wrong not to have made him king. Obviously they had to get rid of the father, who was mad, but the boy has done no harm. It would have been much wiser not to have taken the crown away from the real heir apparent. It's not easy to see why the Swedes should have gone to the trouble of choosing a French general whom they didn't even know, and who really was of no ability, even though he may have possessed more than the Emperor gave him credit for.

"I wanted to marry Désirée, who had been my first love. She was much surprised and annoyed when she learned of my marriage to Josephine and, at the time, reproached me bitterly. I wanted to marry her to Duphot, of whom I thought highly and who was later assassinated at Rome. Upon my return from Egypt I would have married her to Desaix, if she hadn't, in the meantime, married Bernadotte while the expedition was on. In all probability I would have married her off before my sister Caroline, who later became Queen of Naples. Désirée had ability and she was bound up with my fortunes."

The Emperor vomited his dinner and his medicine, as the result of having taken some of it two or three hours after eating his dinner. At nine o'clock he dismissed the doctor; at ten o'clock he called for him again. Someone went to fetch Dr. Antommarchi while he was attending Mme. Bertrand. He went to the Emperor, who failed to receive him; yet at two in the morning Napoleon sent for him again and, when he arrived, made a scene which lasted for two hours.

"It was high time that the Grand Maréchal had him appointed first lackey to Mme. Bertrand," Napoleon cried. "Antommarchi is nothing but a great rogue, a rascal, a good-for-nothing. In fact he is a cazzo of a valet."

After this Napoleon rang for Noverraz to make him a cup of tea, and he repeated in French everything that he had said in Italian about the great [. . .] He told Antommarchi that he could leave with Abbé Buonavita. The doctor replied that he would do whatever the Emperor desired, but that he felt that he had nothing for which to reproach himself. The Emperor then patted him and gave him a slap on the shoulder.

At noon Antommarchi went to see Mme. Bertrand. He was quite put out about the whole incident. He told the Grand Maréchal that when he went to see Napoleon, he must be prepared for a scene. The Grand Maréchal went to see Napoleon at the usual time. He found him asleep. The Grand Maréchal returned at three o'clock. Napoleon had gone into the salon and was again asleep.

The Grand Maréchal chuckled all evening over "he is a cazzo of a valet." He found it exceedingly funny. It is only home truths that hurt. Mme. Bertrand remained indifferent to the Emperor's nonsense. The Governor talked to Abbé Buonavita about his departure.

General Montholon went into Jamestown and had a talk with Montchenu, the French Commissioner. That day the Grand Maréchal didn't see the Emperor, who wasn't well and who didn't go out at all.

January 24—Napoleon told the Grand Maréchal the result of General Montholon's conversation with Montchenu.

"He says there is talk of making Belle Isle into a residence for the Emperor. That would mean taking a grave risk. The English could no longer have the custody of the Emperor. They will never let him go to Austria. Besides Austria doesn't want him, it would be awkward for her."

The Austrians are no longer going to march on Naples. The Russian Emperor won't permit it. Russia has left the Holy Alliance, which has been dissolved. Russia supports and foments European events. She will march on Constantinople.

M. Decazes should have returned to the Ministry by now. He is a favorite the King is unable to dispense with. After M. Decazes left, they wanted to give the King another favorite, but he would have none of them. He no longer received M. de Martignac, who was too old and boring. He liked young people who could chat and tell him things. It was thought that the King should have sent M. Decazes to Russia, but he didn't want to.

On the subject of Belle Isle, the Emperor believes that the intention of the powers would be to keep him there under the same conditions as at St. Helena, with a governor, a garrison, and a cruiser, just as we have here. But the Emperor will never consent to that. He would be at the mercy of the Congress of Aix-la-Chapelle, which would be able to have him assassinated there. He would never agree to it. England would have to give him up before such a thing could happen, and she would never do that. It would be necessary to obtain the Emperor's consent, and he would never give it.

Or perhaps they want to give him Belle Isle as a place of refuge, with a battalion of his own as at Elba? That would be a different matter, but it would be unwise from the point of view of the Bourbons, on account of the present state of unrest in France. It would be possible to communicate with Paris quickly and without delay. In Boucheseiche, there is a map of Belle Isle. According to what Montchenu, Boucheseiche's geography, and French statistics say, Belle Isle is an island about the same size as Elba, but with only half the population.

Montchenu said that the King of France had never approved of the Emperor being taken to St. Helena; that personally he liked the Emperor very much indeed; that the King is not sufficiently well known, and that if his orders were seen, there would be a considerable amount of surprise. Montchenu says that he himself would not be here at St. Helena if he had 100,000 francs, or an income of 5,000 livres; then he would be independent.

The Grand Maréchal finished Labaume's second volume concerning the French Campaign. Three or four times he let the book fall from his hands in disgust. Some of the battles were well described, but many of the views expressed were so un-French, the actions of the Emperor so often scurrilously misrepresented, and so many crying injustices done, that it was difficult not to feel indignation.

"The greatest mistake of my campaign was in not having taken Vitry the first time. It would have been easy to have surrounded such a small place with my immense artillery, and then success would have been certain. It is from then on that all the misfortunes of that campaign date.

"The second mistake I made was in marching on Laon after the Battle of Craonne. I should have returned to Rheims at once and immediately done what I only did several days later. Then we would have had peace. The Austrian Emperor was thoroughly disgusted. My successes had greatly discouraged him. He saw no end in view and said: 'If Napoleon has one more success, I will accept the Frankfort conditions and make peace.'

"I was unfamiliar with the position of Laon. I took my decision after receiving advice from Dulauloy, who came from Laon and whom I had consulted. I should never have dreamed that he would be unfamiliar with his own part of the country. According to him, Laon wasn't a fortified town. But when it came to the point, he didn't even know the outskirts of his own town. Apparently only hunters really know them.

"I believed Marmont to be quite near and, as a matter of fact, he was, judging from the map. But he was very far away indeed when one realized that he was separated from me by a marsh that made a big detour necessary. For a long time we were without news of Marmont's Army. He was inclined to be full of fire when the enemy was imprudent, but less so when the enemy was present in strength. He forged ahead and then lay and waited for the enemy to attack. His artillery park was captured. Those thirty or forty guns had a tremendous effect on the mind of the enemy.

"Under the circumstances Marmont did not pay much attention to the loss of the guns; those guns, at the moment, were less than nothing to him. Although we were without an army, we nevertheless had plenty of guns. We masked them with a thin line of troops, either cavalry or infantry, but mainly cavalry because at that time we had some that was fairly good and proportionately more numerous than our infantry. The artillery alone enabled us to carry on the campaign and fight the enemy, who was under the impression that we possessed very strong forces, judging by our guns. . . But it was a small infantry attack that decided the issue. Marmont's gross mistake, of being held up at Saint-Dizier and which lost France, therefore cannot be attributed to me. The Marshal and the Cavalry General de Ségur had said that the whole army was there, so I was forced to believe them and to march on Saint-Dizier.

"On two other occasions I could have retrieved the situation.

The enemy couldn't fight with Paris at the back of them; so they had decided, if I advanced, to evacuate Paris and take up positions on the heights on the other side of Paris. General Kleist told me this and, in any case, it made sense. What general would dare to fight a battle with a city the size of Paris behind him which might rise up and which, if it barred the way, would lay his army open to the risk of being wiped out? The betrayal of Marmont averted this."

The Grand Maréchal was of the opinion that once Paris and Lyons had been occupied nothing further could have been done. What would the Emperor have done afterwards? Become a partisan? Or possibly the leader of some guerrilla band?

"My Guards would have remained faithful to me," the Emperor said. "But in the end they would have ignored me, if they had come to feel that the war was without point, and that I was the only obstacle to peace."

It was not Laharpe, as Labaume states, but Pozzo di Borgo, who made the enemy decide to march on Paris. He knew Paris and the Revolution. He had been a deputy to the Legislative Assembly in 1792. He had also accompanied the Emperor on his trip through Corsica, at the time when Bastia was being fortified. "Nothing is of any importance," he said, "if the enemy retains Paris." He maintained this point of view before the Conseil; and rumor had it that the Grand Duke Constantine, who disagreed with the idea of a march on Paris, had seemed embarrassed: "You will answer for this with your head," he is reported to have said.

Caulaincourt showed that he lacked ability. It was only a question of holding out against the surrender of Antwerp and of playing for time. To retain Antwerp was the only thing the Emperor cared about. It was just possible that he might have considered parting with Mainz; about which he cared nothing. He knew that he could retake it when he wanted to. It would have meant sustaining a siege, and with eight or nine hundred pieces of artillery at his disposal, in a matter of two or three weeks he could have recaptured it without breaching the walls, crossing the moats, or any of the other trappings of a siege. Merely by digging some first and second line trenches and by advancing to within two hundred toises [600 ft.] of the fortifications . . . From a distance of six hundred feet bombs could have been lobbed by hand into the out-works they wished to attack, and then the enemy would have been cleaned out. It was largely a question of money. Ten thousand vehicles . . . Ten million francs would have settled the matter.

Whereas at Antwerp it was a different situation altogether. The docks would have been destroyed and the ships taken away. The Emperor didn't want, indeed he couldn't afford, to sacrifice his naval squadron. In any case, he would have preferred not to have been forced to part with either Antwerp or Flushing.

Caulaincourt blundered over his ultimatum. The question of the Prince of Neufchâtel, or even of Talleyrand, could not possibly arise when the prime interests of France were at stake. Quite possibly the Emperor didn't want to have anything to do with the former frontiers. At first he had thought that he might have ob-tained the Rhineland frontier, and in this he all but succeeded. Moreover, he wrote as much to Emperor Franz of Austria: "Neither the Republic nor the Empire could guarantee the former frontiers. Only the Bourbons could do such a thing . . ."

"I had nothing whatever to do with the Treaty of Fontaine-bleau," Napoleon said. "I did not ask for the Island of Elba. It was suggested, because they thought that I would ask for Corsica. Which, indeed, had been my intention. I hesitated before decid-ing to abdicate. I did it for my friends, and to place France on a national footing so that everyone could obey the Bourbons without fear. They have been told this often enough since their return to power.

"But for that to come about I had to abdicate, not only for my-self, but for my son and for my family. Moreover, my abdication was a personal matter and I didn't want there to be any question of it in the Treaty. My return from Elba and the Treaty are quite separate from the Abdication."

One final accusation by Labaume: "After Waterloo, it would have been wiser to have called the Legislative Assembly together and to have defended ourselves inside Paris; then at least we could have negotiated. But it was precisely that which the Emperor re-fused to do."

"That was a very hard thing to say," the Emperor remarked "and the nation was very cruel and unfair . . ."

January 26—Conversation about the Emperor's divorce and remarriage.

When the Emperor obtained his divorce, it was his intention to marry a Russian princess. The idea had been mooted at Ehrfurt by no less a person than Talleyrand. This marriage failed to take place because of a scurrilous joke. A pretty dirty one in fact. The story runs that some writers of libelous witticisms had said that Bon-a-parte stood for *bon-à-rien*, good-for-nothing. Then someone had revived an old joke about a soldier of the Army of Italy; when it was said that he had no children, the comment was: "But isn't it obvious that he carries his b——s in his head!"

It was the Empress who gave substance to this rumor. In fact she herself put it about. This was one of the reasons why Madame Mère disliked her. No mother likes to have such things said about her son. This explains why Mme. D[uchâtel] burst out laughing one evening at Malmaison and said to the Emperor: "Aha, so the Empress says that you are no use at all, that it's just like so much water . . ."

It was impossible for Josephine to say that the Emperor did not look like other men. . . . But she remarked that Crescentini [famous Italian soprano] had also looked like a man and had nevertheless produced *nothing*. . . .

The Prince of M[echlenburg?] took it upon himself to interview the Empress on the subject, but he did so in such a stupid way that she was quite shocked, so much so indeed, that Talleyrand advised the Emperor to have the Prince removed from court. He said that everyone was talking about the story and the sight of a foreign Prince consulting the wife of the Emperor on such a subject was supremely ridiculous.

"Do what you please," said the Emperor, "you have all the means at your disposal. As for me, I will have nothing to do with the matter. It would be the height of absurdity for me to do so."

Talleyrand then sent for the chargé d'affaires of the Prince, and told him that his business had been completed and that it would be advisable for him to leave within the next few days. When the Prince announced his forthcoming departure at the next levée, the Emperor simulated surprise. The Empress had explained to the Prince what she had already told Mme. Duchâtel; namely, that the Emperor was *no use at all*, that she had had children by her first husband, and that while she was still a comparatively young woman she had married the Emperor who had been able to do *nothing*.

The Prince, in turn, told this to the Dowager Russian Empress. After the divorce had been made absolute and the question of the Emperor's remarriage came to the fore, the problem of the *nothing* arose. When Emperor Alexander mentioned the subject to the Dowager Empress, she expressed considerable repugnance. She said that the Emperor was *no use at all*, and that such a thing would be a disgrace for his wife. . . .

Emperor Alexander replied that she was mistaken, the Emperor Napoleon was as other men, and that what she had heard was nothing more than scurrilous gossip. She replied that on the contrary it was actual fact. Prince M[echlenburg] had heard it from Josephine herself, and that the Emperor could write and ask him.

Alexander sent a messenger to the Prince, who replied in the affirmative. When Alexander received this answer, the French Ambassador objected that the Emperor already had a child by Mme. Walewska. "Yes, yes," exclaimed Alexander, "but everyone knows what young Polish women are like. She probably had other lovers." All the objections raised could be brushed aside, as, indeed they were. But nevertheless it put people off. No one had any further doubts on the subject. The Austrian princess was proposed at the time and was accepted. Such, in a few words, was the history of this great incident.

"I would never have thought that my divorce from Josephine could have caused any difficulty," said Napoleon, "because it was based on reasons of State in which everyone, even Josephine herself, had an interest. That is why I never felt any concern about it.

"There were people who would have liked it if I had not had Josephine crowned. Why not, I said? Isn't she my wife? This had nothing to do with the divorce. I did not pretend that I had been living with a concubine, but with my own wife. To have her crowned was to recognize that fact, though it in no way altered the reasons for the divorce.

"The painting of the coronation is really the coronation of the

Empress, not mine. That was just one of Josephine's little intrigues with David. The pretext being, of course, that it made a better picture.

"Josephine, who was afraid of the divorce, thought that she had achieved something by this petty trick. There were some who pointed out that the painting was unsuitable. It was the coronation of the Emperor that should have been shown. I paid no heed to them and let the 'finer' picture be painted.

"Upon my return from the campaign of Wagram I was at the height of my fame and power. I was forty, and I was afraid that if I waited much longer, I might not have any more children. I discussed the matter with the Empress. I explained to her that unless I had a child, my dynasty was without any foundation. My nephews couldn't replace me, the country wouldn't understand such a thing; while a child born to the purple, to the throne, in the Palace of the Tuileries, stood, in the eyes of the nation and of the people, for something quite different from my brother's son, who would naturally be of much less interest to them. Reasons of State and the continuation of my dynasty forced me to have a child. After all she had hers. But when I married her she was unable to have any more. In a word, she had been unable to give me any. I had not taken her in the flame and passion of her youth, and it was unfair that she should deny to me that for which every man longs. She could be sure that I would always treat her well. Her interests and those of her children were identical. If she wanted posterity to look upon her as an Empress, and to assure the future of her children, my dynasty must be firmly established, and for that to come about I, the Emperor, must have heirs.

"'The divorce is necessary. It will take place because I desire it. There are, however, two ways of going about it. Either with your consent or without it. Choose! I am convinced that you have no reason to hesitate.'

"The Empress felt faint. I sent for Mme. d'Arberg, her lady-in-waiting. For three days Josephine pretended to be ill, and refused to take any food. I ignored the whole matter. Then one morning Josephine sent for me. I found her attractively dressed as was her wont. She told me: 'I have made up my mind. I agree to the divorce.' In the course of our first conversation she had asked me:

'Tell me, whom is it you wish to marry?' 'Good heavens, I have no idea,' I replied.

"It was the Empress who had wanted Prince Louis to marry Hortense. I would have preferred to have given her a dowry without mixing the two families. But Josephine, who had something else in mind, and who feared the divorce, wanted the marriage to take place. To her, my objections merely seemed evasive . . . She insisted, and I finally gave in."

January 27—The Emperor has read Benjamin Constant's pamphlet on the Hundred Days. He pointed out that Constant says: "Above all, it was the peasantry that wanted the Empire." Indeed! So the Army wasn't for Napoleon? The author agrees, I take it, that the Emperor didn't want a House of Lords. The Emperor believed that the country didn't want such a thing.

"What France wants above all is equality," said the Emperor. "What she doesn't want are the pretentiousness and the arrogance of the aristocrat. It was that which made the aristocracy antipathetic to the present order of things. They had preserved an almost feudal arrogance, which cut them off from the people even when they were no longer in office. This reminds me of an old soldier story: 'Who are these Bourbons we hear so much about nowadays? Do you remember those old marquises in our village whose goods were sold? Well, the Bourbons are the old marquises of France.'

" 'Oh, now I get it. So the old marquises want to recover their belongings, and the Bourbons want to recover all their former privileges.'

"The main objection to the Bourbons is that they were once really the masters of France. They have said so themselves, positively. We all know that. Everyone knows it. Louis said it often enough in case we might forget it. That is the precise reason why we don't want the Bourbons.

"It appears that Benjamin Constant is of French extraction. His family had to flee from France at the time of the revoking of the Edict of Nantes. He was born a Protestant. It is even thought that he may have written the Brunswick Manifesto. He is an intelligent man. But being a writer he has to write and to indict. At one time he was the lover of Mme. de Staël. He was an ardent supporter of the 18th Fructidor and the 18th Brumaire. At that time he frequently came to see me. He saw me every day, or at least very often . . .

"Mme. de Staël and her friends went out of their way to be very nice to me when the Tribunate was being formed. Constant, too, assured me many times of his friendship. Sieyès didn't want to give him an appointment because he thought that he was an intriguer. But I persisted and Constant received his appointment.

"By the second day I was astounded to hear him speaking against me along with Duveyrier on something of no importance: the means of communication between the Council of State and the Tribunate. Something that was not of the slightest interest to me and to which I had barely paid attention. Duveyrier said: 'From where I am standing I can see the rostrum from which Camille Desmoulins, etc.' I blew Duveyrier up properly. He had formerly been a contractor to the Army of Italy, and I knew him. 'What do you mean by your rostrum of Camille Desmoulins?' I said. 'Are you trying to compare me to Louis XIV? Have you come here with the intention of preaching insurrection against the government?' Duveyrier apologized profusely and said that I could count on him—that I knew quite well how it was when one was in the tribune, and how one sometimes got carried away when speaking in public (he recalled Mirabeau's reprimand)—and that in spite of everything he was completely devoted to me.

"After that incident I refused to see Benjamin Constant. Mme. de Staël was beside herself with fury. 'Do as they do in England,' she screamed. 'Over there they make speeches against the government.' 'Very good, but after that you won't expect me to favor you or to make up to you.'

"After the return from Elba, when it was proposed that Constant should be recalled, people said that he would try to run away. 'Oh, tell him not to worry,' I said. 'I will receive him.' Under the Empire, Constant had always tried to draw closer to me, but it was I who had paid no heed to him.

"He belonged to Mme. de Staël's circle, which would have liked nothing better than to have overthrown me. There are some things too serious to joke about."

In the evening the Emperor told Antommarchi that General Montholon had been to see the Governor to ask for some medicine. He told the doctor that he could remain as a surgeon if he liked, but that if he preferred he could leave with Abbé Buonavita. Antommarchi replied that he would never leave the Emperor so long as there was no one to take his place.

The Emperor dismissed the subject. The conversation then turned on how difficult it would have been to have restored the High Courts of Justice.

"I would undoubtedly have been willing to have restored them, but I was unable to do so," the Emperor said. "What exactly were the High Courts of Justice? Which section of them could I have re-established? The sale [of public offices], perhaps? Such a thing was not to be thought of for a moment. That was much too far removed from the ideas not only of the times but of the Revolution as well.

"The old legal families? Without a doubt it would have gratified me to have been able to appoint some of the old wealthy families. I did find places for some of them. But almost all of them were hostile to me. The High Courts of Justice had the policing of the upper classes, and the police in general. They had the power to arraign before the courts a lieutenant general or a marshal of France. Such ideas were no longer acceptable to us. The police should come under the executive body and not under the jurisdiction of the law courts. It was one of the fundamental principles of the Constituent Assembly and of the Revolution that the administration of justice should be independent of either the executive or the police. Thouret and the lawyers who were members of the Constituent Assembly were hostile to the *parlementaires*. All our laws were designed to split authority and to prevent the judiciary from encroaching on the authority and jurisdiction of the executive.

"The recording of laws? But the [former *parlementaires*[2]] no longer belonged to the Legislative Assembly. That was another kind of encroachment to be tolerated even less. I knew quite well that the High Courts of Justice had convicted Marshal Turenne.

[2]Members of the High Courts of Justice.

That it was they who had created an unbridgeable gulf between the throne, the royal family, and the people.

"Moreover, the conduct of Parliament had been ridiculous. What kind of a body was it that vetoed everything, yet made no suggestions? That almost inconceivably refused to sanction a land tax which would have weighed equally upon everybody, and which was fair and universally popular, as well as a tax on registrations. At the very least it could have said what it was that it wanted. 'We don't want any stamp taxes.' 'Good! But what do you propose to introduce in their place? Forty million francs must be found which could be procured by the above tax. Would you add this sum to the forced loan?'

"It is at this point that helpful advisers become somewhat involved. The objections raised are quite reasonable; but try and put them into practice and suggest a better way of coping with expenditure. There you have some of those vague, half-baked ideas of which the public is so fond."

General Montholon went to see the Grand Maréchal to tell him about his visit to the Governor. The Emperor spoke to him about it later. Montholon inquired whether the Governor would consent to give money in return for promissory notes signed by the Grand Maréchal, in view of the fact that he was no longer able to issue bills of exchange. Since Mr. Baring had sold out, he had nothing left. They would prefer not to draw on Mr. Holmes, because they didn't know him, and because Sir Hudson had said that his business was in poor shape. Either the Empress Marie-Louise or Prince Eugène would be applied to for further funds. If the monies were not paid, the Emperor would sign a promissory note. Sir Hudson replied that he didn't want to have to pay the money quarterly. The treasurer had difficulty in meeting his commitments at the end of each month. Nevertheless, he would send Mr. Ibbetson to see Count Bertrand in two or three days' time.

General Montholon mentioned Dr. Arnott and said: "The Emperor would like a French doctor. He leaves it to the King to choose one for him. Let the Ministry suggest one or let Desgenettes or Larrey be consulted. In short, permit them to send a kindly man, at the very least. The Emperor will be satisfied with that, and he will accept him. He spoke with contempt of the three who had just arrived from Europe, and was peevish about the Grand Maréchal. Sir Hudson Lowe said that there had been talk of having him replaced by D[aru?], who wanted to come. The French Government had no objection to sending him. Had this request been made two years earlier, we would now have all that we could wish for. The two cooks would arrive shortly and he had been told to expect lots of books as well as other things."

The Emperor had begun to read a book about English jurisdiction, written by a lawyer who had been sent to England to study the question. This book confirmed the Emperor in the opinion he had always held about England. Compared to ours, their legislation is barbarous. Over there everything is done for the upper classes, while with us everything is done for the people. There the people are of no importance; only the riff-raff is arrested. It is for the same reason that they have press-gangs, which is a matter that only touches the rabble.

Montholon's servant asked him if it were true that in France common soldiers could become generals; that soldiers were decorated and that they weren't beaten, saying: "If that is so, why don't the peasants become soldiers instead of tilling the soil?" The English are beginning to realize, as a result of their Army being in France, and of the ideas that their soldiers and peasants have picked up there, that a big difference exists between their institutions and ours.

January 29—After having to wait for some time, the Grand Maréchal was shown in to Napoleon. Marchand told him that the Emperor had not been well during the night, and that he was feeling weak.

"I am very unfortunate not to have a doctor," Napoleon said. "If Madame had only spent two, three, or six thousand livres, she could have sent me Vacca or Locatelli. Vacca was brought up in France and speaks French.

"But Antommarchi is uneducated. He is a most unreliable man. He repeats what he hears, which is a violation of the first principle of his profession. He puts Mme. Bertrand's back up. If I should say to him: 'How is the great Count?' he would at once repeat it in such a way as to make it sound an insult.

"Besides, it is his misfortune, poor man, to be an indifferent doctor. Also he fails to grasp any of the finer points of a conversation, and he doesn't know French. One day Mme. Bertrand said to Montholon, in Mlle. Raucourt's tone of voice: 'Well, well, since you have been taken into favor, we no longer see anything of you.' That remark was entirely due to Antommarchi, who sets her against General Montholon."

The alleged details of the birth of Gustave IV of Sweden are nothing more than a tale. The fact is, he was his father's son, just like every one else. If he had been the son of the Duke of Sudermania, as it is claimed, he would have said so. After all, Gustave reigned for seventeen years, and no mention was made of such a thing during that time. It is all a pure invention, dating from about 1809.

Charles XIII has always been looked upon as the son of his father. Gustave wanted children; and he made up his differences with his wife. Of course, it is just possible that his son may be the son of a peasant or of a servant, which is, after all, a thing that may happen to anyone. That is quite beside the point, and nothing but backstairs gossip. A man is nonetheless presumed to be his father's son. He has no less a right to his inheritance; he is none the less the legitimate heir to the throne. This was generally recognized, and so people assumed a divorce and another marriage, but there were no proofs forthcoming. Had it been so, the Duke of Sudermania would have admitted it. It's no more than a story told about Gustave, like all those told about the Emperor, which are completely without foundation.

The Emperor believes that Gustave was a better man than the book that he is presently reading would lead one to think. He undoubtedly possessed many qualities. The Swedes, by accepting money from all the powers, were very rash. In the same way Catherine the Great subjugated all her neighboring states with her gold. It was Gustave's madness which occasioned the loss of Finland and cost him his throne. Once peace had been made between France and Russia, Gustave was never able to make his own peace with the Emperor Alexander. The misfortunes to Sweden, which were a direct consequence of this, caused him to be deposed. Nevertheless, the Swedes should have transferred the crown to his son, who had a right to it. Had the Swedes done this, everything would have been settled, and Sweden would have been secure. At first, the Duke of Sudermania put forward as candidate a prince of his own house, which was right and proper. But the Swedes were prepared to accept a French general, which was absurd. They should have accepted the son of King Gustave. No one was more illegitimate than Bernadotte. If he doesn't succeed in marrying off his son, he won't reign. Russia would probably like to give the throne of Norway to Oscar, and that of Sweden to the son of Gustave IV, so as to weaken all her neighbors.

"Then you believed Mme. Dillon to have been an honest woman?" Bertrand asked.

"As honest as any other," the Emperor replied.

"Do you know exactly what Mme. Dillon was? For fifteen years she was the mistress of the Prince of Guémené. At the time of his bankruptcy, the whole of Paris turned against her."

"That is quite true, yet your memory is at fault. It is the first wife of 'le grand Dillon,' who was Mlle. de Rothe and mother of Mme. de la Tour du Pin."

"No, you are wrong; it was the Empress Josephine who told me this."

"She must have been mistaken."

"It was the mother herself who sent me a report on her circumstances, and that prevented me from giving her a pension of 12,000 francs. See on what slender threads a person's fate may hang! Had the Empress told me that it was not she, I would certainly have granted it willingly."

"But it is only a few months ago since I myself told you about it, and that you questioned me on the subject."

"Montchenu must have told the story to Montholon during his last conversation, when he went to see him to discuss the latest news."

January 31—Antommarchi asked the Grand Maréchal to come and see him. The Emperor had sent for him at one o'clock in the morning and had told him that he would have to make up his mind. He could stay on as a surgeon if he wanted to; however, the Emperor was writing to ask for another doctor, and he showed him what he had written. At the same time the Emperor also intended to ask for a surgeon. Most of the unpleasantness that he had had to endure had come not from his potions, but from Antommarchi's conduct. He would have to see General Montholon. If Antommarchi wanted to be in favor with the Emperor, it would be wise for him to be in Montholon's good books. He should pay court to him, and no longer visit the Grand Maréchal in the evening. Antommarchi would be allowed to pay him a medical visit every morning, for half an hour at most. The Grand Maréchal and his wife were leaving shortly anyway; also he was rude and would do well to express himself more politely [. . .]

Antommarchi said nothing in reply and the Emperor gave him until midday to make up his mind. The doctor then wrote a letter in which he requested the Emperor to send for someone of greater ability than he, adding that he would remain at St. Helena until that person should arrive.

The Grand Maréchal advised him to act quite differently. The Emperor was not asking Antommarchi to do anything against his conscience. He only asked him to make sacrifices, and these should be made. "I would make them, if I were in your position," Bertrand added. Everything possible must be done to please the Emperor. Antommarchi's position forced him to ask the Emperor for lodgings. In future the occasion for such quarrels would no longer exist. In fact he would only mention the matter to Mme. Bertrand privately, and even then, not for several days, as at the moment she was threatened with a miscarriage and must be spared any kind of upset. If the doctor remained at St. Helena, the Emperor would insure a brilliant future for him, the more so when he returned to professional practice. After all, he had only been at St. Helena for a year; he had behaved honorably and he should continue to do so. The doctor appeared inclined to act on this advice.

At one o'clock the Grand Maréchal went as usual to see the Emperor, who was asleep. Napoleon woke up at about three-thirty, and then they talked of one thing and another.

The Governor had had the railings removed. He came to see them and to offer the new house. Montholon made three requests: 1) that the railings should be removed and a wall built at the bottom of the park; 2) that shutters be put on the windows; 3) that lodging be found elsewhere for the captain for two months, by which time there might be more news.

The Emperor wanted to go out, but the weather was bad.

"If the Emperor Alexander takes Constantinople," he remarked, "he will threaten India. It is impossible to say whether or not his activity over towards Persia is intended to frighten the English and to keep them quiet while he moves on Constantinople. The English ask for nothing better than to clear the passage to India, which is their lifeline. Possibly they will take Egypt for themselves. France will get nothing. If England is able to arrive in time, and if she can put a fleet into the Mediterranean that is capable of landing 100,000 men at Constantinople—25,000 Dutch, 25,000 English, and 50,000 French troops—it might be possible; but you will see, it will all boil down and be settled quite differently."

That evening Dr. Antommarchi said that at two o'clock he had sent his letter to the Emperor. He had rewritten it with the help of General Montholon, who had told him that he had behaved extremely well. The Emperor expected the letter, and he would use him well. He would give the Doctor all that which he had formerly had at Florence, possibly more. The Grand Maréchal was much surprised to learn of Antommarchi's action.

"He will soon be leaving. He will have benefited from the situation. He says that fundamentally one is forced to be a slave here; that he prefers a little more happiness and peace of mind to honors; and that he will write his book in Europe."

CHAPTER TWO

February 1821

February 1—At midnight Mme. Bertrand called for assistance. Dr. Livingstone went to see her and gave orders for her to be bled. Dr. Antommarchi took 4 ounces from her and throughout the night she slept heavily. During the day, Mr. Ibbetson brought the Grand Maréchal twelve thousand francs for expenses incurred during October 1820.

February 2—At nine o'clock in the morning Antommarchi again bled Mme. Bertrand and took another 2 ounces of blood. . . . The Emperor called on Mme. Bertrand.

February 3—Mme. Bertrand vomited throughout the day, and again in the evening there was repeated vomiting. . . . The Governor sent three newspapers that had been left by a passing ship. They were those of October 7, 16, and 17.

February 4—In the morning Mme. Bertrand had suffered from spasms and passed a clot. She ate some dinner at four o'clock in the afternoon and managed to keep it down, but during the evening she felt somewhat restless. At four o'clock the following morning she had further pains, and at five o'clock Antommarchi went to see her.

At ten o'clock Dr. Livingstone was sent for. At eleven o'clock she had violent pains which were accompanied by much loss of blood. Dr. Arnott went to see her at eleven forty-five and Dr. Livingstone at two o'clock in the afternoon. By then she was having a terrible hemorrhage that was plugged.

By that time Fanny was exceedingly pale and weak. She hovered between life and death until five o'clock in the afternoon, when she revived a little. Her mind was full of sad thoughts and she left final instructions for her children and Arthur. Then she had fainting fits, and had they continued, there was every reason to have feared the worst. Finally, at about five o'clock, she was delivered of the foetus without further complications; Fanny was out of danger. What a relief this was for me! Several times I had been to see my wife, concealing the fear that oppressed me. Was it perhaps to be the last time that I was to see her? Might I not have to reproach myself with her death? Montholon had not left the house while she was ill, and he went immediately to tell the Emperor of the good news. An hour and a half later the Grand Maréchal also went to see the Emperor. Dr. Antommarchi had told Montholon that Fanny was in a dangerous condition and that she would not survive.

February 6—Lady Lowe came with the Governor to see the New House. She sent for news of Fanny, who had passed quite a good day but felt very weak.

February 7—Admiral Lambert stopped his horse at the door of Mme. Bertrand's home, to ask how she was. The Grand Maréchal told Mme. Bertrand he had informed the Emperor of what Dr. Arnott had said, and that today the Emperor had remarked that it was impossible for her not to leave St. Helena, although the thought of it pained him greatly. However, he would see that she was well provided for, and he would do the same for the Grand Maréchal. There was no one of whom he thought more highly, though at times he had said unkind things about her. He thought that she would be well advised to go to Rome.

Fanny suffered a great deal, and had pains as though she were in labor. Dr. Livingstone and Dr. Arnott both paid her a visit, and she was delivered of the afterbirth. Every evening and throughout most of the night she was exceedingly irritable, ran a temperature, and had a violent headache. She was unable to sleep.

February 8—The Emperor had read some two hundred pages of *Paul and Virginia*. He talked to the Grand Maréchal about Bernardin de Saint-Pierre and Jean-Jacques Rousseau. "They both had much in common," he said. "They both professed a great love of ethics, and neither of them was at all admirable."

The Emperor had reckoned up the probable income of the heroine, Mme. de la Tour. She lived in a cabin with her daughter and an old Negro called Domingo, who tilled some twenty acres for them. The Emperor assumed that she paid the Negro something. She would have had a pension and possibly a few diamonds that she had sold. An income of about a thousand *écus* a year was what the Emperor attributed to her. Yet she ate off banana leaves, although tableware was very cheap. "What is the point of that man [the hermit] who lived all alone?" the Emperor asked. "A fine kind of happiness, that is! It's very boring to live by oneself" (the Emperor knows this only too well, even though he lives surrounded by people). "Suppose the man fell ill," he went on, "who would look after him? He cooked his own dinner. What did he eat? . . . The whole thing is absurd," he concluded, "and it gives people false ideas.

"Bernardin de Saint-Pierre was a bad man," the Emperor continued. "He married the daughter of Didot the printer and made her extremely unhappy. I once gave him twelve thousand francs, but that was all that he ever got out of me. But he received a lot of money from Lucien.

"Laplace was the first to say anything against Bernardin to me. He was unable to forgive him for having attacked the natural sciences. What Bernardin wrote about the tides and other things, in *Les Harmonies de la Nature*, was nonsense. If he had stuck to writing tales and stories such as *Paul and Virginia*, well and good. He did that sort of thing extremely well. But he should have left geometry and science, about which he knew less than nothing, alone. As for Jean-Jacques Rousseau, he was simply ridiculous. He played at being a parasite. He ate and slept at the house of Mme.

de Montmorency, who was a whore. He had his children sent to the Foundlings Association and refused to accept a pension from the King of England or from the Queen of France. He returned the game sent to him by the Prince de Conti, because he would have had to part with a couple of crowns.

"Surely it would have been the obvious thing for him to have lived on the income from his books like Voltaire, who was a much more reasonable person, and who became quite well off and was able to help other men of letters. Voltaire's fortune was the result of his own efforts, than which there is nothing more admirable. Of course, it has been said that he stole, but there is nothing to prove it, and personally I don't believe it.

"He loved money? Well, of course he did. That's obvious. Money means everything. Sieyès loved money, but he was nevertheless an honest man and quite incapable of taking any. It's all so simple."

February 9—Mme. Bertrand was a little better this morning, though she still had a terrible headache. General Montholon called on her. Thirteen days ago the Emperor was reading a book written by a French lawyer, on English legal administration. The Emperor spoke to Bertrand about it.

"He explains everything very well, indeed," the Emperor said. "I knew nothing whatever about the subject. We are so keen to learn Greek and Roman history, and yet we know next to nothing about England, which is on our doorstep. The truth is that we don't know England at all, and a book of this kind will make it better known.

"Through reading this book I have been confirmed in the opinion I already held on the subject of the English aristocracy," the Emperor said. "In England, everything revolves around the upper classes. Everything is done by and for them. Whereas in France, everything is done for the sake of the people. It is members of the English aristocratic families who make all the laws, because all the most important institutions have been founded by them. They hold most of the important posts. No one complains at the way in which the law is administered, because it is only there to keep the rabble in order. It is highly improbable that a member of one of the great noble families would be condemned.

"Parliament is a fine institution, and an honor to England. It is the only thing that will survive. There is, legally speaking, no such thing as freedom of the press in England, but on account of Parliament the English can afford to laugh at the censorship, so freedom of the press does, in fact, exist."

Another time, the Emperor had been thinking over the achievements of the Egyptian Commission. He said to the Grand Maréchal: "The Egyptian Scientific Commission accomplished nothing. Denon, alone, did quite as much as they. He arrived there with a fixed plan and he carried it out. The Commission had not even been able to reach a decision on whether the 'waterless river'[1] would reach Alexandria. They barely recognized the fact that the Nile had seven mouths. They didn't succeed in clearing up a single geographical or historical point. On the Island of Mercury and in the Nubian Desert monuments have been discovered that are in as good a state of preservation as those of Thebes. Yet there is no mention of them in either Herodotus or the works of any other historian.

"Then how," Napoleon asked, "did such cities come to be built? They would appear to be holy cities, which, after all, implies some form of established art, as well as a great nation. Were those countries formerly made fertile by rain? Could there possibly have been some form of revolution in nature since those days?

"I believe that a powerful race once existed in Central Africa. Who destroyed those cities? Why is it that nothing is known about Abyssinia and the interior of Africa? This is inconceivable, for it would seem to have been so easy. Egypt should be the starting point of any expedition into the interior. If the African Society in England had had the money, it would soon have remedied this, but it appears that they lacked the necessary funds.

"The first step would be to explore Abyssinia and become familiar with it. To make this possible, it would at first be necessary to send out ten different people. Some of them to travel via Egypt, while others passed through Suakim—why have we no resident agent at Suakim? It is a place through which all caravans pass on

[1]On modern maps known as Wâdi en Natrûn (Valley of the Lakes). The Wâdi was formerly a distributary of the Nile. See Carte générale de l'Egypte; Dépôt général de la guerre, 1807. (Napoleon's own map.)—Translator's note.

their way through Africa to Arabia. It could also be reached from India, by sea. Once on the spot, there would be plenty of information available. Then it would be possible to join one of the caravans passing through Suakim on its way to Timbuktu.

"The world is old," the Emperor continued, "but mankind is young. Everything tends to prove this because it seems those ancient ruins are of no greater antiquity than Biblical history. The idea that the Chinese are a much older race than we are appears to have been abandoned. The Chinese didn't calculate the ecliptics for as far back as has been asserted.

"The Egyptian Commission has been preparing a large infolio on the Zodiac of Dendera, but it now seems that Visconti had already proved it to be modern. . . ."

February 10—Mr. Ibbetson came today and brought two months' money owing from the previous year, which amounted to twenty-four thousand francs. He also brought a draft of the receipt to be used for the quarterly payments. After having examined the proposed form of receipt, the Grand Maréchal said that, of course, it was purely a matter of form, and a thing that could easily be rectified, but in the receipt as it stood, the name Napoleon had been used; whereas he, the Grand Maréchal, was unable to refer to the Emperor other than with his full titles. Sir Hudson Lowe apparently did not wish to return the papers in which this question had been raised. Obviously, it would be better not to refer to the matter again, and it was to avoid doing so that the Emperor had suggested that he use an assumed name. As a result of this the Emperor dictated another draft form of receipt, together with a letter to Mr. Ibbetson, one to Mr. Baring, and another to Prince Eugène.

The Governor told General Montholon that the new house would be finished the following week, and that the furniture for it would arrive from England in March. He offered to have some planting done, or any other small things carried out that might be wished. He would have the stables built wherever they were wanted. He also sent over two newspapers of October 22 and 29.

February 11—The Emperor made a few alterations in the letters he had dictated the previous afternoon. He was not well during the night.

He had to send for the doctor in the evening and again in the morning. He suffered pains in his spleen and in his kidneys. Everything was happening just as he had predicted that it would. Certain almost imperceptible things had already arisen to alter his health for the worse, and they would ultimately carry him off. He felt weak and frequently quoted Lusignan [Voltaire]: *To look again on Paris, I may no more pretend.*

Then the Emperor would say: "I shan't last out the year, or another year, at the most."

He has been reading more of Virgil's poetry. The Emperor prefers things that are genuine and well written. Lebrun disliked the style of Jean-Jacques Rousseau.[2] He thought it affected. According to him, Bossuet was a model of good French prose. The Emperor has been reading the third volume of his *Egyptian Correspondence*. In it are several letters to General Dugua that explain many things. "Furthermore," said the Emperor, "it makes very fine reading, and when posterity rereads this correspondence, it will be able to quote many pages of history."

Napoleon read out one or two more of his letters to the Grand Maréchal and then made him read the letter he had written to the Grand Vizier from Alexandria, after the Battle of Aboukir. This was the letter of which mention had been made to explain the evacuation of Egypt, but which, surely, could in no way justify it.

"From the first day of reaching Alexandria," the Emperor said, "I wished to negotiate. I had already written to the Grand Vizier. It is always advisable to negotiate. It gives one a means of learning what is going on, and it slows down any preparations for war. Furthermore, I had agreed to all the proposals that had been put forward, except the evacuation of Egypt, which could have been placed under the rule of the Sublime Porte by paying tribute to the Turks. I was prepared to agree to almost anything in order to keep Egypt. There exists a confidential letter from General Reynier, written probably to the Directory. It is surprising that it has not been published among all the English documents; probably no one read it."

2Charles François Lebrun: third Consul after 18 Brumaire.

February 12—Napoleon had made himself familiar with the details of the Battle of Maida, fought by General Reynier.

"The Army was far too much dispersed," he commented. "With a large body of men, that is the surest means of being unable to oppose a resistance anywhere. By splitting up armies into groups of forty thousand men, as so often happens, and as was done under the Directory, there ceases to be an army. Fortunately, there were fifteen thousand men assembled for the Siege of Gaeta who were ready a few days after the Maida incident, and they forced the English troops to re-embark.

"There is one curious thing to be found in the English version of the Siege of Gaeta. A two-piece gun battery protected by a tower on Cape Licosa, in which were twenty-five men, was attacked by the *Pompey*, a ship under the command of Sidney Smith, a frigate mounting thirty-eight guns, as well as another frigate. They fired broadsides from four hundred feet and almost exhausted their ammunition. The battery kept up an uninterrupted fire. Finally, although its strength remained intact, negotiations were started, and the battery surrendered.

"The battleship had forty cannon balls in its hull and its mizzen-mast snapped off; a lieutenant, a midshipman, and five seamen were killed, and there were thirty wounded. After the second shot had been fired, the mounting of one of the guns gave way, and it could be fired only by leaning it upon the gun port. All the mountings of the carronade on the frigate *Hydra* were put out of action and had to be repaired at Malta—all this damage was done by a single gun!"

February 13—The Emperor has read a few pages about Murat's landing at Naples, after Waterloo. There was a ten-page proclamation written by him. The Emperor recognized the kind of straits in which Murat had found himself.

"The whole thing was sheer madness," the Emperor said. "Murat landed at Naples with only twenty men. He didn't even wait for the escorting ships of his flotilla to come up with him. If, upon his return from the Island of Elba, the Emperor had been able to have everything on board the *Inconstant*, he would have done so, for there are so many hindrances and unforeseen events that can happen at sea. He would have greatly preferred to have had a single, more powerful ship that could have transported everything at once."

February 14—Mme. Bertrand is still very ill. The Emperor had the Grand Maréchal read aloud the chapter on Egypt written by General Menou, then he dictated a few corrections. The article on General Menou in *Victories and Conquests* was a libel on Menou, and appeared to have been written under the influence of General Damas. The article on General Kléber was very poor. He received much praise, yet at the same time, the transactions of El-Arisch were severely criticized. This article may possibly have been written by General Soulier.

February 15—Mme. Bertrand is somewhat better. The Grand Maréchal reread the remarks in the chapter on General Menou. They are very fine. The lessons in warfare given to the English for their landing technique will not be wasted on them. The Emperor would be unwise to have *The Eighteenth Brumaire* printed.

Napoleon spoke of the way in which his family property had been administered, and of the way in which everyone's estates should be handled.

"The first, and most important thing for happiness," he said, "is never to incur any debts. The second is to spend no more than two-thirds of one's income. A man who isn't well off with an income of twelve thousand francs will never be rich. One should cultivate tastes in proportion to one's income—and like to have his servants well paid." Napoleon affirmed that it would be possible for him to live on twelve thousand francs a year even now, although he admitted that it would not be easy.

"It is most important," he continued, "to live in surroundings suitable to one's means. Should one only have an income of 12,000 francs, it would be advisable to live at Châteauroux or some small provincial town, where one would be socially prominent. And yet," he enjoined, "don't think that it would be possible to spend the winter in the country, on that money. To be really comfortable there, one would have to be more affluent. Furthermore, no matter where one lives, social intercourse is a pleasant form of relaxation in winter.

"With an income of twenty to thirty thousand francs a year," he said thoughtfully, "it would be possible to set up in a city such as Lyons, Marseilles, Bordeaux, or Rouen. With fifty to sixty thousand francs a year, Paris becomes possible. Of course one can live in Paris on twelve thousand francs a year, but it means privations and at the very least one would have to take lodgings in the Marais quarter.

"What's the craziest form of expenditure?" Napoleon asked. "Why, to indulge a passion for building. It's even worse than laying out gardens. The house and garden of Malmaison were no better, possibly less so, for having had millions spent upon them. It is very doubtful whether Grignon was much improved by the huge sums Marshal Bessières spent on it. If it had been kept just as it was, without any kind of building upon it, he might have spent quite as much money maintaining the estate in the condition in which it was found.

"Women's clothes," continued Napoleon, "are a quite ruinous expense, and a very bad investment. It is enough for a woman to be clean and decently garbed. I'm not speaking of the Court," he interpolated, "which is quite a different matter. After all," he went on, "what does it matter if your wife wears a shift made of linen or of lawn? If you are alone she won't dress up for you. Therefore, she only dresses for others, which is sheer coquetry or a matter of pride. It is possible every day to invite two or three friends in to share one's dinner, which is much the best form of entertaining. There should never be any formal dinners or parties. No one will thank you. It is merely a form of pleasurable self-satisfaction. It's quite enough to give one big party in a lifetime, when marrying one's daughter. Never otherwise.

"In my family," Napoleon continued, "it was a matter of principle with us not to spend money. We never bought anything that wasn't strictly necessary, such as clothes, furniture, etc. But we spent practically nothing on food, except of course such groceries as coffee, sugar, and rice, which didn't come from Corsica. We grew everything else. The family owned a communal mill to which all the villagers brought their flour to be milled, and they paid for this with a certain percentage of flour. We also had a communal bake-house, the use of which was paid for in fish. The wine was vintaged. The milk was brought to us, and the goatsmilk cheese; even meat from the butcher was never paid for in cash. Instead we had an account with the butcher, and in exchange for our meat, we gave him the equivalent in sheep, lambs, goats, or even oxen. The main thing was not to have to part with a penny. Money was very scarce. It was a tremendous undertaking to pay cash down.

"There were two olive groves in Ajaccio. One belonged to the Bonaparte family and the other to the Jesuits. Since then they have increased considerably. It was the custom in those days for the near relatives, such as uncles, aunts, first cousins or grandfathers, to come and collect their supply of olive oil at the time of the harvest. On Sundays, which was the day on which the peasants brought their goats, cheese, milk, and other produce into town, there were great junketings which, in winter, lasted all the next day and the next. In summer we gave presents to the relations of all the things that wouldn't keep. But no one thought of buying a present. That would have been looked down upon.

"The family also vintaged its own wine. It was a point of honor with my family," the Emperor said, "that we had never bought any bread, wine, or oil. 'Never,' old Uncle Lucien would boast proudly, 'never has the Bonaparte family bought bread, wine, or oil.' I remember some Genoese cherries that were extremely good. I don't think that I have ever eaten any others that tasted quite so delicious.

"We also bought macaroni and noodles, although they were made at home, as well."

February 17—Napoleon is not well. He is unable to eat any meat. This morning he tried some arrowroot and found it very good. It appears that the English have recently flooded all Europe with this product.

February 18—The Emperor went out for a drive in a carriage. The tackle came undone, and the coachman had to cut the traces. The Emperor was in a rather bad mood and waited anxiously for news.

February 19—The Emperor was in his garden when Marchand showed him the picture he had just finished of Longwood. The likeness of the Emperor was less good than in some of the previous pictures he had done, because the Emperor had ceased to dress, and Marchand had got out of the habit of seeing him other than in his dressing gown. Marchand would have liked to have sent the drawing to his father.

It is rumored that the Emperor may be sent to England. But he thinks that under the circumstances the English will not wish to be rid of him.

"France and Italy are in much too great a state of unrest for England to be able to dispose of me," the Emperor remarked. "The English have a Bill of Parliament which enables them to do what they like. They could keep me on a very large estate; there are many such in England. True, I could then escape more easily than from here. Yet it is a much more feasible idea than Belle Isle. A safe place could not be found for me so close to France, not one where I could be interned and yet enjoy a certain amount of freedom, as I do here; that would be most unwise on their part. They cannot hand me over to the Congress of Aix-la-Chapelle without my consent, which I will never give.

"It is obvious that in England the free press has succeeded in arousing about one hundred thousand citizens into making an appeal to Hunt, which shows that it would be quite impossible to have a free press in France; the government wouldn't last a day. If one hundred thousand men unite, who can withstand them? Who could hold out against thirty placards posted up every morning?

"Only the aristocracy is unchanging and in a position to laugh at liberty and at freedom of the press. Which is why I sought to create an aristocracy. I worked at it for fifteen years, and if today there exists a certain amount of stability in France, it is due to that. It would be a European disaster if the English aristocracy were to disappear; if it were handed over to a London mob.

"Only a republic could now give France the freedom and the energy that she requires. The Figaro and fools of Paris and of the universe are only interested in the gaiety and wealth of Paris and of the capitals. I saw this during the Terror. When I asked the extremists of the Convention where they thought they were going, what they hoped to accomplish, and how it would all end, they replied: 'It will last as long as it can; in the meantime let us make merry, for tomorrow, if need be, we die.'

"Everyone had accepted the thought of death. It was present every day, before our eyes. They had grown used to the idea. Marat and most of those who had played a part in the Revolution were determined to kill themselves. Marat had chosen suffocation as the easiest form of death.

"While we were in Egypt, Joseph heard the men of the Manège, Lamarque and Andreossi, congratulating themselves on our reverses, which they thought would surely overthrow the Directory and bring the Manège into power. Then they would enjoy power as well as the money and amusements of Paris, for a time, at least.

"That is where Tom, Dick, and Harry always lead to. Yet who can resist them? They have ability, a passionate intensity, and nothing to lose; so they stop at nothing."

February 20—The Emperor considered the Aeneid much inferior to the Iliad. He told Bertrand:

"Homer must have been to war; all the details of his battles ring true. On every page can be found the very face of war. The night before the Battle of [omission in the text], I felt as though I were again on the eve of Jena or of Austerlitz.

"There is the same nervous tension at the approach of a great undertaking. The emotions that stirred Homer were those with which all soldiers are familiar. The timing is always right. It is the very picture of truth itself.

"The Iliad covers only forty days, whereas the Aeneid lasts for years. In it there is no unity either of place or of incident. The Siege of Troy should have taken three weeks. The city had an entire army within its walls that the Greeks had never beaten. This army had all its equipment and resources intact, and it had forced the Greeks to raise the siege. Then, in the course of a single night, the town is captured and sacked. It would have taken at least three weeks to have burned a city like Troy. The burning of Moscow lasted for two weeks; for the first four or five days, I was able to remain there. The sacking and burning of all large cities takes about the same length of time. The plundering of Rome by the Barbarian hordes lasted for a week.

"How does Aeneas learn of the Fall of Troy? It is summer, when the nights are short, and he has fallen asleep. In his dream he sees Hector. The noise does not disturb him. He goes out on the terrace and sees the flames. He leaves the city. He returns. He has time to go a considerable distance, and all in the course of a few hours. It's utterly lacking in common sense. By comparison with Homer, Virgil is an amateur.

"The brick gates had to be knocked down, according to Virgil. With what? How long did that take? The whole thing was the work of a few hours. Troy was a large city with a great many gates. Merely to go from one gate to another would have required a certain amount of time. An army doesn't thrust into the center of a capital city in such a fashion. The Palace of Priam alone should have withstood a siege of several days. There is no house, however small, that cannot be defended by a hundred men, especially today when projectile weapons are so powerful, and which could not hold out for at least twelve to twenty-four hours. While a king's palace, big, solidly built, and defended by stalwart Greek soldiers, was consumed in a couple of hours! The general doesn't exist, however brave or however stupid, who would dare to make such an attack.

"No doubt Virgil is a good writer, that is a matter I refuse to discuss, as I don't know Latin. But the composition of this second canto, which is supposed to be the masterpiece of the whole poem, lacks plain common sense. It may be said, of course, that Virgil was not a military man and that all this had no bearing on the essential beauty of the poem. To which I would reply; then why does Homer do it differently? Why in his works, does one always find the necessary passage of time; the probabilities, events, and all the details that go hand in hand with an act of war? It is impossible for Homer not to have been a soldier. I don't believe the stories that are told about him.

"The chapter on the loves of Dido is not beyond criticism. Was Aeneas married or not? What did he mean by the torch of Hymen? Was he a married man or an adulterer? His conduct with Dido wasn't very pretty. That alone would have sufficed to make a poem. Virgil should have stopped there.

"The tale of the wooden horse was absurd. How did they manage to pull that contraption inside the walls of the fortifications? Apparently it was done by a handful of heroes. If one took the trouble to calculate the probable weight of that tremendous machine, all the wood and iron that went to build it, and the men it contained, it would be seen that its weight would have been enormous, and that it would have taken a week and much strength and ability to have got it into the city, and then to have transported it for a mile. Of course, it could be said that the silly tale of the Trojan Horse was not invented by Virgil, but was a popular legend. Nonetheless, there is nothing of the kind to be found in Homer."

February 21—The Emperor had some turtle soup for lunch and felt quite well after it. Some of the soup was sent over to the officers mess. The Grand Maréchal had been reading Carnot's correspondence. The Emperor wrote in the margins of several of the letters that they were false, and written after the events.

"It is annoying that a man should allow his character to be tarnished by false documents," he remarked. "Lies serve no good purpose. It is true, of course, that the book doesn't carry Carnot's signature, nor has it been published under his name. Yet he hasn't disowned it. It was published with his consent, probably by some friend of his, with the intention of giving him a character he doesn't possess. One must be truthful, and I have never received any such letters. They would appear to have been written by a stupid yet honest man. After receiving the first one, I would have gone up to Carnot and said: 'What the devil do you mean by writing to me like this, M. Carnot? Am I in need of tutelage? You see me two or three times a day, and yet you write me balderdash like this. I have better things to do.'

"He would never have done it again. He was very pleased to be made a Count. He was an honest man, but he needed money and he would willingly have gilded his fortunes. Not only did he not seek to teach me my business, but he was very respectful to me. He was continually asking my advice, not only for the sake of having my opinion, but to call attention to himself. He was frequently unfamiliar with new systems, ideas and precedents, and he would ask: 'What does that mean?'

"Lafayette had a spurious letter printed in which it transpired that he didn't want to become a Senator; which was quite untrue. In the first place I never received any such letter, furthermore, there was no foundation for it. I never had the least intention of making him a Senator. Lafayette wanted to be one, would have been delighted. He didn't play up to me much because I didn't give a damn for him. I had no respect for him, and I paid him little attention.

"What could be done with a man who still clung to the ideas of 1789, according to which rebellion was the first duty of all? How, with such principles, could a government be reorganized? If rebellion was the primary duty, why, then, did he march on Versailles against the sovereignty of the people?

"Although Lafayette didn't pay court to me, he did to my brother Joseph. He was perpetually to be found in his waiting room. I only saw him once, when he wanted the estates to which he laid claim, at Cayenne I believe, returned to him. As he was asking for something that was against the laws of the country, I was unable to grant his request. Lafayette had destroyed his own fortune during the Revolution. He now wished to retrieve it and to leave it to his children. Everybody has children to be settled in life; and one doesn't write in such a fashion to someone who has it in his power to dispose of everything."

Bernadotte's letter is false. This is obvious if one takes the trouble to compare the dates. At that time Sweden was still negotiating with the Emperor through the medium of the French Consul in Dresden, and a sovereign does not use such a tone when writing to another while negotiations are in progress between them. If the Emperor were in England, there would be no need to put all this in writing for, in the course of a private conversation with Lord Bathurst for instance, he could demolish with a word all this dubious correspondence. A writer who knew his job, who could write up such a conversation and get it published, would suffice to put an end to this flood of spurious documents.

There ought to be a man of letters among the Emperor's entourage. Either Arnault or General Denon would do; who could exercise his profession and find glory enough in that. Mme. Montholon had already written to her husband on this very subject: "None of you know how to write. Yet you are placed in an amazing situation. You should note down all that you hear. You ought to keep a diary. It's most important."

Curriculum Vitae. Biographical Sketches—"I was born in 1769, and I left Corsica in 1778," Napoleon said. "It was in either August or September, I don't well remember which.

"Joseph and I were together; Father was taking us to school in France. Madame drove in the carriage of M. de Marbeuf. Such a procession of carriages made a great impression on me. We spent our first night in a poor inn at Bastia. An old man came into the room and laid out mattresses on the floor. There weren't enough to go round. Then on the second day the three of us went down to the harbor, where we embarked. We arrived at Marseilles. While we were passing through Villefranche Father remarked: 'How stupidly proud we are of our country. We speak grandly of the Main Street of Ajaccio, and there in a single French town is a street every bit as fine and broad.'

"We were both entered as pupils at the school of Autun. Joseph was supposed to have remained there to finish his studies, as he was intended for the Church. M. de Marbeuf had promised him a living worth a thousand crowns, as soon as he should have become a subdeacon. This was a fine thing as it would have put him on the way to fortune, and yet cost nothing. It also opened up a career to him, but Joseph wouldn't hear of it; he liked women too much. He protested no matter what arguments were used, continued to show a great repugnance for the ecclesiastic state, and absolutely refused to give in.

"At the end of two months, my father had obtained a scholarship for me at the Brienne Military Academy, and I left for there in the company of M. de Champeaux, who had also succeeded in entering his own son at the same school. M. de Champeaux was a gentleman from Autun. He was a fine man, of middle age, who treated me as though I were his own son. So far as I can recall, I must have reached Brienne before the end of December, though it may even have been in November. I know that the weather was uncommonly fine for the time of year, so it may have been during the St. Martin's summer. I don't remember much about our arrival at Brienne. One day, in the middle of winter I was much surprised to find ice in my water jug. 'Oh,' I exclaimed, 'who has been putting glass in my pitcher?' Everyone laughed and made fun of me. Then the supervisor came up and reprimanded the children. 'Why do you make fun of Monsieur?' he asked. 'He comes from a country where there never is any ice. This is the first time he has ever seen any.' 'What,' they cried, 'do you mean to say that there is no ice where he comes from? Dear me, how very odd!'

"I remained at school," Napoleon continued, "until 1784, when I left Brienne to enter the Ecole Militaire in Paris. One of the fathers of the Order of St. Francis of Paula conducted four pupils together, to Paris. We crossed the bridge of Lesmont and spent the night at Arcis. I saw that town again during the 1814 Campaign. We went on to Nogent and then by evening we were in Paris, where they accompanied me to the Latin quarter; then we were taken to the Ecole Militaire.

"The first night of communal life was horrible. The whole tone of the school was quite different from that of Brienne. The classes were under the command of four officers who wore the Cross of St. Louis, and of eight sergeants who were very high-handed and military in manner of speaking. Imprisonment was the accepted form of punishment. Cadets were treated as though they were officers. I was then extremely young, being only fifteen years old. I only remained at the Ecole for a year, possibly somewhat less. I was immediately placed in the mathematics class for those intended for the Artillery. I passed into the Ecole Militaire second from the bottom.

"Among the young pupils with whom I had traveled from Brienne to Paris was, I think, Ville-sur-Arce, an uncle of Marmont's. I was intended for the Regiment de La Fère, then in garrison at Valence. Upon leaving the Ecole Militaire, I think that I went to see General Rossi, who wanted to show me Paris, the Opera, etc., before I left the city. I arrived at Valence in 1785. I went there with Des Mazis, the one attached to the State Furniture-Repository, who had been received with me. At Valence, in the officers mess, there were two tables for lieutenants. One was more expensive than the other, as it was intended for officers who were well off, and cost sixty-five francs; the other cost only forty-five francs. Des Mazis wanted to sit at the first table, so I felt that I had to do the same. We were very well looked after. Also at the same table was Sorbier, who was rich. He was the son of a surgeon attached to the Invalides. He had an income of twelve to fifteen thousand livres, a gig, and three or four carriage or saddle horses. At the second table were Lariboisière and Phélipeaux, who was a small, rather insignificant officer, who was killed later at Acre. The fourth was, I believe, Pecaduc, who served in Austria, was taken prisoner several times, and never applied to me to be sent back to France. The Austrian Emperor mentioned him to me. He is at present in command of the Remount Depot. A good man, but of small ability.

"I look back with pleasure on my stay at Valence. I was accepted by the officers. I was then sixteen years old. I dined and lived well. Shortly after my arrival there I was invited to make up a game of reversi. I sat down to play with four women, one of whom was the Countess de Tournon. I lost twelve francs, and at the end of the game the Countess tried hard to make me take them back. I was scandalized, and refused to do so. 'But my dear boy . . .' the Countess said. 'Madame,' I replied, 'I have not the honor of belonging to you.' I put the twelve francs down on the table and left the room. No one talked of anything else for the rest of the evening. All the officers highly approved my attitude. Count d'A . . . asked Mme. de Tournon to explain to him just what had happened. He too approved of my conduct. I had played and lost. If she had lost, I would have taken her money, therefore it was only right that I should pay my debts. Mme. de Tournon forgave me, saying that I was little more than a child, that obviously I didn't understand the game, and that I had lost because I didn't have a proper grasp of it. I had been pressed into playing, and I had done so only to be obliging.

"One night the call to arms was sounded. With some difficulty, the entire regiment was got under way in twenty-four hours. There had been trouble at Lyons. The Regiment reached the city and marched through it. It was a fine turn out, all complete. The Regiment was quartered in the suburbs, because the city of Lyons enjoyed the privilege of not having troops quartered upon it."

Napoleon then transferred to another regiment, and in 1787 he was at Auxonne. He was still there in 1789, when he learned of the events that had taken place during the night of August 4, which caused a great stir. Rulhière, who had a sister living in Paris, received details from her. He was made to stand on a bench near the church and read her letters aloud; they excited great interest.

Old General du Teil commanded the Regiment. He was an excellent artillery officer, with a sane outlook, and the first to say that an artilleryman's greatest merit lay in being able to bring two guns into action; the scientists of the Corps, the officers in command of the munitions dump and the artillery parks, could not be compared to an officer who knew how to lead his guns into position, who could direct their fire quickly and accurately, who knew how to handle his gunners at such a critical moment, and who could hold up a column. That was the really brilliant part of the job. The genuine artillery officer was a man who could bring into position eight guns, and order them to take aim and fire accurately, and at the right moment. This was the most important, the most difficult, the thing most noble and most to be respected in the entire profession. A general of artillery was a mere nobody. There were, of course, some generals like Drouot who knew how to lead thirty guns into position. But they were rare. Most of the really competent artillery officers, like Sorbier and Dommartin, came from light artillery regiments.

In 1789 Napoleon obtained some leave and went to Corsica. General Rossi, who was really not an army man at all, and who had formerly been a lieutenant colonel in a Provençal regiment, had been appointed Lieutenant General in command in Corsica. It was he who approved of, or who organized, the Corsican National Guard. One day General Rossi told Napoleon that he had just received instructions that might be of advantage to him. He had been ordered to organize three or four battalions of the National Guard in Corsica. He had also been told that he might take officers from the regular army for the ranks of major and adjutant. These officers would retain their rank and pay in their former regiments, and Rossi thought that it would be a good thing for Napoleon to apply for command of one of these battalions. Napoleon agreed with him, and obtained command of the Ajaccio Battalion. In the meantime, Paoli had returned to Corsica. He was given a triumphal reception at Bastia. Before he became a major in the Corsican National Guard, Napoleon had been granted an extension of leave which enabled him to wait for the National Guard to be formed. He had been advised to do this very nicely, by his superior officers. These older men played the part of fathers to the younger officers and did everything in their power to help them, never losing an opportunity of obtaining a favor for them.

Napoleon doesn't clearly remember through what combination of circumstances he found himself in Paris in 1792. He was there, however, on August 10. Shortly afterwards he went to St. Cyr to fetch his elder sister, whom he accompanied back to Corsica, under the protection of his National Guard uniform, and it was then that the adventure of the black cockade, recalled in an article in the *Edinburgh Review*, took place at Toulon.

It was after this return to Corsica that the expedition of Rear Admiral Truguet left for Cagliari. Admiral Truguet had neither an artilleryman nor an engineer with him. The Town Major of Corsica went with the expedition, and he would have been glad if Napoleon had been in command of the artillery. But Napoleon had refused on one pretext or another, as he thought that the expedition appeared badly organized. At this time the incident took place in which a monk was hung by two sailors, and later four or five sailors were killed fetching water from the town. The whole thing was patched up through the mediation of Napoleon and his uncle Lucien. At about the same time the Sardinian expedition got under way, in which Napoleon commanded his Corsican battalion as well as the artillery, and in which Villantroys and a captain of the regiment, a fine man and the soul of the undertaking, also took part. As a result of these events Paoli, who had been ordered to appear at the bar of the Convention, and who was afraid of being guillotined if he went, decided to raise Corsica and place it under the protection of the English.

Napoleon had several conversations with Paoli, who had been much impressed by his qualities. It was on this occasion that he murmured several times: *Tu sei un uomo di Plutarchia, un uomo antico*. [Thou art a man of the age of Plutarch, a man of antiquity]. Napoleon refused to share Paoli's ideas, and a conference was held at the Convent of [omission in text]. He felt that it was in the interests of Corsica to remain a province of France. Corsica was a small and very poor country that could accomplish little on its own. It had already benefited immensely from its union with France. It was of necessity a dependency, and if it were a dependency of Genoa, Tuscany, or Sardinia, it would be much less to the advantage of France. The Corsicans had now become citizens like the French; they were no longer subjects as in former times. If there were excesses and guillotinings in France, they must be prevented from reaching Corsica, which would be an easy matter. Napoleon stuck firmly to his opinion, and in the morning he left the Convent with his uncle Lucien, whom he had taken with him. His brother Lucien urged him to make absurd denunciations, and Lucien himself denounced Paoli to the authorities [at Toulon]. Whereupon Paoli issued orders for a march to be made on Napoleon's house. Madame had time to flee, and I believe that she went to Corte. Napoleon asked Representative Lacombe-Saint-Michel for a corvette in which to go and get her, which was granted. Napoleon boarded the corvette [chebeck], went and got Madame, and took her and all his family on board the corvette to Toulon.

Before this incident, Madame had been in close touch with Paoli, but under the circumstances all further relations with him were broken off. Sometime later, Napoleon rejoined his company, which was then stationed at Nice. There he found Dujard, who had become a colonel. He lived in Dujard's house, but didn't take his meals with him. The events of May 31 and of the Federalists took place. They were then sent to join the Army of Italy and to supervise the delivery of gunpowder. Napoleon saw General Brunet who was in command of the artillery. He had as first aide-de-camp, a certain X [omission in text], who was later guillotined with him, and who at that time ruled the roost, and was general factotum. (He had formerly been an ordnance officer in Corsica, where Napoleon had met him. Having picked up the knack of assessing positions in mountainous country, X played the oracle and gave himself airs). Napoleon had been quite taken with him for a few hours, but in the end he became bored, as he found the man puffed up and superficial, and he dropped him. "Go and see him since you already know him," old Colonel Dujard said, "he might be of use to you."

"Fear of seeing the ammunition run out, for it was said that supplies were being held up by the people of Marseilles, was the reason for deciding to send an artillery officer to hurry them up," Napoleon explained. "So they chose me. The Representatives gave me my orders and a hundred and fifty thousand francs. I bought a post chaise and left to speed up the delivery of gunpowder, bullets, ammunitions, etc., that were required by the artillery services.

"I left for Avignon and Marseilles, and as I carried some weight with the People's Society, my mission was successful. All the letters I received expressed satisfaction; everyone seemed pleased with me. I gained confidence and in pursuance of my activities, I went on to Lyons and Auxonne. When I saw that everything I did was approved, I went on to Paris. It was during this trip that I wrote the Avignon pamphlet on the Federalist War called: *The Conversation of a National Guard.*

"Upon my arrival in Paris, I learned of the betrayal and surrender of Toulon to the English. The Committee of Public Safety had asked the Ministry of War for an artillery officer capable of directing the siege. The Artillery Division of the War Ministry had at its head a certain third lieutenant by the name of Boiteux, who was assisted by a commission composed of a lieutenant from each of the artillery regiments, which amounted to seven or eight lieutenants in all. This third lieutenant was, therefore, in charge of all the officers of the Artillery Corps. He was down on the older officers, though he did single out several whom he knew to be patriots and whom he happened to like. I went to see this officer to report and to receive further instructions. He suggested sending me to Toulon. I was made a major on the spot, which, as I was a captain, surprised me very much. I replied in the affirmative.

"I received the appointment and was given traveling expenses. Therefore, in the course of a single night I had received my appointment, my orders and money, and I was off!"

I think that it was while Napoleon was at Auxonne that an 8th Artillery Regiment was formed. This caused much movement and promotion throughout the entire Artillery Corps. Napoleon had been made a captain, and it was in this capacity that he had gone to Grenoble, I believe. He reached Toulon and went to find Carteaux. Artillery officers in Toulon wrote to Paris: "Since Bonaparte arrived everything is quite changed, and things get done." It is well known that the Artillery always has great *esprit de corps* and many connections, so Napoleon received plenty of support from the officers in Paris who had appointed him, and who saw that he was being successful.

Lyons capitulated. When Napoleon reached that part of the Army that was actively engaged, he found an old artillery general in command of Lyons, who had acted very well, for him. It was felt that he ought to be left in command of operations. "Quite right," agreed Napoleon, "but I have been ordered here by the Government to take over the command. Either I command or I leave." The old general, who was a good man, but who no longer posessed the necessary ability, and who was able to judge Bonaparte's capacities, wisely stepped down and retained some kind of honorary command; indeed, Representative Gasparin, who was very pleased with Napoleon, immediately grasped the difference between the two men, and wouldn't let him go. Thuriot fell in with this arrangement, and the rest is history.

"At Auxonne, I had my younger brother Louis with me. I paid for his lodgings and we ate with the officers. I think that I only paid forty francs for him, although most of us were paying sixty francs. Probably the innkeeper didn't ask any more. Louis wore the regimental uniform, but without epaulettes, instead a small silver stripe; this was the result of an arrangement made with the colonel of the Regiment. I sent him to the School of Mathematics. Lombard gave him lessons. I didn't pay him, but I paid for private coaching. This created a good effect in the Regiment. They all thought highly of me for the care and money I was spending on my brother's education.

"There was a difference of about ten years between us. Louis was very handsome, and women were always taking a peck at him. One day while playing cards, he lost four francs. I allowed him only six francs per week or per month for pocket money, so I advised him to say to the woman who kept his lodgings: 'Madame, would you care to go halves with me?'

" 'Done,' she replied; after that he regularly won thirty or forty sous. It was common knowledge that she cheated."

February 22—Napoleon, who for several days has not touched either bread or meat, was able to eat a little meat today.

The Grand Maréchal had been reading Bernadotte's correspondence: letters among which were those inserted at the end of his *Mémoires*.

"For a good Frenchman, there are things in these letters that ring untrue," Napoleon remarked. "He claims that the Meeting at Abo brought on hostilities with Russia, but he is wrong. The Meeting only took place after the Battle of Witebsk. He says that he should have demanded the Auland Islands. Whereas, what he really should have asked for was a principality for his son Oscar.

"It was Bernadotte who set the Swedes against me. They had chosen him as a means of drawing closer to me. It was the charm of Désirée that got him the appointment, besides the fact that he was Joseph's brother-in-law. The Swedes were greatly surprised at the tone Bernadotte adopted, as well as to discover that he was so ill disposed towards me that he forced them to make a complete break with France. The thing that made Bernadotte adopt this strange attitude was the fear that Russia and England would run him out of Sweden, whereas he knew that he could count on me. He knew that whatever I did I would never hustle him off his throne. That no matter how badly he behaved, he had only to send Désirée, Julie, or his son Oscar to see me for the matter to be settled. As a matter of fact, he openly declared himself against France only after the Battle of Lützen, when he knew for certain that Austria was fighting us, and that he had nothing to risk.

"I well understand the institution of commissions of the peace as they exist in England by comparing them with those of Corsica. Suppressive institutions are never established by any one man, but are constituted by events. Anyone who possesses an income of twenty-four hundred francs a year puts his name down on the commissions of the peace. This is a relic of feudal times. All nobles or landowners are justices of the peace. There are as many justices of the peace as there are landowners, which shows it to be a relic of feudalism.

"In Corsican jurisdiction, the leading men in the country head all law-giving institutions. They are more interested in them than anyone else. Therefore it is the most important men in Corsica who settle all disputes, adjust differences, and, in a word, see to the public peace."

February 23—Napoleon had read several articles in the dictionary of natural history. "It appears," he commented, "that furse is the best type of pasture to grow on artificial meadows. Everyone says that it is better to put sheep out to graze than to keep them in sheepfolds."

The thing that characterizes the Emperor's type of mind and . which is its most outstanding feature is his ability to focus his attention on a single idea, to examine it from every angle, abandoning it only after he has exhausted the subject and when—according to his own typical expression—he has "grasped it by the head, the seat, the hands and feet, and by the head." In other words, when he has sucked it dry. Not giving up the subject until he has thoroughly examined it from every angle. Finally, it is not unusual for him to spend ten or twelve hours on a single idea [. . .]

February 24—In the night Napoleon vomited all he had eaten during the day. Two days previously he had declared that whatever he had accomplished—at the Siege of Toulon, while in command of the artillery; with the Army of Italy; at the Saorgio Incident; at the Laono Meeting; on the 13th Vendémiaire and while in command of the Army of the Interior; in the early moments of his Italian command; at the Battles of Millessimo and of Montenotte; at the capture of Tortone; at the crossing of the Po; at the Battle of Lodi —had not made him feel superior to other men.

"But the moment in which I became conscious of the difference there existed between other men and myself, and when I had a glimpse of the fact that I was called on to settle the affairs of France, was several days after the Battle of Lodi.

"I had already returned from Crema and Melegnano and had entered Milan, since Melzi [d'Eril] had arrived at the head of a deputation from Milan to offer me the keys of the city. I had just received the order from the Directory to march on Naples with part of the Army, and to hand over the Italian command to General Kellermann.

"I was pondering over this letter, while in my mind's eye I saw the Army of Italy lost through this senseless order, and I was drafting the letter that is to be found among my correspondence in which I said that one bad general is worth two good ones. At the time, I was sitting by a fire laid on the hearth in a corner of the room, and although the weather was mild a fire had been lighted. Apparently it had been raining. I was absorbed in my thoughts, when Melzi was announced.

"From this precise moment dates my conception of my own superiority. I felt that I was worth much more and was much stronger than the Government that had seen fit to issue such an order; that I was better fitted than it was to govern; and that the Government was not only incapable, but also lacking in judgment on matters that were so important as ultimately to endanger France. I felt that I was destined to save France. From that moment I glimpsed my goal and I marched directly towards it."

Today Napoleon felt weak and barely spoke. The Grand Maréchal mentioned a pamphlet to him that he had just been reading. It was about a judge who had resigned four or five years previously in Corsica. He had wanted all the judges as well as all the Corsican police to be French. He proposed that two courts should be set up, because in winter communications throughout the country were difficult, and this would have halved the costs of litigation. Indemnities had to be granted to witnesses who were sometimes obliged to travel anywhere up to a hundred miles to attend court. The Corsican judges could have been found posts in France.

"But that wasn't the real point at issue," Napoleon said. "Corsica is a ruinous expense for France. She costs her three or four millions a year; under the system proposed in your pamphlet, she would have cost seven or eight million francs. In my day, Corsica cost France nothing. It is a matter that should be tightened up.

"Corsica is a nuisance to France; but there she is, like a wen on her nose. The Port of St. Florent is on the doorstep of Toulon; if France doesn't occupy it, the English will. M. de Choiseul once said that if Corsica could be pushed under the sea with a trident, it should be done. He was quite right, it's nothing but an excrescence.

"The writer of the pamphlet speaks airily of the potential wealth of Corsica. That is something that remains to be proved. Corsica is and always has been a poor country. In the first place, the people are destitute. On the whole, it is rather an odd thing that the coast-line should be uninhabited. There are no inhabitants at the junctions of any of the rivers, not even at that of the Liamone. Ajaccio shouldn't be where it is; the city lacks water. There are no villas, no small estates near it.

"What caused this? Was it due to the cruelty of the Barbarian hordes that the coast remained uninhabited? Or was it because the population was poverty-stricken? Was it perhaps owing to the lack of water in summer? Possibly it was because during the heat the temperature was much more agreeable on the slopes of the mountains, which is quite true. Just calculate how many shoes Corsicans buy, and then it will be plain just how rich the country is. No doubt the production of Balagnia oil and Corsican wine could be doubled. But that wouldn't make the country rich. It would barely be sufficient to provide shoes.

"The pro-English Corsicans used to say: 'You can't make anything out of the French. They don't want your oil, wine, figs, and raisins, as they have plenty of their own in Provence, whereas the English need all those things. The English would come and settle in Corsica for the sake of the wonderful climate. They would acquire vineyards and buy up all your fruit.'

"In Corsica," Napoleon continued, "there were no established political parties. No Royalists, Imperialists, or Republicans. There were, in reality, only two parties, the pro-English and the pro-French. The present government of France can have only one aim, to throw out the pro-English party. But how can it do this when it is 'English'?

"If it were possible to expel from Corsica all those who were in the pay of England, it would be a very good thing. The English paid out large sums of money to their Corsican supporters. Under the Empire, the Peraldi family retired to Tuscany. Peraldi, with Pozzo di Borgo, had formerly been a deputy to the Legislative Assembly. It was he who received orders to arrest Lafayette. Since then he threw himself heart and soul into the pro-English party. The English paid him an income of twelve thousand francs. Very wisely, he realized that there were only two parties in Corsica, and as the pro-French party, therefore the Emperor's party, had obtained a decisive victory, he decided to sell his property in Corsica and retire in Tuscany. In this he was very wise. It would have been a good thing if many others had done the same. Pozzo di Borgo received between twenty-four and forty-eight thousand francs a year from the English.

"In Corsica," the Emperor went on to say, "there were several fine buildings, houses or structures that had been put up more or less by accident. The Jesuits built a lovely place near Ajaccio. A Bishop had built a seminary at Bastia that was a huge place. Genoese nobles sent to Corsica as governors or commissioners, also did some building.

"For this reason Great-uncle Lucien upheld the Genoese cause, and maintained that it was more to the advantage of the Corsicans to be subject to Genoa. The commissioners sent to Corsica by the Genoese, had always been extremely rich. Genoa had been wealthy for a great many years. She never paid the commissioners she sent to Corsica, but she always selected rich men, who went there primarily to display their wealth. They would fall in love with a local girl or married woman, shower presents on her, and then build a house for her.

"Whenever I saw a very handsome house in Ajaccio or elsewhere, I would say to my old uncle: 'Who built that?' 'Oh,' he would reply, 'I'll tell you all about it later on.' He would then have his dinner and afterwards he would settle down to tell the story. Some Genoese noble had fallen in love with a woman and had either married her or kept her. He had then left the house to her family. That was the kind of thing that frequently happened with the Genoese, Uncle said. It would never happen with a Frenchman. A French noble would never come to Corsica and build.

" 'Yes, Uncle,' I would reply, 'but the French build roads, reclaim land, and put up barracks. They maintain a garrison here which means that the soldiers spend a great deal of money in the country. On the whole, the troops have made Corsica prosperous, and it is they who have kept her on her feet. Of course, the cloth for their uniforms and all their clothing and equipment, etc., is brought from Marseilles, and, so it seems, are things like flour and meat. Nevertheless, under certain circumstances, as when the winds were contrary or the foodstuffs failed to arrive, they were forced to take whatever was to be had in the country.' The Corsicans, Uncle Lucien among them, would then seize the opportunity to charge a good price for their beef. Wood is one of Corsica's main products, and a good deal of it was shipped to Marseilles.

"There were a great many Corsican officers serving the Venetian Republic. They would do their job, make their money, and return to Corsica with fifty or one hundred thousand francs and build themselves a house."

No doubt the Corsicans should be disarmed and severely dealt with. Though the Emperor doesn't think that they would take easily to being disarmed, and neither would French judges be sufficient. The French were too frank and open for the Corsicans, who are much more sly and clever. In Corsica there are also to be found such incomparable men as Castelli, who was President of the Court at Ajaccio and a completely honest man.

February 25—The Emperor felt better today. He was less nervous than usual. At 6 A.M. he drank three glasses of Burgundy. Then at eight o'clock he fancied a small glass of Armagnac as medicine, which was unusual for him. He then took some soup, sieved food, fried potatoes, and custard. He said that everything tasted greasy, except the custard.

"Old Arrighi, grandfather of the Duke [of Padua], whom I met when he was eighty-six years old, once said to me: 'Well, well, my house has been burned down seven times, and now they want to burn it down again.' That had been during the War of Paoli in 1793. Arrighi had belonged to the pro-French party. Despite that, Paoli, who had known him for years, took care of him and saw that his white hairs were treated with respect.

"In Corsica there were three kinds of aristocracy, the old nobility, the *caporats*, and the foreigners. There were not many of the old nobility, who belonged to the ancient feudal families of Corsica, such as the Colonna and the d'Istria. I lived in the house of a Colonna d'Istria when I was a major in the Corsican National Guard. I was given a large room in a great tower that had been preserved by the family at Corte as a symbol of their former greatness. While I was there I met an Abbé Colonna, whom I asked: 'Why was this tower not destroyed during the civil wars?' 'I don't know,' he replied, 'but it remained untouched.'

"Years later I made that same abbé, Bishop of Nice. He was a Jansenist, and when his family went to see him, in the hope of reaping some benefit from his new position, he sent them all packing, saying that he would give them nothing as he was keeping everything for the poor.

"The *caporats* were families who, in the tenth and eleventh centuries, had roused the whole of Corsica against the old nobility, and had sought to throw off their yoke. Among these were the Casabianca and the Arrighi. Finally, the foreigners were those who came to Corsica from the Continent; from Tuscany and Genoa, like the Bonapartes and almost all the other families that settled along the coast at Bastia, Ajaccio and Calvi, etc. In 1400 the Bonapartes were mayors of Ajaccio. At that time the location of the town was altered, and it was moved from the interior of the Gulf towards the exterior. Since those days, a Bonaparte has always held the office of mayor in Ajaccio. At Sazana there is a painting in which a Bonaparte may be seen signing the Treaty of Tuscany with Genoa, I think it was. Uncle was always telling everyone about it. Personally I have never given much thought to a piece of authentic parchment which on the whole amounted to very little, but the Germans made a great fuss over it. The King of Bavaria wanted absolutely to work out my genealogy, but I didn't give a damn."

On the subject of Sweden, as far as he can remember, the first time that an overture was made to the Emperor was at Donauwörth in 1809, while he was advancing on Vienna. The Swedes wanted the Imperial approval so that they would have nothing to fear from the Russians. The Emperor replied: "I have a lot of things to attend to, such as Spain and a new war with Austria. It would be better to wait and see how that turns out." "Oh," replied the Swedish envoys, "that business will soon be finished, it is certain to be a walk-over." The Emperor then advised them to draw closer to Denmark so as to make common cause against Russia. The following year Count Fersen arrived in Paris to offer his congratulations on the Emperor's marriage, and so far as the Emperor can recall, he then broached the subject of Bernadotte for the first time. "Since Prince Eugène is unable to become a Protestant,"

Count Fersen said to the Emperor, "would it be agreeable to you if we chose Bernadotte?"

It appeared that the Emperor had already advised the Swedes, or if not he did so then, to make the Duke of Sudermania regent for the King and to select the son of Gustave, who had done nothing to forfeit his crown, to succeed him. "In this way you will wind up all your affairs speedily and without trouble, whereas to change from one dynasty to another is always a tremendous undertaking," the Emperor told them.

It appeared that Bernadotte was strongly seconded by Desaugiers, then Swedish Consul General in Paris. He was one of the patriots of the Manège, where he often went, and it was there that he had met Bernadotte. He swore that everyone would be very pleased. The Swedes thought that they were gaining the protection of the Emperor Napoleon, and they cherished the hope that this would make it easier for them to retake Finland. On the other hand, they had some scruples about proposing Bernadotte. They asked the Emperor whether it would suit him; and whether he feared that this might offend Russia, by giving rise to a misunderstanding and by interfering with Russian policy. Later they were amazed when they saw Bernadotte adopt and carry out their own national policy towards Russia and England. Bernadotte had decided that he could never recover Finland, and so he had turned towards Norway, which was a fortunate thing for Sweden.

What caused Bernadotte to take a stand against the Emperor was his knowledge that no matter what he did, the Emperor would not go against him, whereas he felt that he himself had everything to fear on the part of Russia and of England. Also, Bernadotte didn't openly oppose the Emperor until after the Battle of Lützen . . . when he judged the Emperor to be finished. This attitude of Bernadotte's made it quite correct to assume that the letter written by him to the Emperor, and bearing the date of August 15, was false and that it had been written at some later date, which was nothing less than an impertinence, because up till then Bernadotte had been negotiating with Napoleon, and had therefore used, as he should have done, the tone of a negotiator.

After the Russian events, the Emperor should immediately have concluded a treaty with Ferdinand of Spain and sent him back there. Then he should have recalled the three hundred thousand seasoned troops he had in Spain. Added to what he already had with him, the Emperor could then have sent Marshal Soult to march on Danzig at the head of one hundred fifty thousand men, while he himself could have marched on Warsaw with two hundred thousand troops, and all would have been over. Had Prussia declared war, the Emperor could have given Silesia to Saxony and carried the King of Württemberg to Berlin. Nothing more could have been done in Spain; what was needed there was a man. Although Joseph was highly educated, he was quite incapable of ruling. . . . He never paid any attention to the Emperor, or flattered the generals, because he considered himself to be their equal, and therefore in no need of them. It was at the Meeting at Erfurt that Marshal Lannes had ridden in the carriage of the Russian Emperor, who had kept the flies off him for fear that they should wake him. . . .

"Well, you see," Alexander had said to the Emperor, "I need generals, and so I tame them. You are lucky not to have to depend on them." Napoleon told Joseph this and added: "So you see, the Emperor Alexander has more sense than you. Whenever he recognizes a man of merit, he ·tames him and flatters him. He is far from thinking that he is as good as his own generals, even though he was born to the throne."

"I made a great mistake," the Emperor said, "in leaving Joseph in command of Paris in 1815. Through his weakness all was lost. To recall this, nowadays, must pain him very much. Since it was he who was in command, he shouldn't have permitted Marmont to parley. Had he been there when the Emperor arrived, all would have been over. But just because he saw a regiment of Hussars or Cossacks making a detour around Paris, he believed that the road to Neuilly was cut off. Yet by putting up a show of resistance with his troops and by retreating with the last troops, what possible reason had he to fear a regiment of Hussars? It must, however, be said that Clarke the Minister of War, who was also a soldier, and others besides, had all given him the same advice.

"Lord Castlereagh covered himself with ignominy through making public the scandal of the Queen of England. To have let the country run the risk of revolution, all for the sake of an old hussy of fifty-two! And, of all things, the English Government, usually so staid . . . !

"The French Court had found itself in trouble for having made public the affair of the queen's necklace. And yet, that was a very different matter. It was done out of a feeling of generosity, of a form of indignation that had made the King and Queen of France wish the whole incident to be publicly tried and judged, according to accepted legal formalities. They could have had Cardinal de Rohan tried as a Grand Officer of the Crown. Parliament had covered itself with shame by failing to find the Cardinal guilty. A man who had been convicted of having tried to sully the Queen, of having aspired to sleep with her, who had believed that he had received a rendezvous and a promise. Yet the person of the Queen should have inspired only respect. It may truthfully be said that the audacity of the Cardinal had grown out of the very low opinion which he held of the Queen. Since others had been intimate with her, why not he? [sic]"

At the time of Moreau's trial, Cambacérès wished to prevent the Emperor from taking the matter before the Court. "You will suffer for it. Remember the affair of the Queen's Necklace," he had said. "Hand Moreau over to a military commission consisting of generals, men whom you can trust and who have an unimpeachable reputation in the Army, men who are firmly attached to the Revolution. As soon as it has been proved that Moreau saw Pichegru and George, he will be lost in the eyes of the public, and that will justify everything. In this country, when one once comes up against the mentality of Paris, of the salons, it becomes impossible to prove anything because THEY don't wish to believe it." In the middle of Moreau's trial, Cambacérès reminded the Emperor of this.

February 26 or 27—Napoleon went out in a carriage in the morning, but during the day he didn't feel at all well. A ship had arrived from England bringing the news, so it is said, that Queen Caroline had been acquitted, and that Lord Castlereagh and Lord Liverpool had resigned from the Cabinet, which was to be reformed. Upon hearing this news Napoleon made the following comments:

"It will have been popular feeling and popular demonstrations that frightened the aristocracy, rather than the innocence of Queen Caroline, that brought this about. Nothing is more cowardly than an aristocracy that is afraid, nothing more terrible than when it has nothing to fear. I have seen the oligarchies of Venice and of Berlin. Nothing could have been more insolent than they when they were on their own estates, yet when the nobility of Berlin feared the rage of the populace they invoked me and sent messenger after messenger posthaste to me. What do these oligarchies want? It is easy enough to see that they fear Revolution, and that they think they will be beaten up by the mob. Yet when prosperity returns they are just as insolent as before. . . .

"Should I regain my former powers, may misfortune fall on the heads of the Berlin nobility! The wretches have ignobly pillaged Huningue and Alsace, so I have been told. I would have their castles burned and razed to the ground.

"There are no people more impudent or more demanding than the Swiss. Their country is about as big as a man's hand, and they have the most extraordinary pretensions. They wanted, indeed they pretended to demand, that we restore their manufactories. They demanded this as though it were a right. 'But I don't want to,' I told them. 'You are joking. What on earth do I owe you? Why should I let French manufacturers suffer, so as to develop yours?'

"It looked as though France were under some obligation to Switzerland. Yet what did France owe the Swiss? From time immemorial it is the Swiss who have taken French money, with which they have built towns and châteaux. During the Revolution they owned a great many of the mansions in the Faubourg St. Germain.

"It seems that for the past few years, despite bad times in England, their cotton mills have increased considerably, and that from 1805 to 1820 the number rose from four or five millions to eighteen millions. This was because the English first captured the trade in Russia and Northern Germany, then in Italy, and finally in the American colonies. England will probably wipe out the textile works in Saxony. France should adopt a protectionist policy on this matter. She should forbid the importation of all cotton goods and even of all yarn, importing only raw cotton. Surely in Paris, even today, there are people who will try and impose some such prohibition? The trade interests of Bordeaux, Nantes, and Marseilles are in opposition to the interests of the manufacturers.

"Who can tell what will become of your children? What the future has in store for them? Who would have thought that when M. de Choiseul united Corsica with France a little gentleman from that island would one day take the place of Louis XV and prevent his family from reigning? Although the Bourbons have since returned to the throne of France, for a time I had quite got rid of them and they had lost all hope.

"It was I in reality who upheld the Directory. Without the victories in Italy, the Directory could not have been maintained. It may be said that without me, the French Revolution would have been wiped out on the 13th Vendémiaire. Any other general would have been defeated.

"The Convention was saved by the forty pieces of cannon on the Sablons. When I asked General Menou: 'How many troops have you at your disposition?' he replied: 'Five thousand.'

" 'That's not many. And what about your artillery?'

" 'There are forty guns.'

" 'Where are they?'

" 'On the Plain des Sablons.'

" 'Take a detachment of one hundred fifty to two hundred fifty men,' I ordered. I went out immediately and called the cavalry officer. A handsome young man, a squadron leader, appeared; it was Murat.

" 'Take two hundred horse,' I ordered, 'and go at once to the Plain des Sablons and return with the forty guns and the artillery park. They must reach here. Use your swords if need be, but bring them. You will be personally responsible to me for this. Now go!' I had put him on his mettle.

"Murat replied that he would return with the guns. He came back at the same time as a detachment of the Le Pelletier section which, seeing the detachment of cavalry, had not dared to do anything. With those forty guns I was master of the situation. Although the placing was a simple matter, it required tact. To be able to put two guns into position, one has to have done it oneself."

Berruyer commanded the patriots of '89 in the Dauphine blind alley, which was the critical point because there was shooting from the windows. Barras, who would have liked having the honor himself, pushed Berruyer to the fore and wanted to heap on him the credit for the outcome of the day. He behaved quite well on the whole, but after all, it was General Bonaparte who was in command. As soon as a decision had been reached General Bonaparte was called on to appear before the Convention. He came in, with his pock-marked face, and was received with cheers. Fréron, who had known and appreciated Napoleon at the Siege of Toulon and who wished him well, made a motion proposing that Napoleon be given command of the Army of the Interior; the vote was passed by acclamation.

On the 18th Fructidor, Napoleon also had a great influence over events. Without the happenings of that day, the Counter Revolution would have continued.

"It was the name Napoleon Bonaparte that united the Corsicans. General Eliott had written to say that he was no longer master of the situation in Corsica, that they were all out of hand. I had my house at Ajaccio, which had been turned into a barracks, rebuilt, and Madame returned to live in Ajaccio. Mouron, the contractor for the fortifications, was put in charge of the reconstructions, which cost me eleven hundred thousand francs, and the building was completed in six months.

"Upon my return from Egypt, I stayed in that house with all my staff. There was a big gallery, and I had a dinner laid in it for forty people. Everyone was quite at ease. I spent six or seven days there waiting for favorable winds. We had just come from Egypt, and everyone had felt cut off from the world during the crossing; accordingly, everyone found the country charming. 'But,' they would exclaim, 'what have people been saying about Corsica? The town is pretty, the houses are handsome and well built, the women are charming, and there is good food and good wine.'

"It was at the end of September, during the wine harvest. The grape was excellent. I sent basketfuls to my Guards, as well as other fruits and wine. Wine only cost two sols a bottle, and they drank a great deal. It was the season for pears, which in Corsica are admirable and make rare and delicious eating. The most famous hunters in the land, all of whom were peasants, killed two wild boar for us every day. 'Now is the time to show what you can do,' I had told them.

"Then I set the town in order. There was dissension everywhere, and the prisons were full. It was claimed that a conspiracy existed to bring Louis XVIII back to the throne.

" 'Are you quite mad?' I asked them. 'You and your conspiracy. Who the devil thinks about Louis XVIII over here? Do you imagine that you have any influence over the destiny of France or over European politics? You are too absurd.'

"By reason and ridicule, I managed to calm them down, and they were all much embarrassed. I brought some of them back and scolded the others on the stupidity of their conduct. I didn't dare go very far afield, because we were waiting on the winds and had to be ready to leave three hours after receiving the signal."

February 28—Napoleon passed a very bad night. He sent for the doctor at three o'clock and again at 5:00 A.M. The Governor sent over three newspapers, which said that the Bill of Parliament in favor of Queen Caroline had been passed by a small majority, and that it had then been withdrawn by Lord Liverpool. Our hopes and conjectures on the possibility of a new government wore us out. One hopes that Lord Grenville will be in the new Cabinet and that then we shall be moved from here. Mme. Bertrand has visited the Emperor; this is her first outing.

CHAPTER THREE

March 1821

March 1—When Bonaparte assumed command of the Army of the Reserve, he left the title of Commander in chief to General Berthier, as otherwise the Republicans would have taken fright. The post of First Consul was considered a civil and not a military one, and above all it was considered undesirable for the head of the Government to be a general. For this reason Napoleon never wore a uniform, but always dressed as a civilian, wearing the red coat of the city of Lyons. At that time great dinners were held at the Tuileries, in the Gallery of Diana; dinners at which two hundred guests were seated. The places of the most important people were indicated, while the rest sat where they pleased.

One day the First Consul had invited Lady Dorset, who was the wife of the English Ambassador, Lord Whitworth. She had retained her title of Duchess of Dorset from her previous marriage. On this occasion she kept everyone waiting for so long that Napoleon finally ordered dinner to be served and they sat down, her place remaining unoccupied. On arrival, Lady Dorset was forced to accept the slight insult of having to walk the entire length of the long Gallery of Diana. After taking her place beside the Emperor, she tried to make up to him. However he pretended not to notice her, and continued to talk to the woman sitting on the other side of him. Then, at the end of several minutes, Napoleon exclaimed: "Ah! so there you are, Madame!" Empress Josephine, who was always kind hearted, had greeted Lady Dorset, but the English were much put out that she should have made herself appear so ridiculous.

Mr. Fox having been invited to dine, his wife was presented to the First Consul, although there had been some difficulty about this, as she had not been presented at the English Court; possibly because she was a divorcée or for some other reason. Fox very much wanted his wife to be presented to Napoleon, but it had been impossible to approach the English Ambassador on the matter. Therefore it had been necessary to present Mrs. Fox through some other channel. Under the circumstances it had not been very hard to find a lady willing to introduce her. The English Ambassador would have liked to protest at her not being presented through the Embassy; but, as was pointed out to him, although it was generally accepted that people should be presented by the ambassador of their own country, in reality it was no more than a custom and not a matter of right. In any case, Lady Dorset probably would have preferred not to have presented Mrs. Fox. "No," the Ambassador had been forced to admit, "she would not have done it." "So," he was told, "it was a good thing you were spared the embarrassment."

March 2—Napoleon went out for a drive in the morning and again in the afternoon. He experienced great difficulty in digesting his food. For the past fortnight he has eaten no meat. He asked for a piece of toast dipped in gravy, and two pieces were brought to him, of which he managed to eat one. He said afterwards that he had had great difficulty in digesting it. "It was like the wedding feasts of Gamache," he said. After having made up his mind to shave himself, he commented that it was "like accomplishing one of the labors of Hercules. How exhausting!" Nevertheless, he rinsed out his mouth and finished dressing.

March 3—A ship put in from the Cape and brought a mail bag that came from England on board the *Repulse* [?]. This brig, which sailed from England at the end of October, had been believed lost.

Montholon had written to the Governor in the morning to ask for more newspapers. Sir Hudson had the *Morning Chronicle* up to November 15. There was still no change in the English Government. The Governor forwarded a case of books from Lady Holland, which contained upwards of fifty volumes. Among them were the nineteen volumes of *Victories and Conquests*. Ten volumes of Napoleon's *Correspondance inédite*, and the *Mémoires* of *James II*.

March 4—Napoleon has been reading the Siege of Toulon. "It's very badly described," he remarked to Bertrand. "There is hardly any mention of me. On the subject of the Army of Italy, next to nothing is said about the Saorgio incidents; obviously the authors knew nothing about them. The Italian Campaigns, which have been lifted from Jomini, are good. In that account I appear to them as a hero and a giant among men. The 13th Vendémiaire is good, and the honors go to Barras, which is as it should be; he was in command. Whereas the 18th Fructidor is less admirable. My addresses to the Army of Italy are badly reported, and the Champagne Campaign is very badly described. There is hardly any mention of Dumouriez; it is only a question of that idiot Kellermann, which is disgraceful. Dumouriez was a great man and one of our ablest generals. It is only just that this should be said of him. Of course, later he behaved badly, but that doesn't wipe out his previous services."

March 5—The Emperor has been reading the Egyptian Campaigns in *Victories and Conquests*. He told Bertrand that they are not badly described, even though they do not give the same version as the Emperor does of the Cairo events. The writer didn't make General Dupuy enter the Divan, but as he was on the staff of Dupuy at the time, it is possible that things did take place like that. On the other hand he makes no mention of the levy, or of barriers that were done away with. He doesn't know what caused the Cairo uprising. He omits to say that the leading men in Cairo had already approached the Emperor, and that they were with him at Gaza. The Battle of Aboukir is well told. The account makes use of information drawn from English sources, and it situates the anchorage of the English squadron much further from the Island than was shown on Nelson's map. So the English are boasting again as usual: it wasn't such a difficult undertaking after all, to have passed between the squadron and the Coast. Probably their account of this battle is more exact than ours.

"I was only shocked to find," the Emperor remarked, "that [on the subject of the plague-stricken men of Jaffa] Desgenettes said that he had quarreled with me at a meeting of the [Egyptian] Institute, because I tried to make him say: 'if it hadn't been for the plague, the General would not have evacuated Syria.' He also said that I had not forgiven him the fact that he, Desgenettes, backed up by the Army, had mentioned the matter to me, despite the presence of two soldiers, etc.

"It is untrue to say that I ever had two soldiers stationed in front of my chair, or that any such discussion ever took place. All this is obvious. At the time of the evacuation of Egypt, Desgenettes told Wilson that a mysterious meeting had been held at the Institute, and that it had dealt with the question of the poisoning of wounded men at Jaffa.

"In Paris, when I came across this in Wilson's report, I should immediately have dismissed Desgenettes. I wanted to do so, but in my usual easy-going way, I agreed to his being made Chief Medical Officer to the Army. No doubt when the editor of this book asked him to explain just what the meeting at the Institute concerned, which he had mentioned to Wilson, Desgenettes produced this version, which had nothing whatever to do with the Jaffa inquiry."

The facts of the row with Desgenettes were as follows: Desgenettes told Larrey that the men were not suffering from the plague. The Emperor visited and touched the "plague-stricken" men at Jaffa only because he didn't believe them to have the plague. Upon the General's return, Berthollet told him that it had been most rash of him to pay such a visit. The Emperor had no business uselessly to endanger his life or to let the Army run the risk of being without a leader, without valid reason or genuine advantage. Napoleon replied that he had been assured by Desgenettes that the men were not sick with the plague. Whereupon Berthollet affirmed that they were indeed, there could be no doubt about it; Desgenettes had caused the Emperor to make a very grave and perilous mistake; if the General didn't believe him he could ask Larrey. Napoleon then sent for Larrey, who confirmed the fact that the men indeed were sick with the plague. Then Napoleon sent for Desgenettes; there followed a very animated discussion on the subject between Desgenettes and Berthollet, in which the Emperor took no part. Desgenettes was jealous of Berthollet who was a doctor and who, like Monge, dined with the Emperor. This mortally offended Desgenettes, who did not.

"The entire session of the Institute is untrue." Napoleon said. "There must be people still living who could bear me out. I never took any Guides with me to the Institute; that again is untrue. I don't believe there were ever any poisoned men at Jaffa. When we left there, all those with the plague were dead."

March 6—Mme. Bertrand went to visit the Emperor. He is sad, and has lost all hope of any change in the English Government. His health is growing worse. His stomach refuses to retain anything. He has experienced pain on both the right and left sides of his abdomen. He has been reading some French newspapers of the previous July, as well as some scurrilous writings forwarded by Lady Holland. He has read *Victories and Conquests* with great interest, although finding it devoid of talent. In the evening the Emperor went out for a drive in a carriage.

March 7—The Emperor went out for a drive in the morning. Afterwards he had a discussion with Bertrand on the subject of the parties of the Guelphs and the Ghibellines, which divided Italy from the twelfth to the fifteenth century.

The Ghibellines were on the side of the German Emperor and the aristocracy, whereas the Guelphs were for the Pope and the popular parties. The clergy were essentially of the people and opposed to feudalistic ideas, because to become a priest it was not necessary to be noble; it was a career that was open to men of every class. A great many popes have been of very humble birth; among others, Pope Gregory VII, who was the son of a hat-maker. Florence, Bologna, and Pavia were Guelph cities, whereas Milan and Pisa were Ghibelline.

Admiral Lambert would be greatly surprised if, upon returning to

England one morning, he were to find London in the hands of a mob barricaded against the cavalry. There are so many ships in the Port of London that it would always be easy matter to lay hands almost immediately upon two thousand guns. They could be served by five or six thousand sailors, all of them good men, as well as by the gunners. Should the Tower of London be captured and the people armed, it is probable that the Government would not long survive. Had the Emperor landed in London, he would have had the great advantage of having been able to set up a people's party in opposition to the aristocracy. It would have been easy to have founded a very powerful party.

The Governor, Sir Hudson Lowe, has been to see General Montholon. He said that he has no papers other than those he has sent over already. The Emperor has been reading a book on the Convention, printed by Le Normand.

"This book," he said, "is aimed at vilifying men of the Revolution who could still be of some use, such as Lanjuinais, Fouché, and Carnot. . . . It's a thoroughly scurrilous piece of work, utterly devoid of talent."

The English have had the iron grill removed and taken away, as at Plantation House. They are building a lodge for the Captain.

March 8—Mr. and Mrs. Russel, arriving from India, called on Mme. Bertrand. Mrs. Russel is of French parentage; her husband has been chief administrator of the State of Nizam, bordering on Golconda, which is the richest state in India. Mr. Russel is related to Lord Whitworth. The Nizam, who is a Mussulman, rules over five or six million subjects. He maintains an army of seven or eight battalions of infantry and several regiments of cavalry. He possesses an income of three million pounds, of which half is spent on maintaining the Army.

Almost all the officers are English and they are paid by the Nizam. Mr. Russel lived in Nizam as administrator for ten years. The capital, where he lived, has a population of two hundred and fifty thousand. The country and all the people are Indian. There are some Mussulman workers, but almost the entire population of Nizam consists of soldiers. There is no civil administration. Everything is military, even the legal administration.

Napoleon has been reading the Spanish Campaigns in *Victories and Conquests*. "On the whole, the book demonstrates the reasons for the War in Spain quite well," he told Bertrand, "but it fails to mention the protest of King Charles IV, which is an important point.

"King Ferdinand has behaved very badly. If anything should ever happen to him, he will have deserved it. He was exceedingly guilty. It was inadmissible for him to have written to the sovereign of a foreign power without the approval of his father, King Charles, or to have got married without telling him. It was I who saved him, for his father was furious and would have liked to have had him executed.

"Canon Escoïquiz and the Duke of Infantado are responsible for all the misfortunes of Spain. Escoïquiz especially. The *prince de la paix* was far from being a clever man. He should never have allowed a foreign army to cross the Pyrenees. He should have drawn closer to Portugal, and he should have been very suspicious of the enemy. A steel fist was what was required on the Pyrenees. The French Army should never have been allowed to cross them.

"Survival is the primary law, therefore he should never have introduced a French army into Spain. And then, how idiotic to have laid claim for himself to a principality inside Portugal! Or to have imagined that under existing circumstances a principality would have been tolerated in Portugal! He must always have foreseen the possibility of the death of King Charles and assumed that he might be forced to leave Spain. Therefore, he built up a personal fortune abroad. Unlike us!"

March 9—Mme. Pauer [?] and her husband paid a visit to Mme. Bertrand and expressed the desire to meet her and all the other inhabitants of Longwood. They expressed regret at not having called before.

Napoleon read the account in *Victories and Conquests* of the Wagram Campaign. He thinks it good. He would not have been in a position to write it up himself, because he would not have had access to the same information. He remarked to Bertrand:

"It is easy to see that the authors have had access to books written by the Austrians. They are familiar with their movements down to the least detail, which was something I never knew other than through guess work, or from what I could judge on the battle-field. They bring the strength of the Austrian forces up to 550,000, which agrees with the information I had and with what General Andreossy always said.

"According to both the writer and myself, the Battle of Eckmühl was the finest thing I had ever done. There was such huge dispro-portion of strength between the forces engaged. The army opposing me consisted of 180,000 men, while that confronting Prince Eugène consisted of about 60,000. When Masséna reached Eckmühl, he asked me where the enemy was. 'Over there, without a doubt,' I replied, 'Davout is there.' 'But how can you be so sure?' Masséna asked. 'Let me get down and fall on my knees. It is truly admirable, one can only bow down in admiration.'

"As a matter of fact, it was, possibly, the finest maneuver that I had ever carried out.

"The Battle of Raab effaced the defeat of Essling. It created a great effect on the enemy as well as abroad. It was the greatest service Prince Eugène ever rendered me. He behaved well. He came up without loss of time, which Masséna would certainly not have done. In the preceding campaign he had not followed Arch-duke Charles, but had remained behind to make money. Whatever should I have done had Eugène done likewise and had I found myself confronted by Archduke Johann as well as Archduke Charles?

"There is nothing like having friends in time of war, my dear Bertrand. One doesn't need many. Above all there must be friends. They take the place of so much else.

"Macdonald and the others were good while they were well in hand and under my orders. But at a distance it was a different matter. The same may be said of Masséna when he was in Portugal, where, for instance, Chabot had increased his dirty tricks. If Masséna had had Thiébaut for chief of staff, instead of Noguès or Reynier, he might have been successful. Eugène did me a great service at Raab. In *Victories and Conquests*, the writer says that there were 36,000 men there.

"Bertrand, were you in command of the placing of the battery that set fire to Vienna?" Napoleon inquired.

"Your Majesty sent me there with a general artillery officer, either Lariboisière or another, I don't recall which."

"The writer fails to mention your achievement. He barely refers to it. He describes the Spanish Campaign quite well. In the course of a single night, I embarked 200,000 men. How different it all would have been, had I not left the army at Astorga! Soult would then have attacked alone, as he had not sent for Ney to come with him. I had no means of knowing that the Austrians would be so late in making their attack."

At the time of the peace negotiations at Châtillon, the Emperor had wished to retain only Antwerp. He would rather have conceded Mainz. He knew quite well that he could always retake it when he wanted to. In the first place, Mainz was of importance only to Germany and not to England, who was the principal and most important power. Belgium, because of its coastline, was of more interest to England. England was blockaded by the Belgian coast. Their most direct and quickest means of communication with the Continent was through Belgium. The Channel ports and those of Belgium are the nearest to England and therefore represent the greatest threat to her. If Mainz were retaken after a period of several years, it would have been just as much use as at the time it was surrendered. But the same could not be said of Antwerp, where the Emperor had roads, bridges, docks, and locks that he would be unable to recover, as England would have destroyed them all. It was therefore very important not to let the enemy gain a foothold there, and to defer such a moment for as long as possible.

"In five hundred years' time, French imaginations will be full of me. They will talk only of the glory of our brilliant campaigns. Heaven help anyone who dares speak ill of me! It will not be well received. I myself am filled with emotion upon reading an account of these campaigns. All Frenchmen must feel courageous when reading them."

Mr. Gorrequer talked with General Montholon for two hours on the subject of the New House. He said: "Lord Holland has been spoken of as a possible Prime Minister. The Governor will then pay him a great tribute—wise man. The Governor is a schemer. The English don't want to keep the Emperor any longer, and yet they don't want to hand him over to the other powers. The Emperor may therefore entertain hopes of going to America."

The Governor sent the money for October.

March 10—Mme. Bertrand went to see the Emperor, who was most gracious to her. He felt much better and toyed with the idea of doing some riding. He hopes soon to leave St. Helena.

The Emperor believes that the English won't want to be rid of him. But that they would keep him in England on some large private estate, and that they would accept his parole not to leave the county in which he was living without the Government's permission. Otherwise he would be quite free. What have they to fear? They are well organized. What could the Emperor do, beyond writing to the Five Signatories, who would not reply to him? He can't see what the English have to fear.

If the Austrian Emperor were to write and offer him asylum in his States, and if the Empress would also write to him, then he would go to Trieste with no mistrust, so as to be with his wife and son. He would go there, for it has a government of honest people who do not favor assassination. Napoleon is loved and respected in Austria rather more than elsewhere, because he was more formidable to them than to others. He did them no harm and he had no wish to cause them to revolt. . . .

Possibly some form of court intrigue might raise obstacles. There might be some people who would have reason to fear the ascendancy that he or the Empress might have over the Austrian Emperor. Metternich might be afraid that his credit would suffer.

"All such questions are so complex that it is difficult to form an opinion. If I had the choice I would go to America. But the English fear for Canada, which is extremely pro-French, and my name must carry considerable weight there, as for the past twenty years they have heard a great deal about me.

"It would suit me very well indeed to live in America. First I would restore my health—then I would spend six months traveling about the country. Thirteen hundred miles of territory to be explored would take me some time. Among other places I would pay a visit to Louisiana; after all it was I who gave it to the Americans. I have been reproached with having sold it to them, but I would have given it to them for nothing, for with war on the way I could not have kept it, and then the English would have taken it.

"There is great indecision in Austria over my affairs. The reason being that Austria had to wait for the approval of St. Petersburg. Nothing proves more conclusively that Austria is no longer a first-class power. She obeys St. Petersburg. It is there that the fate of Europe is decided."

Napoleon worked the entire day. He was pleased and had hopes of finally being able to leave this miserable island. The Governor kills him. He isn't tired of his job, but he would be no loss to the devil.

Napoleon has been reading La Rochefoucault's book on America, but he finds little in it. The country alters so rapidly that one should have a more recent book of travel. A journey of two thousand miles over such country would be very pleasant.

Napoleon finished Pradt's book on the American colonies. He made a note on the commerce of Tyre, which had traded through India, via the Red Sea, and from there through the Mediterranean and not through the Persian Gulf.

"Upon our arrival in New York, I would have sent a messenger to my brother Joseph. The British Consul would have been sent for to come aboard ship, and we would have asked him to say nothing. Then a few hours later Joseph would arrive and we could have landed.

"We would have taken some of Joseph's servants. It seems that his house is situated on the banks of a river, at Trenton, twenty-five miles from Philadelphia, and fifty miles from New York. I would soon have gathered many French families around me. . . ."

March 13—Pierron intends to go into Jamestown, and during dinner he told the Emperor that a storeship had arrived from England.

"Oh," Napoleon exclaimed, "why did no one tell me this before? Now I can eat my dinner with a better appetite."

He sent for Montholon, who knew nothing whatsoever about the arrival of the storeship. The Captain also knew nothing about it. Mr. Darling arrived from town and said that it was quite true; the storeship had made the trip in seven weeks. It was said that the ship had left England on January 24.

At seven o'clock the Governor sent over the *Morning Chronicles* for November 27 through December 21. No change of Government. The French elections were not liberal. This news was a great disappointment to everyone, above all to the Emperor, who had flattered himself on better news.

"We have been building castles in Spain," he commented.

The Governor wrote Monseigneur Buonavita in the morning that a ship was available on which he could obtain a good passage.

Napoleon went for a drive in the morning and again in the afternoon, as on previous days. He is weak and depressed and makes no reference to the news, either to Montholon or to myself.

March 14—The Grand Maréchal went to see the Emperor at seven o'clock and remained in attendance. At three-thirty the Governor sent over some books bought by the English Government for Napoleon. There were in all about twenty volumes, which included Marbot's reply to General Rogniat; a volume of *Mémoires concerning the Empress Josephine* and the *Mémoires of Madame Rolland.*

The *Mémoires* about Josephine were written by Mlle. Lenormand. But she dares not let this be known, for there is little doubt that Prince Eugène would have her brought into Court, as she has made the Empress speak in a most improper manner, which was quite unpardonable. It is difficult to see the point of this book. Was it written to make money or to give Mlle. Lenormand some importance? It is not precisely a libel, because it contains a certain element of truth mixed up with a lot of untruths that are *blatantly* untrue, and this is sufficient to discredit the entire book. After all, things that are matters of history are so very well known.

The Emperor assumes that Madame de Château-Renaud, Mesdames Tallien or de Rémusat, or a personal maid Josephine had kept at Malmaison supplied most of the tittle-tattle; it is quite impossible for Josephine to have credited her husband [Beauharnais] with being in command of the Army of the Alps, when he never got any further than the Rhine. The writer doesn't even know the cause of his death: that he was accused of failing to relieve Mainz, that he handed in his resignation, and then was arrested and condemned.

"The writer appears to say that the Empress Josephine had as lover the secretary of Barras, who was an old man. In reality, the man was an insignificant adjutant on the Staff of General Bertrand, with the name of Charles. He had the face of a womanizer, and I had been forced to give him several lectures. It was in his company that Josephine crossed the Mont Cénis. I learned this from a maid who had been sacked for sleeping with General Junot, which Josephine had thought frightful.

"The writer will have it that Josephine made my fortune. Yet before meeting her, I already had the 13th Vendémiaire and the siege of Toulon to my credit, and I was General in command of the Army of the Interior.

"In her book Mlle. Lenormand has made out that Josephine and Mme. Tallien were aristocrats opposed to the 13th Vendémiaire, whereas in reality on that date Mme. Tallien was bandaging the wounded at the Convention, and Josephine and Barras were dining together.

"It was said that Josephine spoke to me about the Duke of Enghien, which is quite untrue. Like everyone else, she wept and said that she had spoken to me about it, whereas in actual fact she never mentioned the matter to me. She took no interest in anyone. She asked for nothing, not even for her own son. There was much that she might have done. . . .

"She was kind in the sense that she would have asked any one to lunch, even Mlle. Despiaux and the Raucourt woman. She gave freely. But would she have gone without something so as to have been able to give? No. Would she have sacrificed anything in order to help someone else? That is real kindness. She gave, but then she merely put her hand back into the bag again.

"I was wrong to have given her three million francs after the divorce. A million would have been sufficient. The rest was stolen and only served to enrich the people around her.

"Knowing this, while we were with the Army of Italy I opened her letters—as you know I am rather inclined to do this—and I found that she was sending bills of exchange up to three or four thousand crowns in payment of her debts. In other words, she was robbing me.

"So one day I said to her: 'Let's put an end to this. Surely you realize that you are making me look ridiculous. Tell me what your debts amount to and I will settle them?' But she had always been like that. Forever in debt, and forever denying or hiding them.

"I really loved her, although I had no respect for her, as she was far too great a liar. But she had something, I don't quite know what, that attracted me. She was a real woman. She had the sweetest little arse in the world. On it could be found the three Islets of Martinique.

"I had much more respect for Marie-Louise, though I loved her perhaps somewhat less than I loved Josephine. Frequently I would have liked to divorce her. Her conduct was not always above reproach, but she was very fond of me, and in return I liked her because she never wanted to leave me.

"The thing that displeased me most was that Josephine arrived at the Château de Marracq accompanied by Mme. Gazzani and Mlle. Guillebault, obviously with the intention of providing me with mistresses. This was the advice of some depraved old woman, Mme. Rémusat or another. When the Empress had played the part of the Rosière de Salency, it had its funny side—she herself was just the opposite. But in providing me with a mistress, Josephine hoped to keep me, and by such means, to prevent the divorce. Frankly, I didn't care for such conduct. For this reason I was very glad to be able to send Mlle. Guillebault about her business. As I had come across a letter from the mother to the daughter, which contained advice on how to seduce me, how to give herself to me, and then how to reap the benefit of the situation, I had been outraged at such infamous behavior, and I had sent her packing the very same day.

"To tell the truth, I only married Josephine because I believed her to possess a considerable fortune. She herself had said so, but it was not true. Also I wished to make myself appear more mature. Nevertheless, before our marriage I knew what to expect. Father Patrault had made me go and see a Deputy, a M. Emmery, who was a merchant living at Dunkirk, and who had settlers in St. Domingo. I asked him about Josephine's fortune. Emmery told me that it was not important. Her mother, Mme. de la Pagerie, whose only daughter she was, owned a plantation worth about 50,000 francs a year. The family was a respectable one and Emmery was authorized to draw between 20–25,000 francs a year at Josephine's request. In consequence, Josephine usually cashed a bill of exchange for that sum, either in Bordeaux or on him. The sum was always paid on the simple statement that the reserve had not been exhausted. Ten days before I had paid my visit to Emmery, Josephine had withdrawn 10,000 francs. Her first husband had been a Revolutionary general of gentle birth. On the whole, the marriage was an excellent thing for me. A good French family suited me very well, as I was Corsican by birth."

Mlle. Lenormand pretended that Bonaparte had consulted her. She also said that when they met he never spoke to her, but that as he knew her quite well, he always made her a little sign.

In the evening, the Emperor handed me Marbot's book, in which he had refuted the remarks of General Rogniat, and said:

"That is the best book I have read for four years. It is the one that has given me the greatest amount of pleasure. Marbot had no access to my own refutation of Rogniat, but I would be glad to let him have it for a second edition. He has expressed some things better than I did, he was more familiar with them because, on the whole, he was more of a corps commander than I.

"Then there are large sections in which he doesn't come anywhere near me; things that he doesn't know. For instance, the section on *Artillery* is much inferior to my own version. But when he talks about companies drawn up in a single row and of battalions formed up on three rows with three companies . . . there he is on his own ground. Invariably I agree with him, as he had succeeded in bringing me round to his point of view. In one passage he says that one can't be a corps commander to nine thousand men, but one can be their general, which is quite a different thing. In speaking of a corps commander, one means a man who enters into every detail and who knows every individual soldier.

"Throughout the book he never refers to 'the emperor.' He wanted the King of France to give him an appointment with the rank of colonel; that is quite obvious. He uses 'emperor' once, so as not to look as though he were afraid to do so, or to appear cowardly, and another time he uses 'Napoleon.'

"He mentions Masséna and Augereau frequently, and he has

described the Battle of Essling better than I could have done it myself; not only was the destruction of the bridges not a military ruse, but he shows that it could not possibly have been one; that had it been possible, the enemy should have blown up the bridges on the first day, when 20,000 men had crossed over. It would have been quite an achievement to have taken prisoner 20,000 Frenchmen, after what had happened at Eckmühl.

"I should have liked to show my appreciation to Marbot by sending him a ring. If I ever return to active life, I will have him attached to me as aide-de-camp. He is an educated man, who expresses himself simply, well, and correctly in writing."

The Emperor dictated a letter to Cardinal Fesch for Abbé Buonavita. In it he said that he would procure a living for him, but that until it had been granted, Madame would pay him a pension of three thousand francs. The Emperor would see that he was given three thousand francs to cover his traveling expenses.

March 15 or 16—In the morning, the Grand Maréchal took Arthur Bertrand with him to see Napoleon.

"So there you are, my boy," the Emperor exclaimed. "Don't you like me any more? How stupid you all are. [The Emperor had already made this remark a couple of days before, and he now explained his thought.] How very stupid of you all to say that he resembles the King of Rome."

The Grand Maréchal failed to understand his meaning, and later he asked his wife for an explanation.

"Oh, didn't you know?" Madame Bertrand replied. "Mrs. Russel said to me that Arthur looked like the King of Rome, and that Colonel Hudson had repeated this everywhere. I told this to General Montholon, and added laughingly that they had come to the wrong address."

"You are wicked," Montholon replied.

Madame Bertrand then said to Mrs. Russel: "No, it's not Arthur who is supposed to look like Napoleon II, but Henri, who is fair. Anyway, neither of them really look in the least like him. Their eyes are black, while the eyes of the King of Rome are blue. It is their long hair which has suggested the resemblance."

In the evening, the Governor sent two boxes of new books. He stated that the two cooks have reached the Cape and that they left a fortnight before Dr. Buttini. They were bringing with them four times as many books as had come by this last ship.

The Emperor has looked through the first lot of books to arrive; some two hundred volumes in all. The Grand Maréchal had given Monseigneur Buonavita a letter for Lord Liverpool as well as one for the Cardinal. The two priests and Dr. Antommarchi had dinner with the Grand Maréchal.

Napoleon has read the *Mémoires of Madame Rolland*, which fail to come up to his expectation.

"I thought," he told Bertrand, "that in them I would have found all about the Gironde. But that was not so. They were full of details concerning Mme. Rolland, her husband, and her family, all things of no interest to the general public. Then there was the everlasting question of her love affairs. Only Jean-Jacques Rousseau has been able to make such details interesting, but it takes his gift for writing to do it successfully. What do we care about Mme. Rolland's romance? No doubt it is useful to know that her father was a merchant—well and good. But after that she should have got down to real events.

"Why rave so over the courage of the Girondins? Of what did that extraordinary valor consist? Was it not they who overthrew the Constituent Assembly? Who ruined and then destroyed the King? Was it not they who condemned him to death? They accomplished all that without intending to, for they neither desired to overthrow the King nor to condemn him to death. They were most unfortunate. They had ability, and yet it is probable that they would not have saved France in the way *La Montagne* did.[1]

"Mme. Rolland amuses herself by examining her act of accusation; which is quite pointless, as it was common knowledge that she was innocent. What, after all, had most of those who perished done to deserve death? Nothing. It was a period of Revolution. Then again, she was much more guilty than many others, because after all she had contributed something to the events that brought about her death.

"Those who should be pitied are the wealthy people who had

---

[1] *La Montagne* was the name given to a group of backbenchers of the Convention who voted for the most extreme Revolutionary measures.—Translator's note.

taken no part in the Revolution. The merchants who had interfered with nothing, and whose sole crime lay in their great wealth.

"The book, by M. Guizot, although it is strewn with bombastic phrases, is the work of a man of intelligence. It is well done, but it can be refuted in a word. He says that: 'The Revolution could be governed, but that the counter-revolution can not.' In this he is wrong. A distinction should be drawn between Revolutionary *interests* and Revolutionary *theories*. The theories came first, while the interests only came into play on the night of August 4, after the suppression of the nobility and of the payment of tithes. I retained all the Revolutionary interests because I had no reason to destroy them. This was one of the sources of my strength, and it also explains why I was able to set aside the Revolutionary theories. Everyone felt reassured, because everyone knew that the Emperor did not and could not wish for a counter-revolution. Under my rule, freedom of the press was unnecessary; added to this was the fact that everyone had had enough of the Revolution, of Assemblies, of unrest and of internal dissensions.

"Whereas the Bourbons, on the contrary, have an interest in counter-revolution. They do not seek the interests of Revolution. The nobility merely wish to regain their property and their tithes. Under the Bourbons, the only means of guaranteeing the interests of the Revolution are through the theories of the Revolution, such as freedom of the press, Assemblies, and municipal administrations elected by the people, etc., all of which are the subversive principles of government.

"The only use of the Revolutionary theories is to destroy counter-revolutionary theories. On the contrary, through my propensity towards a monarchic form of government, I had preserved the Revolutionary interests while banishing the Revolutionary theories.

"With the Emperor as head of the Government, everything that M. Guizot says, will become true. But let the Bourbons remain in power, and it all becomes false.

"The Bourbons have only one principle: to govern through counter-revolution, with their own ministers and their own law-courts. And yet not to go too far or to lay hands on national property. For otherwise the ten million rentiers would rise up against the émigrés. Masséna put it very well when he said: 'After all, what have I gained through the return of the King? I formerly had an income of 50,000 francs a year, whereas now, if I had only 18,000, I would be more than content. I have got nothing out of it at all. . . .'

"The creation of my own nobility," Napoleon went on, "was one of the best means of consolidating the interests of the Revolution. Without that, my government would have been swamped by members of the old nobility, whom I would naturally have preferred to the bourgeoisie. Whereas, as I was surrounded by the Dukes of Bassano, Danzig, and d'Istria, I had no reason to accept any others, who in turn had no valid reason to re-establish the tithes, or to return the national properties; or, in other words, to have attacked the interests of the Revolution.

"On the whole, it was a very good idea. The Empress Marie-Louise realized this. She liked the Duchesses of Bassano or of Montebello quite as much as the Duchess of Montmorency, for instance. To her they were all the same. I made no member of the Ancien Régime a Duke."

The Emperor has read the chapters on *Egypt* in the five volumes of Strabon, which reached him in the last consignment of books from Lady Holland.

Monseigneur Buonavita left Longwood and went aboard ship on March 17.

March 18—Mme. Bertrand went to see the Emperor and told him what Mrs. Russel had said about the resemblance with the King of Rome. "What an idiot Bertrand is," he observed.

The Emperor is far from well. He went to bed at five o'clock.

In the course of the morning he looked through several of the new pamphlets that the Governor had sent him on the previous day. Among them were *The Expedition of Hoche to Ireland*, and *The Battle of Austerlitz*, etc.

In her *Mémoires*, Mme. Rolland said that on the evening of the 31st Messidor, she went into the Convention; she found the audience chamber empty, and asked a patriot how the provinces would react to the events of the day. "Bah," the patriot had replied, "the provinces always approve of anything that is done in Paris.

Was not Paris responsible for the Fourteenth of July and the Tenth of August?" He was quite right.

On the subject of M. Guizot's book, the Emperor remarked that it is true, of course, that in the Charter the King has preserved the Revolutionary principles, but he has only given the Charter as a form of bait, because he believes that he can rescind it. Actually, at present the Bourbons are badly ensnared. There can no longer be any doubt as to the true sentiments of the King of France. The expression *Chambre introuvable* suffices as a description and would mislead no one.[2]

March 19—The Emperor experienced a kind of trembling, a sort of feverish shiver or convulsion having a nervous origin, the doctor said. He is weak and eats very little. During the night he sent for the doctor, as he had had difficulty in breathing. The doctor said that he had wind in the stomach and in the lower abdomen.

March 20—The Emperor slept in the morning. The book by M. Guizot was obviously an offspring of the pamphlet on the Bourbons that was issued from here.

"Of its nature," Napoleon told Bertrand, "the clergy is of the people, because anyone may reach the highest ranks without having to show proof of good birth. A priest may bring up his brother or nephew, and educate him. This young man then abandons his plough and has to do something to fill a position in society. In this way the Tiers Etat has acquired many men of talent, who are well-informed and who may, according to circumstances, also have influence. The clergy has therefore, out of its very nature, contributed to the placing in society of a considerable number of men of humble birth who would otherwise have accomplished very little. This is a big point in favor of the clergy. In this book the idea has been badly expressed, but it is nevertheless an important one."

The Grand Maréchal waited three hours to see the Emperor. He was very coldly received.

The Emperor is still far from well. Bertrand went three times

[2]*La Chambre introuvable* is the ironical name given to the ultra-royalist Chamber of Deputies of 1815–16, which passed in blind complacency the most reactionary measures.—Translator's note.

to ask for news of him, but he didn't have himself announced.
Same as on the previous day.

March 23—The Grand Maréchal saw the Emperor in the morning.
He had sent for him at 4:00 A.M. The Emperor believes that if his
temperature keeps up, he will be dead within a week.

In the evening the Grand Maréchal went to the *coucher* of the
Emperor, and at four o'clock he had his pledge to see Dr. Arnott.
If only the Emperor would consult him!

Bertrand spent five hours with the Emperor in the morning.
His condition was unendurable. It was much worse than during
the previous night. At six in the morning he sent for the Grand
Maréchal. At four o'clock he was better, and he even allowed his
big room to be cleaned. . . . He required nothing. The doctor
wished to give him some small enemas. "Let them give me some
broth, otherwise I want to be left in peace," the Emperor said.

In the morning he sent for the Grand Maréchal, who read aloud
to him the commentary upon Hannibal's expedition and his crossing of the Alps. The Emperor feels better. In the morning he was
given several small enemas.

March 26—Dr. Antommarchi held a consultation with Dr. Arnott,
who is of the opinion that the fever is not a dangerous one; that on
the whole there are very few fevers here, and these not of a type
likely to be dangerous to a strong man, with symptoms such as
those indicated above; the Emperor is not delirious, and the fever
will just have to take its course, but it ought not to last for more
than fifteen to twenty days. He advises Antommarchi to see that
the patient's bowels are kept open, and to administer a small
dose of opium, about three or four grains, three or four times daily
. . . and to have a blister placed on the lower abdomen. This
illness had no connection with the old liver trouble.

March 27—Napoleon told the Grand Maréchal that he is much worse.
"If I should end my career now," he said, "it would be a great
joy. At times I have longed to die, and I have no fear of death. It
would be a great joy to me if I were to die within the next two

weeks. What have I left to hope for? Except possibly, an even more miserable end.

"The only thing to fear is that the English may wish to keep my body and have it buried at Westminster. They must be made to return it to France. Let the Prince Regent be informed of this in such a way that they may not be tempted to keep my ashes. After having murdered me, the very least they can do is to return my ashes to France, which is the only country I have ever loved and where I wish to be buried. See that two or three copies are made of the letter to the Prince Regent.

"Were I in America, no doubt I could continue to vegetate. Anyway I don't want to die. I don't wish to die, but nowadays I hold life cheap. I have made mistakes, but I have committed no crimes with which to reproach myself. Surely it were better that I were dead than to continue to vegetate here as I have done for the past six years?"

"But Your Majesty, you now have the help that was lacking for so long," Bertrand protested. "You are still strong and I hope that this attack will save you."

"And I," replied the Emperor, "I too don't believe that I am at death's door."

His temperature rose again at about eleven o'clock; at 4:00 A.M. it had considerably abated.

"I am very glad that I have no religion," the Emperor remarked. "I find it a great consolation, as I have no imaginary terrors and no fear of the future."

March 28—In the course of the day Napoleon felt better. He saw no one except Dr. Antommarchi until one o'clock. He had been advised to take several gentle purges, but he paid no attention to what the doctor had said. The doctor had given him one which had had no effect.

"It is the same with my body as with my mind," he said. "Nothing is to be got from it by force; but only through kindness and good treatment."

His temperature rose again at 3:00 A.M., and declined at 2:00 P.M.

"So much for their good twelve hours' sleep," the Emperor observed.

At four o'clock he said to the Grand Maréchal: "Does a sharp frost prevent drilling?"

"It makes it more difficult," Bertrand replied.

"But is it impossible?"

"No, drilling can be done through rock, therefore all the more so through ground that is frozen, but it is a very slow process. Earth freezes to a depth of from four to five feet."

"Was the last frost we had as deep as that?"

"I believe so; water freezes to an even greater depth."

At five-thirty the doctor gave the Emperor two rhubarb pills. After retaining them for about five minutes, he threw them up with a good deal of mucus. Still, he was undiscouraged and said that he would try and take some more.

March 30—The Governor called on General Montholon. He said that no one had seen the Emperor for the past twelve days. Only the other day he had been going to visit him when he learned that Dr. Arnott had been called in to attend him. Nevertheless, Dr. Arnott had not actually seen the Emperor, and it was absolutely necessary for the duty officer to see him. It was said that the Emperor was ill, but he had not been informed of it. Montholon replied that the Emperor was indeed ill, that the officer on duty had been told, and that he could have no doubts on the subject. Whereupon the Governor replied that the word of General Montholon sufficed for him, personally, but that as the representative of the Powers he was obliged to have the testimony of an English officer on the subject of Napoleon.

"The Emperor is ill," Montholon had replied, "he is unable to go out, therefore he cannot be seen. Do you wish to break down the door of his room?"

"Yes," replied the Governor. "If it should be necessary, the door of his room will be battered down and an entry made by force."

"But that would kill him."

"No matter, I would have it done."

"But you are responsible for him."

"I am responsible for him in the eyes of the Courts. I not only am the agent of the English Government, but I also represent the Powers."

According to Montholon, Sir Hudson Lowe spoke with a harshness Montholon had not yet heard him use. Although his features had expressed irritation, there had still been a semblance of good manners. Two hours later he returned to obtain a reply from General Montholon. Montholon told him that the next day would be the thirteenth of the Emperor's illness, and that therefore it would be a bad day. The Emperor had a temperature and he would certainly not speak to him at all. The Governor held Montholon personally responsible. In the morning Reade had been to see the Captain.

It had been agreed with General Montholon that no one should say anything about this matter to the Emperor. But that someone would induce his consent to see Dr. Arnott. Although the Emperor had spent a restless night, the day had been fairly quiet. The Grand Maréchal suggested [to Dr. Arnott] that he should see the Emperor.

March 31—Dr. Arnott saw Dr. Antommarchi. General Montholon spoke to Dr. Arnott and asked him if he would give his word of honor to look upon himself as a civilian doctor dealing with an ordinary private person? If he would care for the Emperor as though he were a City doctor attending a London merchant? If he would issue no bulletins or spoken or written reports unless he were so authorized, and would first submit a copy for approval. If he would not speak of the patient other than to say "he is well or ill," without specifying anything about the nature of his illness?

The doctor said of his own accord that Napoleon could send for him through the intermediary of General Bertrand. He assumed that if, in the Emperor's bedroom, he should use another form of address, the Governor would not be informed. He inquired whether, if he should have to issue a bulletin, he must always sign it with Dr. Antommarchi? It was usually the procedure in the case of a private patient, and it was advised by all doctors as it placed the responsibility upon both of them, while giving more weight to the bulletins. He then discussed the Emperor's health with Mme. Bertrand and her husband.

CHAPTER FOUR

April 1821

April 1—The Governor came to Longwood, to the New House, and
had a long talk with Dr. Arnott. Sir Hudson seemed much surprised by the remarks of General Montholon. He said that he had
no wish to receive either bulletins or reports on the health of the
Emperor, and that he had never asked for any, as it was a matter
that concerned the Emperor's medical adviser and not him. He
intended to ask no questions on the subject. Finally he decided
to write a letter to Dr. Arnott, stating that he would leave him
free and independent in the exercise of his functions.

At nine o'clock that night Dr. Antommarchi presented Dr.
Arnott to the Emperor.

April 2—Dr. Arnott saw the Emperor for the second time at nine
o'clock the following morning and again at four in the afternoon,
in the presence of the Grand Maréchal. Dr. Arnott prescribed some
pills with which Dr. Antommarchi did not agree, and which were
intended to help the evacuation of the bowels. The Emperor
refused to take them.

April 3—The Emperor passed a bad night. He felt, so he said, as
"though he had the tunic of Deianira on his back." He then asked

someone find out exactly what he had meant by the tunic of Deianira.

The Emperor had not taken any medicine. The two doctors had succeeded in making up their difference of opinion, and they had prescribed one pill to be taken every two hours, instead of two pills. Both the doctors wrote down their consultation on the Emperor and the proposed treatment. This consisted of pills to keep the lower bowel open, and a quinine mixture to strengthen the stomach and to prevent any rise in temperature.

As the Emperor's temperature had been very high, he decided to take one of the pills. By six o'clock the fever seemed to have almost entirely disappeared.

April 6—The Emperor had a fairly good day. At noon the doctors visited him, and at one o'clock he took his second pill, but he put off taking the quinine mixture as he hoped that the fever would have entirely abated. Dr. Arnott was in the seventh heaven because ever since his third or fourth visit he had found no trace of fever. At 10:00 P.M. the fever returned, or at least a form of restlessness accompanied by an upset of the lower bowel.

The Grand Maréchal proposed to the Emperor that he should sit up several nights with him. Since the day before, his servant Noverraz has been ill. General Montholon spent part of the preceding night with the Emperor; he did so for the first time on April 3.

April 7—Napoleon took a dose of quinine. The Grand Maréchal proposed for the second time that he should sit up with the Emperor. He thought that he had done so with some heat.

"Your Majesty," he said, "devotion and affection can take the place of so much. . . . I have spent many nights with you as aide-de-camp, surely I can spend a few as valet de chambre. I don't mind what I do. It will be sufficient for me to feel that I can be of some use to you. I have a wife and four children, but my wife can always send for me, if need be."

"But this is quite unnecessary, Bertrand," the Emperor replied, "there are Coursot, Pierron, and Antommarchi who don't sit up at night. It is my misfortune that my man is ill."

The Emperor asked Dr. Antommarchi to shave him. He asked Arnott if he knew how to do it. Arnott smiled and said that it was not the custom in England for doctors to shave their patients.

"Oh! that is hard to believe!" the Emperor exclaimed. Arnott replied that it was still the custom in Germany, Spain, and Portugal. But that in those countries, the doctors were poor and very ignorant; barely able to look after people and to pull out their teeth, and quite incapable of dressing a wound.

"Have you ever seen the play *Figaro*?" Napoleon asked.

"Yes," replied Arnott.

Antommarchi thereupon remarked that it was a literary masterpiece. It was the second time this question had been put to him.

The Emperor then said that he had several times seen Larrey himself shaving the soldiers. Larrey was a fine man. After Dr. Arnott had said that he was familiar with his books, the Emperor continued:

"Oh! His actions were far superior to his books. I have seen him in the desert, going into the front line with twenty or thirty water bottles; or bending down from his horse to give a drink to poor tired stragglers, bringing up the rear."

April 8—At 11:00 P.M., Napoleon took a second dose of quinine, and Antommarchi made him take a pill. He left the Emperor at midnight. The Emperor sent for him again from one o'clock in the morning until two o'clock, and again from three to four in the morning.

April 9—Antommarchi went to the Emperor at half-past seven in the morning. Napoleon flew into a rage with him. He said that "Antommarchi should be in attendance on him by six o'clock in the morning, instead of spending all his time with Mme. Bertrand."

The Emperor sent for the Grand Maréchal, who arrived at a quarter to eight. Napoleon repeated what he had just said to Antommarchi and added that the doctor was only interested in his whores.

"Very well, let him spend all his time with his whores," Napoleon said. "Let him f—— them back and front, in the mouth and in the ears, but get rid of that man for me, he is stupid, ignorant, pretentious, and utterly devoid of any sense of honor. I wish Dr.

Arnott to be sent for and for him to attend me in future. Discuss the matter with Montholon. I'll have no more of Antommarchi."

This scene took place in front of Marchand and Antommarchi. The Emperor repeated five or six times that Mme. Bertrand was a whore and he added:

"I have made my will: in it I have left Antommarchi twenty francs to buy himself a length of rope with which to hang himself. He is devoid of honor. If Larrey, Desgenettes, or Percy were here, I would be unable to get them out of my room. It would be impossible because they would remain there despite my protests.

"I am a most unhappy man! None of you knows what it is to be ill. Marchand has never been ill, but Montholon who has, makes a fairly good nurse. I should have been cared for by my mother, but here I have no one. In Europe there are famous doctors who look after their patients and who know what should be done. They would taste the broth and say immediately what I was to eat, and how much of each thing I was to have. There are even doctors like that on this island, but my position doesn't permit me to have them attend me. I have to put up with a single surgeon in their place.

"Ivan would not even have gone into the next room. Antommarchi should have his bed set up in there and never leave the room except to go for a walk in the little garden, to get some fresh air. I forbid him to leave that room. He must be ordered not to. . . .

"Yesterday the valet de chambre told the doctor that I was expecting him, yet he nevertheless went to see Mme. Bertrand. One can't get him away from there, and it makes the servant look ridiculous. Antommarchi will end by spending every minute of the day there. When he leaves me he runs over there like Napoleon Bertrand going to Mr. Nagle for his riding lesson, or like Hortense and Henri when they go to the stables to ride."

After Antommarchi had left, the Emperor told the Grand Maréchal that Dr. Antommarchi was his wife's lover. And he added, in front of Marchand and Ali, that Bertrand was countenancing something that dishonored him as much as it did Mme. Bertrand. Dr. Antommarchi had been lost when he had ceased to see Montholon. and when he had become more intimate with Mme.

Bertrand. The whole thing might have been foreseen, and Mme. Bertrand had ruined Antommarchi just as she had ruined Gourgaud. . . .

The Emperor dismissed the doctor, and afterwards he repeated the same things to the Grand Maréchal, who continued to listen without comment. Napoleon said: "Now go and tell Antommarchi to remain in attendance on me. . . . I myself have ordered it." The Emperor sent for Dr. Arnott who was ushered in alone, without Dr. Antommarchi.

The Emperor told him that Antommarchi was sick. The Emperor then inquired whether there were another surgeon in Dr. Arnott's regiment, and whether he was one of the officers, and if he took his meals in their mess. Dr. Arnott replied in the affirmative. Arnott paid a second visit to the Emperor in the evening, also unaccompanied. The Grand Maréchal acted as interpreter for Dr. Arnott.

The Grand Maréchal and Montholon spoke to Antommarchi and told him to think over his duties, and to be prepared to remain in attendance on the Emperor as he himself had ordered.

Antommarchi replied that he would refuse to do it. He would not and indeed could not act as a nurse, which would tire him out. In such a position, he would no longer have the free use of his faculties. He would no longer be able to carry out his duties as a doctor, and he intended to get some fresh air and to go for walks. Anyway, he had made up his mind to leave St. Helena, and he asked whether he might go to Plantation House.

The Grand Maréchal replied that the Emperor must first be informed of his desire to leave St. Helena, and that he would speak to the Emperor for him, should the doctor prefer not to do it himself. And in any case it was not for him to reply to such an important request. Antommarchi observed that the Emperor had received plenty of warning; after all, he had thrown Antommarchi out and had told him to go to the devil.

Antommarchi took a horse and rode to Plantation House, where he saw M. Montchenu and Major Gorrequer. The Governor was in Jamestown, whither Gorrequer accompanied Antommarchi, who then explained to the Governor that he wished to return to Europe as, unfortunately for the Emperor, he could be of no further use to him. He had finished his book and wished to return to Europe to see it published.

The Governor replied that he was quite right; it was the only thing for him to do. Ships would be arriving from China until the middle of June, and he would notify the English Government of the doctor's desire to leave. Gorrequer asked after Mme. Bertrand. He had heard that she had been seriously ill. After all, she had spent six years on the island and a year on Elba. Count Bertrand was very long suffering. The Governor observed that, on the whole, they were not a very happy lot at Longwood.

At 9:00 P.M., the Emperor had the Grand Maréchal shown in. The Grand Maréchal told him all about Antommarchi's request to leave, and also that the Governor had said that he would see that he had a good passage, and that he would notify his Government.

Napoleon inquired whether the Governor had asked Antommarchi any questions. The Grand Maréchal replied that he didn't know. He himself had been very much surprised at Antommarchi's request, but he had paid no attention to the details. The doctor had been badly advised.

"I think that he advised himself," Bertrand said. "As for me, I only asked him to do two things. First to think about what he was asked to do, and second, to remain in your attendance as you ordered him to do. He refused. If there were anterooms available in which he could wait, he would do so willingly; but he was unable to act as night nurse, because that would wear him out and he would then be unable to fulfill his duties as a doctor. He pointed out that he had been in attendance on Your Majesty from eleven o'clock until midnight; then from one to two o'clock in the morning and again from three to four o'clock. His Chinese boy had forgotten to wake him at six, and he had been much put out at being late. He seemed to me to be very hurt that Your Majesty had told him that you would leave him a rope with which to hang himself."

"He has been in a great hurry," Napoleon remarked. "I was just going to send for you to tell you to put a stop to the whole thing. It is a request that should have been pondered for at least a week. See here, Bertrand, I told Dr. Arnott that Antommarchi was sick. Besides, we must wait and see how the Governor takes it. Possibly he will look upon Antommarchi's request as an unaffected piece of hot-headedness, and as a demonstration of jealousy against Arnott. During the ten weeks that must elapse before the doctor can leave the island, he will have time to reconsider his decision. Between now and then everything will have been settled one way or another."

The Grand Maréchal went from the Emperor's presence to see Antommarchi, who told him that the Governor had not questioned him. He, Antommarchi, had merely told him that he wished to complete his book; in any case, he had only seen the Governor for five minutes.

April 10—Dr. Arnott visited the Emperor twice during the day. At one o'clock Napoleon ate a large *bavaroise* and three or four biscuits. During the morning he was sick three times. He had a fairly large movement.

In the course of the day, the Grand Maréchal told the Emperor that the Governor had not questioned Antommarchi, who had simply asked permission to finish his book in Europe and to see it published there. In the evening Napoleon said again that it was necessary to wait and see what action the Governor would take.

"Did the Governor really believe that it might only be a question of jealousy on the part of Antommarchi?" Napoleon asked Bertrand.

"No," the Grand Maréchal replied, "Antommarchi told him that he got on very well with Dr. Arnott."

April 11—At seven in the morning, the Emperor sent for Dr. Arnott. The vomit of the Emperor had contained some of the *bavaroise* that he had eaten the evening before. The Grand Maréchal was sent for at 9:00 A.M. He returned again at four or five o'clock in the afternoon.

"Could you come at midnight?" the Emperor asked Dr. Arnott.

"Yes," the doctor replied. "If it should be necessary, let them send for me."

Dr. Arnott then asked why Antommarchi no longer came to see the Emperor. Bertrand replied that the Emperor had not sent for him.

During the morning Bertrand realized that it was not a sign of lack of zeal on the part of Arnott if he failed to come, but that very probably he was afraid of the Governor and preferred to be sent for.

"You are a very sick man, not to have a doctor at hand," Bertrand told the Emperor. "It seems to me that Your Majesty ought to see Antommarchi."

"But he asked to be allowed to leave. Therefore, until he goes, I shall see Arnott, who seems to me to be a sensible man," the Emperor replied.

"I have thought over what you said about waiting to see what the Governor would do," Bertrand remarked. "I may be mistaken, but I am inclined to think that the Governor will keep out of the way and not wish to do anything. He doesn't even want to know that you are ill. He was very obliging to Antommarchi, and said that he would see that he obtained a good passage."

"He was lying," said Napoleon.

"He added that there would be good ships available up until June," added Bertrand.

There was a pause which lasted for a quarter of an hour.

"What time is it?" Napoleon asked.

"Half-past ten."

"Send for Montholon, if he has arrived." But he had not. Then a quarter of an hour later:

"Marchand, send for Antommarchi." Dr. Antommarchi entered the room. Napoleon asked him: "What is this dose they are trying to make me take?"

"Five grains of opium and some saline tincture."

"What for?"

"To stop the vomiting."

"Must I take this stuff?"

"Should Your Majesty feel like being sick, it would be better for him to do so before taking the mixture. In the meantime Your Majesty need take only half the prescribed dose."

Fifteen minutes later, Montholon entered the room.

"Did they have to wake you up?" Napoleon asked.

"No, Sire," Montholon replied. "But as I was already up they told me that you had asked for me."

"Go and have your breakfast."

135

Soon afterwards the Emperor dismissed Antommarchi and then Bertrand, saying as he did so: "Since I have consented to receive Antommarchi, the very least he can do is to show his gratitude by his care of me."

At eleven o'clock at night, the Emperor took a pill. At noon he had eaten some toast dipped in hot wine. At three o'clock in the morning he brought up some mucus, but no food.

At eight o'clock in the morning the two doctors paid their visit. Dr. Arnott was late. It appeared that he had been to inform the Governor of all that had taken place.

April 12—At ten-thirty the Emperor passed a large and well-formed movement. At eleven o'clock the two doctors visited him together. The Emperor was in very low spirits, as he had been on the previous evening. He told the doctor that the wine had disagreed with him. His good movement had cost him fifteen hours of suffering and discomfort, which had exhausted him. He asked:

"If this weakness increases, how long can it last?"

"For four or five days."

"How will it end?"

Dr. Arnott said that the length of time the weakness would last was very uncertain. It was quite possible to bring up food and to be weak for a very long time; to live almost without eating and then to recover; or for the weakness to increase while the circulation of the blood diminished gradually until it finally ceased altogether. For that matter, Dr. Arnott said, he didn't think that the wine had done the Emperor any harm, however, if His Majesty believed that it had, he should cease to take it. He should try and find out what his stomach could stand. In weaknesses of this kind, some doctors favored one type of treatment, while others preferred another.

Arnott insisted that the Emperor should take the pills as well as the quinine. The quinine would strengthen and tone up the stomach.

When the two doctors had left the room, the Emperor remarked to the Grand Maréchal: "It looks to me as though they have about reached the end of their tether."

Nevertheless, it appeared that two great results had been achieved: the Emperor's temperature was normal, and the lower bowel was more settled. It was true, however, that the stomach remained weak, tricky, and finicky. Nevertheless, it digested whatever it was given, with the exception of the *bavaroise* he had eaten two days before. The doctors advised quinine, but the Emperor refused to take any.

"Shut up, you bore me," he said.

A quarter of an hour later, the Emperor put an end to the conversation and dismissed the Grand Maréchal. Major Gorrequer came to Longwood and went for a walk in the grounds.

April 13—At two o'clock, Napoleon threw up some of the creamed rice he had eaten at nine o'clock. At ten, he sat up for half an hour and then ate a little jelly and a dish of stewed apples. At eleven o'clock he had an enema, but he was unable to retain it; fifteen minutes later he threw up the jelly and some of the stewed apples, also some of the rice he had eaten the previous evening. At noon, he again vomited some mucus, just as the doctors were about to leave the room.

The doctors found the Emperor much weaker than on the previous day. The Emperor said that he felt weaker; he had slept a little towards morning, but he had been thirsty and so he had drunk nothing but water. He asked whether the doctors could give him something to strengthen his stomach. They found his tongue less coated, and the two movements had been large and quite good, though less so than those of the day before which had been produced by the action of the pills. They said that the dose of quinine is intended to strengthen his stomach. As he was leaving, Dr. Arnott advised the Emperor to take a dose of quinine after the next attack of vomiting. He said that it would be better, in view of the weak state of the patient, to give only half the dose that had been prescribed several days before, and for the Emperor to have something to eat about an hour later. Dr. Arnott said that it was amazing that the Emperor was not even weaker than he was, considering how little nourishment he was taking. If he had been given two different kinds of medicine, he would have attributed the discomfort he was experiencing to the medicine, whereas it was due in reality to the previous upsets, which had brought about the present weak condition of his stomach.

During the night watch, the Emperor had remarked on the fact that he had taken no medicine, that he felt weaker, but that he had been less restless. He said no medicine had been offered to him. When Antommarchi tried to take his pulse, the Emperor drew his hand away pettishly, remarking that he no longer had any temperature. As he was leaving, Dr. Antommarchi said that the Emperor appeared to be out of humor with him. Montholon replied that he was imagining things. The only thing he had noticed was that at six-thirty the Emperor had inquired whether Antommarchi were there, and had then said:

"It seems that he sleeps well."

At one o'clock the Emperor took his dose of quinine. At five o'clock he had a jelly and at nine o'clock some arrowroot. He felt much better after his dose of quinine.

With the help of Montholon he had drafted a letter to the Prince Regent, so as to be sure that his ashes should not be kept in London, but that they should be sent back to Paris. At four-thirty, the doctors arrived. The Emperor was sitting up in his big armchair, wearing his flannel vest, a smock, and his shirt, with the doors and windows wide open. Dr. Arnott asked him if he did not fear the cold.

For an hour the Emperor abused the English governing classes. He said that the English people, after having known victory, had become the most unfortunate in Europe and were now barely able to subsist. The English soldiery was very badly treated; they would be the equal of the French if they were well trained and well treated, but they were too severely handled. The soldiers were made to cry out under the lash of a whip. Dr. Arnott replied that he only saw the men when they were in hospital, where they were very kindly treated.

"Oh, you only take their pulse so as to know how many more strokes of the cat they can stand. That is the reason why they dislike you. One of these days John Bull will turn against the English ruling classes and he will hang the lot. I won't be there to see it, but you will. You will have an even more terrible revolution than ours. The ruling classes are the same everywhere, puffed up and insolent so long as they are at the head of affairs, but cowardly so soon as there is danger anywhere near them. The cowards, to keep an unarmed man imprisoned upon a rock! They are all the same. I saw the ruling classes of Venice on the eve of the day they perished, and they were then every bit as inflated with a sense of their own importance, as the English.

"I have just written to the Prince Regent to ask him not to keep my ashes in London, but to send them to France.

"I have predicted that if he sets up a monument to me, one day John Bull will swear on it the destruction of his throne and the ruin of the English ruling classes. He will live to see that come about. In any case, it would be a monument of shame."

The Emperor wanted to give Dr. Arnott a book on the campaigns of Marlborough, the greatest English general, as a gift to the regimental library. "To show them," he said, "that I honor the brave men of every nation."

Dr. Arnott asked the Grand Maréchal to express his gratitude to the Emperor.

"How many volumes are there in the regimental library?" the Emperor asked.

"About seven hundred," Arnott replied.

"Are all of them in English?"

"There are some French books. . . ."

"The medicines you have been giving me are too strong," Napoleon said. "These doctors treat me like a horse. I am not accustomed to violence . . . my organism is revolted by extreme measures."

Napoleon said that the English Government was very astute.

"I asked Lady Holland to send me some five hundred volumes. The English hastened to send off the letter, and to say that there would be no difficulty about the matter. Later they said that the books had been sent off eighteen months before, though they had not yet reached me. When we asked for the books they pretended to be surprised. They had received them a long time before. And all this because they didn't want me to have them. Cowards! To act like this against a disarmed man. For the past six months they were supposed to send cooks to Longwood, and they have sent them heaven knows where. No doubt they will reach St. Helena when there will be no further need for them.

"My organism needs delicate things. It is not a little like the elephant, which may be led by a string, but not by a rope."

"Yet these medicines are very mild," the doctors protested. "They are the sort of thing one gives to a child . . ."

"It's no use trying to drive me. I won't take any medicine this evening. I hope to have a quiet night. I receive better care during the day than during the night. Therefore I intend to take medicine only in the morning. Which would be best for me to take to-morrow? Quinine or some soup?"

"A pill, without any doubt," the doctors replied. "It is essential to keep the bowels open. When the intestines are settled, the condition of the stomach will improve."

The Emperor dismissed the doctors.

In the evening the Emperor reread his letter to the Prince Regent. The Governor came to Longwood, but only stayed a quarter of an hour. Upon leaving the Emperor's presence, Dr. Arnott remarked that he had never known such a peevish patient. Nevertheless, he had found the Emperor much more lively than in the morning.

April 14—The Emperor sweated heavily during the night and changed his flannel vest ten times. The previous evening, at nine o'clock, he had eaten some jelly and had digested it. At eight o'clock in the morning, he had some chocolate. Antommarchi said that when one perspired one did not vomit, but the fact that the Emperor had not been sick did not mean that his condition had improved. During the night the Emperor ate two wafer biscuits, and twice he had some wine soup diluted with water. He got up for half an hour.

In the morning the two doctors found the Emperor weak, but better. He had had no movements. He had taken neither a pill nor a dose of quinine. He took none the rest of the day, in spite of what the doctors might say.

In the afternoon, he got up for about half an hour. He asked Dr. Arnott what the officers had said about the book he had presented to the library of the 20th of the Line. Dr. Arnott replied that they had not yet had a chance to read it.

"Doesn't some society look after the library?" the Emperor inquired.

"No, it is a commissioner. A Mr. Oakley."

"Have you many reading clubs in England?"

"Don't you also have them in France?"

"I see that he has been told off by Reade on account of the book," Napoleon said to Bertrand afterwards, "but don't tell him I said so."

The fact is that the doctor left the book with Captain [Luytens], who did not dare to take it to the Regiment. Instead he wrote to the Governor to ask for his permission. To have taken it away from Longwood without his consent would have been treason in his eyes. The officers of the Regiment have been much flattered by the gift, and have appreciated this attention on the part of the Emperor.

During the doctor's evening visit, the Emperor was very weak, and his pulse was much slower than on the previous day.

April 14 (continued)—"Tomorrow is Palm Sunday, the Sunday before Easter," Napoleon said to the doctors. "But, of course, you are a heretic and will go to hell." Everyone laughed. "Oh! Very well, Dr. Arnott, there are good people of every kind of religion."

Dr. Arnott noticed that the Emperor has a slight twitching of the lips. He asked him if he had anything in his mouth. The Emperor said no. As he was leaving, Dr. Arnott repeated to the Grand Maréchal his question as to whether this twitching of the lips were habitual to the Emperor. The Grand Maréchal said that it was not. When the Grand Maréchal re-entered the room, the Emperor asked him what the doctor had said, and the Grand Maréchal told him. After a few minutes' silence Napoleon remarked: "That doctor is a very observant man."

Napoleon then told the Grand Maréchal that General Montholon was ill, and that he had admitted that he would be unable to nurse the Emperor at night. The Emperor felt like asking Abbé Vignali to look after him. The Grand Maréchal said that the Emperor could not do better; Vignali was very robust, and he also had some knowledge of medicine. He would make an excellent nurse.

He repeated to Napoleon his offer to attend him, and to nurse him as soon as would be agreeable to him. Bertrand then went out to the garden to fetch some flowers for the Emperor. He had been there two days before and had brought him a rose. This time he picked two bunches of flowers.

He also told the Emperor that his wife Mme. Bertrand would make an excellent nurse. She was quite admirable, and she very much wanted to do it. She would nurse him night and day, and it wouldn't be too much for her. She had almost entirely recovered from her illness.

Napoleon replied that she was over-confident. To nurse him would exhaust her. For six years she had not played the part she should have played. She should have dined with him, or at the very least she should have joined his party of an evening.

"Well," replied Bertrand, "now she is anxious to make amends. She would still like to do so."

In the evening the Emperor ate some fried potatoes and jelly and he seemed better. He went to bed in the sitting room, and the service of Forty Hours of Prayer was discussed. Monseigneur Vignali, Montholon, and Marchand sat up all night with the Emperor.

April 15—Napoleon took a dose of quinine at nine in the morning and had some chocolate at ten o'clock. The doctors arrived at eleven o'clock. Napoleon got up for half an hour. He had had a good stool quite normally, so it was thought unnecessary to give him a pill.

Napoleon asked Dr. Arnott whether he had ever been to mass. The doctor replied: "Yes, several times." Napoleon added that mass was about to be said and made the doctor promise to attend. But Arnott replied that it would have to be on the following Sunday as he was obliged to visit Mr. Brooke, who was ill and who had sent for him.

"You have seen our churches," Napoleon said. "They are very beautiful, are they not? There are paintings and Madonnas in them. Your churches don't look like that, they are more like stables."

"But," Arnott replied, "they are very nice, too, and one can sit down, whereas in your churches one has to remain standing. There are no seats, at least not in Italy."

"You are mistaken," replied Napoleon.

The Emperor was very weak. He vomited some chocolate at two-thirty. He was closeted for two hours with Montholon and Marchand. Montholon said that he had talked a great deal about his death, and of the effect it would have in France and in Europe. He seemed to think that he was near his end.

The doctors returned at five in the afternoon. The Emperor was weak and his pulse was very rapid. He talked a great deal about his illness. He believed that the two principles on which his recovery was based were over-simplified, and that it was insufficient to keep the bowels open and to tone up the stomach with doses of medicine. The illness was more complicated than that, and the doses of quinine were not sufficient to relieve it. The Emperor had hoped that the fever coupled with the lack of nourishment would have saved him and that then it would have been merely a question of time. But his weak condition was not the result of his present illness, because it had existed six months earlier. If his weakness arose from the fever, the treatment he was having would be the right one, and he would already be convalescent.

"Is there any form of natural crisis that can pull me out of this?" the Emperor asked the doctors.

Dr. Arnott replied that he did not see how the fever could have cured him. The sweating was a direct result of his weak condition, and in consequence it would never cure him. He was unable to predict what natural crisis might pull the Emperor out of his present state. If it had been an acute form of illness such as a violent fever, it might have been possible to have spoken more precisely; but this was a wasting sickness. No doubt one could expect much of nature, but it was best to give it a little help, not to despair, and to continue with the treatment. It was not a matter that could be resolved by a couple of pills of quinine. It was necessary to persevere.

"No doubt," Napoleon replied, "but that is not the question. This treatment is inadequate."

Dr. Arnott finds the Emperor proportionately much worse than he was two weeks earlier, when he saw him for the first time. He has begun to share Antommarchi's opinion, who believes the Emperor to be dangerously ill.

Mass was said in the chapel. Mme. Bertrand and her children, the Grand Maréchal, General Montholon, Dr. Antommarchi, and the servants were present. The Emperor was closeted from two to four o'clock with General Montholon and Marchand. Monseigneur Vignali and Montholon sat up with the Emperor the previous night, as well as Marchand.

Marginal Note—Bertrand and his wife asked Monseigneur Vignali what the Forty Hours of Prayer were, what was done in such cases, what was the usual procedure. Monseigneur Vignali replied that everyone could go and pray.

They met General Montholon. Bertrand spoke to him about the Forty Hours of Prayer. Had the Emperor mentioned them to him? Did Montholon know what the procedure was? What would be most agreeable to the Emperor?

Montholon replied that the Emperor had not said a word to him on the subject. Vignali was the only one to whom he had mentioned the matter. For several days now, the Emperor had been seeing a good deal of Vignali, and if he were to become religious, he, Montholon would not be surprised, as the Emperor made a point of calling Vignali, abbé.

Bertrand replied that it might possibly be for the sake of religion, but of necessity there was also a political element in the matter. It would be known in Europe that the Emperor had ordered the Forty Hours of Prayer to be held, and, should the Emperor recover from his illness, the rumors this would cause might give rise to a movement in his favor.

"Finally," Bertrand said, "whether the Emperor has had a religious or a political aim, he should be upheld. If you are agreeable, Montholon, tomorrow at noon and at six o'clock in the evening, my wife and I and our children will go and pray."

Later, finding himself alone with Montholon, the Grand Maréchal told him that he had been very much hurt at the way in which the Emperor had treated him, and at the fact that he did not receive his wife, whom he would most certainly have forgiven had he not been ill. Bertrand said that he believed Montholon to be too upright a man not to act under the circumstances in a simple and straightforward manner.

General Montholon replied that he knew there were prejudices against Bertrand and that appearances were unfavorable to him, while Mme. Bertrand added fuel to the fire, though that could not be helped. On his side he might unintentionally have caused him some disquiet, just as Bertrand had done to him, but that nevertheless, he had always acted like a brother towards him . . . Bertrand replied that he realized that it was not his fault . . . but that at such a time of crisis he had hoped that the ill health of the Emperor would have been the sole preoccupation of every one of them.

The Emperor passed a fairly good night. At half past six in the morning he had some vermicelli soup and at eight o'clock some chocolate.

The doctors came at eleven. The Emperor had been up for about half an hour. Dr. Arnott found the Emperor somewhat better than on the previous evening and much the same as on the previous morning; with a good tongue. At two o'clock the Emperor ate some chocolate.

He was closeted from two to four o'clock with Montholon and Marchand. It appeared that he was at work on his final dispositions. He had sent for Monseigneur Vignali and had spent three quarters of an hour with him.

At a quarter to five the doctors arrived. The Emperor got up for a quarter of an hour. He inquired whether the Chinese packets had brought any news. Dr. Arnott replied that they never brought any. Napoleon asked whether the Emperor of China was still angry. Dr. Arnott replied that a different Emperor had ascended the throne since the ambassadorship of Lord Amherst.

The Emperor said that he had written a great deal, that he had found it very tiring. He no longer had the strength to write. He spoke very little. The Grand Maréchal told the Emperor that he was sorry, at a time when it was obvious that the Emperor was far from well, to broach the subject of his personal troubles, but he was broken-hearted that the Emperor should have seen fit to treat him so harshly.

"No, no, I don't know what you mean," Napoleon said to him. "You will have to explain yourself. I am sick in bed and I don't talk much. You have nothing of which to complain."

"Your Majesty has withdrawn the confidence which he formerly reposed in me," Bertrand said. "I have lost almost without regret the high rank, the fortune, and the honors to which you raised me. But this new misfortune overwhelms me. I cast off my honors as one abandons a borrowed garment, but I thought that I had some claim to your esteem and to your friendship. I am unable to forego this without experiencing great distress. It is not long since Your Majesty said that my conduct had been irreproachable. Yet now you blow hot and cold with me. How can I, in so short a time, have fallen from grace?"

"But I don't know what you are driving at?" Napoleon replied. "I am very nice to you. I have nothing against you. Marchand is the one person whose care I find most pleasant, because it is that to which I have been accustomed. That is all that I can say."

"My poor wife," Bertrand continued, "if the climate is not sufficient to kill her, will surely die of a broken heart. You have forgiven so many of your enemies. Will you not forgive your old friends? No doubt Mme. Bertrand has been in the wrong, but has she not most cruelly expiated those wrongs? Is she not very unhappy? Has she not been the victim of the most atrocious slander?"

"But I have nothing with which to reproach Mme. Bertrand. She is an admirable woman. I am simply not accustomed to seeing her," Napoleon said.

"She would have cared for you with such deep affection," Bertrand went on. "She is sincerely fond of you, more so than you think. Will you see her tomorrow, if only for a moment?"

"But I have already told you, Bertrand, that I find Marchand's care the most agreeable because it is what I have been accustomed to. I gave you to understand precisely what I meant; it would be exactly the same with my mother, had she not been used to looking after me. Nevertheless, I shall see Mme. Bertrand before I die."

"Things have not yet reached that point," Bertrand cried. "We will keep you with us. You often used to say that you were a father, so forgive us as you would forgive your children. Are we not your friends?"

The Grand Maréchal was unable to restrain his tears. He remained another half hour with the Emperor, who said nothing further.

Dr. Antommarchi's bed was put up in the library, where he was to sleep. Monseigneur Vignali was not to nurse the Emperor that night. In the evening, the Emperor had some soup, an egg, some jelly, and drank a spoonful of wine in two spoonfuls of sweetened water, as is his custom. He was very cheerful afterwards and told Montholon to tell him some baudy stories. The Emperor went to bed in the sitting room and rested.

April 17—The Emperor had a disturbed night. He was sick twice although he did not bring up much, but what he did, contained chocolate and some half-digested food. Antommarchi thought that his stomach was at present too weak to throw up everything; that there was a lack of tone.

Montholon told Antommarchi that the previous day the Emperor had been busy arranging the distribution of all his boxes. He had cut out pieces of cardboard and had written on them, afterwards putting one in each of the boxes. He had done all this by himself. He had had inventories taken of everything he possessed, even though that was something that had already been done. He had been busy making his final dispositions and distributions, but he had not as yet made a will, and if he were to die, nobody would get anything.

At eight o'clock Montholon arrived. The Emperor and Marchand were busy writing in the room next to the old bedroom. The evening before, the Emperor had gone to sleep in the room with the clock. He said nothing all morning.

The two doctors arrived at eleven-fifteen and stayed for an hour. Napoleon remained for a quarter of an hour without speaking, then he said:

"I digest nothing, therefore there is no point in my eating. My stomach rejects everything."

Dr. Arnott said that he had only brought up a little, and whatever food he managed to retain would always do him good. The Emperor asked whether he thought quinine could take the place of food. Arnott replied that it could not. It could help the stomach to digest, but it could not take the place of proper nourishment.

"If it were sufficient," the Emperor declared, "I would prefer it to eating. The dose I took this morning weighed less heavily on my stomach than the first ones I was given. Have you no better remedies for weakness? Something else of a similar nature? If you have nothing stronger, then medical science can do nothing, because every day I lose more strength and become weaker from day to day."

"It is true that Your Majesty is weaker," Dr. Arnott replied, "but I have seen many patients in an even weaker state than you make a recovery. You must therefore have hope."

"Words, words and phrases fit for women and children," Napoleon said wearily, "but to men and especially to soldiers like us, you should speak the truth."

"I have told you the truth," Arnott rejoined. "I have said what I think."

"What is the strongest remedy you have? Mercury?" Napoleon asked.

"In certain cases, but it is useless in cases of weakness," Dr. Arnott replied.

"Mercury? Opium? Quinine?" the Emperor repeated.

"Yes, in certain illnesses, but in other cases to let blood is one of the strongest remedies."

"You English, you let too much blood," Napoleon remarked.

"To let blood is excellent for certain types of illness; but no blood is ever let in cases of weakness."

"Are the English full-blooded as a rule?" Napoleon inquired.

"Yes, generally, up to the age of forty," Dr. Arnott replied.

"Nevertheless," Napoleon said, "I had thought them to be of a more lymphatic temperament. You have no sun in England."

"Oh yes, we do," Arnott replied, "but it is less strong than in the Mediterranean countries. In July and August the sun shines warmly in England."

"But Carracioli said that an English sun is not the equal of an Italian moon."

"Who was Carracioli, a painter?"

"No, he was an ambassador," replied Napoleon, who then returned to the subject of his own health.

"If my present state of weakness were the result or the consequence of a fever, of a recognizable cause, doubtless the treatment you have prescribed would have been effective. But as this weakness is not the consequence of a definite illness, but the illness itself, I perceive that you have no means of curing it. It requires something more drastic than quinine."

"But," Arnott protested, "you are so weak that we are unable to give you anything stronger."

"Very well, I won't argue the contrary," said Napoleon, "but no matter what the cause, you can see the effect. I know that I have none of the symptoms of death, but I am so weak that it would not take a cannon ball to kill me; a grain of sand would suffice."

In the morning Montholon met the Grand Maréchal in the antechamber of the Emperor, and asked him whether Mr. Ibbetson had paid the third month of the quarter, as he had only received the first two months. He pointed out that it would be most distressing if a crisis should prevent the Governor from paying that month, as then all these unfortunate people would lose a month's salary. The Grand Maréchal said that he would ask Mr. Ibbetson for the money for the third month.

April 18—The Emperor was sick twice during the night and once in the morning at about ten-thirty. At noon he had some chocolate, while the doctors were present.

"Should I have some sieved food afterwards?" Napoleon asked them.

"Certainly," Dr. Arnott replied. "Since you were able to assimilate it yesterday, you would be well advised to have some more."

The doctors left the room at one o'clock. The Emperor sat up in his armchair for half an hour. He then had an enema, a great part of which he was unable to retain, although he did not lose it completely, as he had done the day before.

"Was there any bile, Marchand?" he asked.

"No, Your Majesty, I don't think so," Marchand replied. At half-past two the Grand Maréchal asked permission to retire.

"Go, my child," the Emperor said to him. "I am very weak. There must soon be an end to this."

Since the Emperor has had to change his clothes so frequently, he has no more shirts, only his flannel vest. When he sat up in his armchair, he placed a flannel blanket over his legs. For the past three days he has constantly asked for the windows to be kept wide open. Usually, as he sat down in his chair, he would say:

"Good morning, sun, good morning, my friend!" Or else he would nod his head in a gesture of welcome.

Yesterday and today, while he was in his armchair, his blister was dressed. It had been neglected for forty-eight hours. Since it had been dressed every day, the blister was discharging much more.

Dr. Arnott commented on the pockmark on the Emperor's right arm.

"Yes," Napoleon said, "that was from the inoculation I had forty-five years ago, when they were just beginning to do such things."

Yesterday and today the Emperor ceased to have any twitching of the lips. He has been sleeping with his mouth slightly open, but this morning his mouth was shut. Antommarchi finds him to be even weaker and thinks that the condition of the Emperor is much worse and that no treatment can save him. Dr. Arnott finds that during the past few days he has indeed grown increasingly weak; he is taking far too little nourishment.

Montholon arrived at four o'clock. The Grand Maréchal talked with the doctors. Dr. Arnott is of the opinion that the Emperor needs to have his mind taken off the thought of death, which seems to disturb him. He asked whether the Emperor is interested in gardens, though of course, for the present such a form of relaxation is not to be thought of. He finds that the Emperor has grown increasingly weak during the past four or five days, but that nevertheless the stomach has gained strength in the past two days. If the Emperor were able to eat more, he would recover. Certainly the little he is eating at present does not give him sufficient nourishment.

At half-past five, the Emperor sent for the Grand Maréchal. He handed him three packages closed with a wafer and sealed with the Emperor's own seal. The Emperor said to him:

"Bertrand, I have made my will. It is written entirely in my own handwriting. Please place your own signature and seal there. Montholon is to put his here, Abbé Vignali there, and Marchand there. You will also sign and seal the three boxes. Do this and ask no questions."

Then they went into the former bedroom and there, together with Montholon and Marchand, they carried out the Emperor's instructions. None of them had his own seal, and the question arose as to whether Bertrand should use his own seal or the seal of Grand Maréchal of the Palace? Bertrand went and asked the Emperor which he was to use.

"The seal of the Grand Maréchal, of course," Napoleon replied. "There can be no possible doubt about that."

The Emperor got out of bed. The Grand Maréchal went to support him, as he had been doing for the past ten or fifteen days.

"No," said Napoleon, refusing Bertrand's arm, while he walked to his chair with a firm step. To those around him it was as though they were seeing Sixtus V, after he had been elected Pope, throw away his crutches and start to chant the Te Deum. Monseigneur Vignali, whom we had been unable to find, then came into the room.

"Ah, so there you are," said the Emperor, and he sent for the doctors.

When they entered the room, Napoleon was quite gay, and spoke freely, without supporting himself over-much on his chair, and he asked for his dinner. When it had been brought in, he ate some hash. He complained that Marchand had not heard him ask for some gruel, and that he had ordered his potatoes to be cooked à la maître d'hôtel. Whereas for supper, the Emperor had asked for some gruel, souffléd potatoes, and no stew.

"Give the butler my order and say I want something that is well cooked and easily digested," Napoleon said.

He ate some hash with croutons of fried bread. He asked for some clear soup and ate several spoonfuls of it. Then he asked whether there was a leg of mutton, and if so would they bring him a thin slice that could be chewed easily. But there was only a roast turkey cock. However, the Emperor asked for a wing to be sent up, and he began to eat it, starting with the skin. Then he threw it down and said:

"Is this good, doctor?"

"Yes, very good indeed," the doctors replied.

Later Napoleon told the Grand Maréchal that if he were having a roast leg of mutton at home to send him a slice. He felt like eating some. A leg of mutton was to be roasted for his supper. The doctors urged him to take a second dose of quinine in the evening. Dr. Arnott said that he could not bring it himself, on account of the distance, but that Dr. Antommarchi would give it to him at eight o'clock. Then the doctors left.

The Emperor sent for Vignali, who came into the room. He handed him the three wills and said:

"There is my will, in my own handwriting. Place your signature and your seal on the three of them, as well as on the three boxes."

Vignali bowed deeply and went into the bedroom to carry out the Emperor's instructions.

Prior to this, Napoleon had told the Grand Maréchal:

"This evening Marchand will bring you my side arms. You will give them to my son, the King of Rome, when he is sixteen years old, because until then it would mean giving them to Austria."

Bertrand told the Emperor that he had discussed his condition with Dr. Arnott, who had found him weaker than during the past few days, but thought that his stomach was stronger. The Emperor thought a great deal about what he was going to eat. If he digested the hash, it would be a very good thing. Bertrand said that two ships had put in from the Cape. One the *Bosnia*, which was a ship on the cruise, had brought no news, but the other, which had come from India, was commanded by Captain Edwards, the husband of the "Nymph." And although she herself was not on board, her sister Mrs. Jordan [?] was returning on this ship to England.

As Vignali had finished, the Emperor dismissed the Grand Maréchal, while Monseigneur Vignali remained with him. Napoleon told Montholon that evening that Vignali had taken the will away with him. Montholon asked what the Grand Maréchal had thought about that.

"Nothing," Napoleon had replied, "he didn't say a word." Then he asked:

"Does anyone in the house know that I have made my will?"

"Not at all," Montholon replied. "No one believes you to be dangerously ill."

Napoleon discussed his condition with Montholon. He knew that Dr. Arnott did not believe him to be dangerously ill, whereas

Antommarchi did. At eight-thirty he took his dose of quinine, and soon afterwards he vomited almost all he had eaten at six o'clock, although he retained the quinine. The same thing happened twice during the night and once at six o'clock in the morning. At ten o'clock at night the Emperor had an enema and passed a fairly good movement.

April 18—At eight o'clock the Emperor ate a little bread and milk. At nine o'clock he had a piece of bread soaked in the gravy of the roast leg of mutton. The Emperor felt very weak. The doctors paid their visit at eleven o'clock. The Emperor asked for some vermicelli. He ate three spoonfuls, then threw it up almost immediately.

He asked Dr. Arnott, "Is the quinine mixture made up here or in town?"

"In town," Dr. Arnott replied.

"Did the chemist come to St. Helena with the Governor?"

"No."

"Was he sent to the Island by Sir Thomas Reade?" Napoleon asked.

"There is no connection between them," Arnott stated. "The chemist is a man who was here before the arrival of the Governor. He belonged to the Company. A thoroughly trustworthy man."

The doctors left the room. The Emperor ate some fried potatoes. The doctors returned at five o'clock. The Emperor complained that he had no surgeon in ordinary, and that his dinner was not ordered for him. He asked Dr. Arnott who should act as head waiter to a sick person, and who should order what the patient was to eat. Arnott replied that it was the duty of the doctor.

"Then give your orders," Napoleon said.

He got up, and then dinner was brought in. It consisted of rice soup, floating island, potato soufflé, and a purée of pheasant. Napoleon ate some of the rice soup and purée of pheasant, some floating island, and drank some Madeira.

Dr. Arnott advised him not to eat the soufflé. As a general rule he advised him to avoid eating butter. The Emperor asked what he was allowed to eat. Arnott replied: "Anything that agrees with you."

"Yes, but what?" the Emperor asked. "I have no mind for such things. I have never known how to order my own dinner, and now even less than ever before."

The Emperor complained to the Grand Maréchal about Dr. Antommarchi. Everything about the man displeased him, even the very tone of his voice. "It's all the fault of Madame, who should have sent me Locatelli or Vacca."

Montholon came to see the Grand Maréchal. In the evening he would bring the Emperor's side arms to Bertrand's house. He told him that the Emperor had been much affected at what the Grand Maréchal had said to him, that he had not wanted to be upset, yet he had perceived the Grand Maréchal to have been very much hurt. As to Mme. Bertrand, he would embrace her. It was not at times such as these, he said, that one could remain vindictive.

In the evening the Emperor's side arms were conveyed to the house of the Grand Maréchal. They consisted of the Emperor's pistols, sabre, sword, and dagger. The Emperor had retained only his rapier, while Noverraz had his hunting knife.

The Emperor passed a quiet night, with little vomiting.

A Captain who was on his way back from China, called on Mme. Bertrand. Four years before, he had been presented to the Emperor by the Grand Maréchal. He recalled all the details, and was much attached to the Emperor. He said that the English people had no wish to keep Napoleon at St. Helena, and they felt that the ignoble way in which the Emperor was being treated was a slur on them. The Captain was told that the Emperor was very ill indeed.

"Then we must make every effort to see that he recovers," he said. "It can not be long before he will leave here, perhaps in less than three months. Probably Admiral Lambert will accompany him back. He is a good man, not very outstanding perhaps, but he is generally respected. It is public opinion that is forcing Lord Holland into the Government, not any political party but a unanimous public opinion. That was what was generally rumored at the Cape, and it was also the opinion of the Governor of the Cape. There, news was even less recent than it is here." There news had been received only up until December, while here at St. Helena the Captain had found news dating from January 12. The trip from the Cape had taken him nine days.

The Grand Maréchal repeated this conversation to the Emperor who said: "It is too late now."

"But the Captain only said at first that such a thing might happen. That nothing concerning your health should be neglected, and every kind of treatment should be tried."

April 19—The Emperor had a good night, and kept down his dinner. At seven o'clock in the morning he had some soup. Then later in the morning he had Marchand read to him the chapter on the Italian Campaigns from Toulongeon's *History of France*.

"It is pathetic," Napoleon remarked, "and difficult to imagine that a man who had no need to write for a living could do such bad work. The writer is even more frivolous than Dumas. He puts Milan behind Turin."

The doctors paid their visit at eleven o'clock. Napoleon had lunch at noon. He ate some sieved sorrel with croutons of fried bread and chewed the wing of a chicken; he then had some floating island and a stewed plum; and drank two spoonfuls of wine in six of water. The Emperor made Arnott taste everything in a way that was a compliment to him, and as he had done during dinner on the previous evening. In future, the Emperor said, he intended to have three meals. At six in the morning, at noon, and at six in the evening. He was feeling stronger than he had felt for some considerable time.

Napoleon got up for three quarters of an hour. After the doctors had left, the Grand Maréchal read aloud until two o'clock Toulongeon's *History of France*, on the subject of the negotiations that followed the Italian Campaigns and the 18th Fructidor. Marchand took over from him at half-past five and read about the affairs of Rome. Then, with the help of Marchand, Napoleon burned many documents.

The doctors returned at half-past four. The Emperor said that he felt weak.

"Then you must eat more," they replied.

Napoleon asked the Grand Maréchal whether any ships had arrived. Marchand remarked to Mme. Bertrand that only good news would cure the Emperor. He had supper at eight o'clock, and ate fairly well.

Montholon told the Grand Maréchal that during the night the Emperor had asked him if he had handed over the side arms to Bertrand. Every time the Emperor had woken up it had been to speak of his death or to give some instruction relating to it. He had burned all the notes to his military works, as he wished no trace of them to remain. He wanted to leave only the best of his military ideas. He himself had picked up military ideas from the Maréchal de Saxe and the King of Prussia. His notes on Rogniat were given to General Marbot, as, on the whole, there were many things Marbot knew better than he did.

Montholon added that four or five days before, on either the fifteenth or sixteenth of April, the Governor had begun to re-assert pressure again, saying that as Arnott was unwilling to give him news of the Emperor's health, he wished to see Napoleon himself. Montholon had replied that Dr. Arnott could tell Sir Hudson whether the Emperor were in good or in bad health.

Today the Duty Captain deposited with Montholon an unaddressed parcel which contained the book on Marlborough. General Montholon asked the Captain for an explanation. The Captain replied that he was unable to furnish one, as he had been forbidden to say anything whatever under penalty of being court-martialed, together with Dr. Arnott and the Regimental Adjutant.

"Here is the letter which I have received," he said to Montholon. "Read it, but don't give me away."

The Governor had written to say that the book must be returned, as he did not wish the Regiment to accept it: 1) because the Emperor's name was on the flyleaf, 2) because it had not been sent through the usual channels. The Regiment was very angry with the Adjutant, who had sent the book to the Governor before telling the Regiment anything about it. Had the officers known of the gift, the Governor would never have dared to proffer such an insult. Captain Luytens was overcome with shame.

"What a cowardly business. The wretch," the Captain exclaimed, "to rebuff a dying man in such a fashion!"

Ward told Montholon that at Plantation House they feared the death of the Emperor, because they wanted him to live for a long time in a sickly condition as then they could feel sure that he would not escape, and also on account of the salaries they received.

Today Dr. Arnott, having been called into Jamestown to attend Mr. Brooke, who is to have a bladder operation, asked permission not to pay his morning visit, should the Emperor feel better and thus permit it. The Emperor had passed a tolerably good night, yet he nevertheless had a pain in his lower abdomen, although he was not sick. He said that he would excuse Dr. Arnott from attending him that morning.

April 20—At seven o'clock in the morning the Emperor ate some semolina soup and munched a round of buttered toast. He had someone read to him the *History* of Toulongeon all morning. At eleven o'clock he ate some more semolina soup, as well as something else. Afterwards the Grand Maréchal read aloud to him the Swiss expedition by Brune, in *Victories and Conquests*.

"That is better and less complicated than Toulongeon's book," the Emperor remarked.

He then had Hannibal's Battle of Cannes read to him. He had been unable to find in *Victories and Conquests* any account of the Swiss act of mediation. He had Bertrand look in the *Bibliothèque Orientale* to see who was the Saracen King who had reigned over Corsica. But it could not be discovered. From this it transpired that in 806 the Genoese had chased out the Saracens. Between 1100 and 1118, under Pope Pascal II, the Romans had chased the Saracens out of Corsica. But no account of this was to be found in the *Bibliothèque Orientale*.

The doctors arrived at half-past four. The Emperor told them that during the night he had suffered a great deal in his lower abdomen. He had had a temperature between ten o'clock at night and three o'clock in the morning. And he had been so thirsty that he would have liked to have drunk three bottles of water in succession, but he had been unable to take anything, for if he hadn't made an effort he would have been sick. The abdominal spasms where the urge to be sick appeared to originate, started from the line which separated the small intestine from the large. At present he was experiencing such intense pain that it woke him up and caused him to cry out sufficiently loudly for the entire household to hear him. And yet, for the past three days he felt almost sure that he had not lost but gained in strength.

At five o'clock the Emperor ate a little semolina and sorrel. He ordered his dinner for nine o'clock at night, and then the doctors left. It appeared that Mr. Brooke was better and that he had not had to undergo an operation on the bladder. Two ships had put in from China; they were the *Canning* and the *Aegea*.

Polybius gives few details about the Battle of Cannes. Although on the whole he described it very much as the Emperor had understood it. Hannibal had 50,000 men, whereas the Roman Army consisted of 80,000. It was nothing out of the ordinary for 50,000 men to defeat 80,000, especially under such conditions. Hannibal had at his disposal excellent and well-seasoned African and Spanish troops, whereas the Roman Army had not been anywhere near equal to Hannibal's experienced troops. Hannibal also possessed great superiority in cavalry. He began the battle by sending his cavalry against the right and left wings of the Roman Army, which were much inferior to him in numbers and in caliber. Then the Roman Army, drawn up in three ranks, while the enemy was drawn up in one, was surrounded by the cavalry and almost completely wiped out. All this was nothing out of the ordinary. The Roman general, Fabius, did not want to fight and quite rightly. So he behaved as any general would have done under similar circumstances, who had only inferior troops with which to oppose an army of good troops. . . .

The Grand Maréchal, who has been doing some research for the Emperor, went to his home for a short time, while Marchand was reading to the Emperor. The Emperor then asked for the Grand Maréchal, and in the evening he made him explain why "he had not returned, as he had been asked for an account of the Saracen Kings of Corsica."

April 21—Napoleon is not sleeping at night. From midnight until four o'clock he dozed and from four to seven o'clock he dictated either to Montholon or to Marchand. Montholon remarked that he was far too restless for it to be a good sign. Marchand told Antommarchi that the Emperor had talked about nothing but politics and the great distress of Mme. Bertrand.

He had something to eat at eleven o'clock at night and again at four in the morning. He then slept from nine o'clock until half past ten. The doctors arrived at eleven o'clock. Dr. Arnott was very pleased that the Emperor had felt like being read to, but he said that he was not to tire himself mentally. Marchand said that if things went on like this, in two weeks the Emperor would be able to go out for a drive. He had dined as though he were back at the Tuileries. He had got up for half an hour, had eaten a fairly good meal at one o'clock, and then had the Battle of Cannes as described by Polybius and Guillaume read to him.

"Titus Livius came nearer to the truth than Polybius, in the account of the prisoners. The victory at Cannes was not surprising. It was a case of good troops against bad ones; numbers were of no importance," Napoleon remarked.

He also had read to him, mainly by Bertrand, an account of Caesar's arrival in Greece on the eve of the Battle of Pharsalia. Napoleon then dictated a note to Marchand that was to be inserted in his copy of the Campaigns of Caesar.

"It was the bombastic Lucain, who said that Caesar, when he saw his armies had not arrived from Brundisium, went aboard a fisherman's sloop and when surprised by a storm in the middle of the night said: 'what fearest thou who carriest Caesar and all his fortune?' Caesar does not refer to this in his *Commentaries*. Such conduct on the part of Caesar was pointless and would be very reprehensible. He was needed by his army, which was confronted by that of Pompey, and he could not abandon it. It was, on the other hand, quite useless for him to have gone to Brundisium, as Mark Anthony was there and he had every reason to rely on his zealousness.

"It was ridiculous of Caesar to have taken a fisherman's boat. Could he not have, unknown to the enemy, fitted out a good boat with twenty crack oarsmen and twenty legionnaires, had he wished to cross? In itself the phrase was puffed up and absurd. What did Caesar and all his fortune matter to a raging ocean that paid no attention to such matters?"

The Emperor slept from half-past two until half-past four, although at about four o'clock he asked to have a novel read to him. The doctors paid their visit at half past four, but Napoleon said little. His condition was much the same as before. He said that he wished the doctors to come in future at half past five.

Admiral Lambert called on Mme. Bertrand. He had been very ill; he was accompanied by his flag captain. They both asked for news of the Emperor. The Admiral said that when he had first come to St. Helena he would have been very glad to have been presented to the Emperor, but that to his great regret it had not been possible for it to be arranged.

"It was his own fault," the Emperor observed, when the Grand Maréchal repeated the conversation to him.

"M. de Montchenu is very ill," Bertrand told the Emperor. "He is unable to ride a horse or to go for a drive in a carriage."

"Then why doesn't he go away?" Napoleon asked. "The poor old fellow could continue his treatment in France. He is of no use here."

The Emperor thought that the ship bearing the cooks must have been forced by bad winds to return to port. At six o'clock he asked for his supper and sent for Antommarchi, who told him that he was to have cream of rice soup, a mutton chop, fried potatoes, and apple meringue.

The Emperor complained at being given a meal so unsuitable to his state of health. The cream of rice was so insipid that it had made him sick. Dr. Antommarchi had himself advised him not to eat meat. He said that Antommarchi was careless. The Emperor made a scene in his presence.

"M [. . . ?] would have handled this matter with a big stick as they do in the Army. You have got yourself involved with a woman," Napoleon said, "and what have you done with your reputation? You are much inferior to Dr. Arnott. . . . I don't know whether he is a good doctor, but he has a good manner, and I will receive him."

The Emperor told the Grand Maréchal that he would have left Antommarchi 200,000 francs, but that now he would not leave him anything in his will. He had left 50,000 francs to Monseigneur Vignali, who at least had made himself respected by his behavior, who had worked, and who had carried out his duties in a proper manner.

In the morning the Emperor had said to the Grand Maréchal:

"No one will be able to say that the doctors cured me. Rather it was they who hindered me from getting well," which amounted to saying what Molière had said elsewhere: "I see my doctor, I listen to what he has to say. I do not carry out his instructions . . . and I recover!"

"I too," Napoleon said, "have not taken their potions, but I have listened to my doctors when they said: 'don't eat such and such; get up, etc.' Nevertheless, I have told Dr. Antommarchi that I was unable to digest my food and that pills and quinine would do me no good, while on the contrary the doctors have thought that they have benefited me, with the exception of the last dose of quinine."

On another occasion Napoleon told Antommarchi that the Grand Maréchal should have prostituted his wife, and that he owed it to himself to make up her mind for her should she have proved refractory. However, the great thing with the Grand Maréchal was the fact that he always agreed with the Emperor and never complained, whereas Montholon did complain. Napoleon had wanted Antommarchi to play the part of Mercury, and to persuade Mme. Bertrand to become his mistress. "But," Antommarchi had protested, "how can I do such a thing? Whatever would the Grand Maréchal think of me?"

Dr. Antommarchi had come to St. Helena filled with respect and admiration for the Grand Maréchal and his wife. Almost the day after his arrival, he had been told that the Grand Maréchal was a nincompoop, and of no use to the Emperor. He had come to St. Helena, not on account of his devotion to Napoleon, but because otherwise he would have shared the fate of Labédoyère and Marshal Ney. His wife, it was true, was pleasant and attractive, but she was nevertheless a fallen creature who went with every English officer who passed her house, and was even to be found in the ditches with them. She was the lowest of women.

Antommarchi had been stunned by what he had heard. He could have had no very great opinion of the moral standards of the Emperor.

At nine o'clock the Emperor had some soup, a jelly, a spoonful of wine and was promptly sick. He remained in the sitting room until one o'clock. The doctors paid their visit at half past eleven.

Montholon told them that the Emperor had had an unbroken sleep from midnight until five in the morning. He had then woken up and asked whether it were midnight, and had afterwards gone peacefully to sleep again. Upon his entering the bedroom, the Emperor had told Montholon that his illness had changed in character. Previously the vomiting had come from the abdomen, whereas it now came from the stomach itself. From nine in the evening, until three o'clock in the morning, the Emperor had woken up every half hour and he had been obliged to drink water to clear his throat. But from three o'clock until nine o'clock in the morning, he had slept peacefully. After nine o'clock he had eaten, though without feeling hungry, but as soon as he had drunk some wine he had felt like being sick. He had no wish to eat anything.

The doctors prescribed a dose of gentian to tone up the stomach. They said that it would be sufficient if he took one or two tablespoonfuls every morning. The Emperor said that he would see. He dismissed the doctors and had mass said: *it was Easter Day.*

Dr. Arnott had some patients to visit and was unable to attend mass. At half past five the doctors returned. They urged Napoleon to take the gentian mixture. He replied that he would try. The doctors found that the movements he had passed were good.

"You see," the Emperor told them, "your pills are still taking effect, and my organism is easy to handle."

Dr. Arnott said with a smile that he didn't think that his pills could have acted on the Emperor's movements today.

"Do you know why it is raining now?" inquired Napoleon.

"No," replied the doctors.

"Because five hundred years ago there was a wind somewhere in Europe. . . . You say that enemas have no effect on the upper regions of the body. But why not? They are able to clear the head and the heart, so why should they not also have an effect on the upper regions?"

"I don't pretend that they have no such effect," the doctor replied, "but it can only be very slight."

"No, no," said Napoleon, "one must be precise. You have said that enemas produce no effect on the upper regions of the body, yet in nature everything is linked together. The wind of today will, in a hundred years' time, cause a ship to founder off the coast of China. By this I mean to say that those who would know what the weather will be like through analyzing what it has been in the past are mistaken. There is no such thing as a periodical return, and it is useless to seek to regularize the weather. That is nonsense."

The doctors again advised their prescription. "A child would take it," they said. The Emperor said that he would see; then he dismissed them.

April 22—The Emperor had the Grand Maréchal remain with him and talked to him from six to eight o'clock about his will and his final dispositions. A separate note on this subject will be made.[1]

At eight o'clock Dr. Antommarchi discovered that the Emperor had a temperature. Napoleon had something to eat at ten o'clock, but he then vomited everything which he had just eaten as well as all he had taken at four o'clock. He passed a fairly quiet night.

Conversation of the evening of April 22—The Emperor told the Grand Maréchal that he had made three wills. The first was not to be opened until it reached Paris. They were to say that Buonavita had taken it with him to Europe, so as to prevent it being found by the English. The second will, was a codicil which was to be opened at Longwood and shown to the English. In it the Emperor had disposed of all the possessions which he had at Longwood, so that the English could not lay hands on them. The third will was intended for the Empress.

Marchand had been intrusted with delivering the wills when and in such manner as the Emperor had seen fit to indicate.

RELIGION—In his will the Emperor declared that he had died in the Catholic faith, in which he had been born. Before his death it had been his wish that Abbé Vignali should administer communion, extreme unction, and whatever else was usual in such cases. Napoleon had asked him whether he quite understood what was to be done.

[1]This valuable note has been preserved. It has been thought advisable to insert it here, in its chronological place. A version was published by M. d'Hauterive in the *Rev. des deux mondes*, December 15, 1928, which followed a fair copy of this note made by Bertrand himself.

In actual fact the Emperor died a Theist, believing in a rewarding God, the principle of all things. Yet he stated that he had died in the Catholic religion, because he believed that to be compatible with public ethics.

BURIAL—It was the wish of the Emperor that Dr. Antommarchi should perform an autopsy on his body, alone or with Dr. Arnott, who had attended him. But that as probably Dr. [Shortt] would be sent to assist them, every precaution was to be taken to see that no nonsense was inserted in the official report.

The Emperor requested, and called upon us all to join in demanding, that he be buried on the banks of the Seine, in the country he had loved so well. By banks of the Seine, he meant, of course, somewhere in France.

He thought that the Bourbons would raise no objection to this. He would prefer above all to be buried in the Cemetery of Père Lachaise in Paris, where his body could be placed between the graves of Masséna and General Lefebvre, and in the center of their small memorial, a column might be put up to him. He would much prefer that to being buried at St. Denis among all the Bourbon kings. If the Bourbons wished to distinguish themselves, they would have him interred at St. Denis, but he thought that they would not have the intelligence to do that. Or else, let his body be buried on an island formed by the junction of the Rhône and Saône rivers near Lyons. Or lastly, let them bury him at Ajaccio in Corsica, which was still a part of France. In that case, let him be buried in the Cathedral of Ajaccio, by the side of his ancestors, where he had had his uncle Lucien interred.

The Emperor did not think that his body would be left at St. Helena. He thought that provision had been made for such an eventuality. But should it happen, he preferred to be buried, not at Plantation House, but near the fountain which had provided him with water throughout his sojourn.

Louis Bonaparte had had the body of their father interred at Montpellier, then after having had it reburied on his estate at Saint-Leu, he had sold the property, which was a thing he should never have done as his father's ashes reposed there. The sisters of Mercy had been obliged to come and collect them. He would have done better to have left the body at Montpellier, where his father had received an honorable burial.

ESTABLISHED FACTS—In his will the Emperor established certain facts and some of the principles on which his Government had been based. For instance the trial of the Duke of Enghien; whom he had had executed, not for the political reasons that the *Manuscript of St. Helena*, which he disowned, had attributed to him, but because there had been a conspiracy in Paris of sixty assassins sent there by the Bourbons. He had had the Duke arrested from a sense of justice and of national dignity. It had been his right so to do, and at present, when he was on the brink of the grave, he remained unrepentant and he would do it again.

THE ENGLISH RULING CLASSES—The Emperor stated that he died murdered by the English Ruling Class and its hired assassins. He hoped that the English people would soon avenge his death. He had been killed first by the climate, then by pin pricks, and finally through lack of exercise. The sentries had been removed from Longwood and permission given for him to go out, only after he had no longer been in a condition to do so. Doubtless the English oligarchy would reply to this, as well as by publishing documents. But the Emperor asked us to refute them. First we would have to say that there had been two types of official correspondence. One which had been open and above board, and the other which had been secret, and they had both been in opposition the one to the other. There had also been hints and insinuations.

TESTAMENTARY EXECUTORS—The Emperor named as Testamentary Executors the Grand Maréchal, General Montholon, and Marchand. Napoleon felt that he owed this to Montholon for the devotion that he had shown him for the past six years. Montholon owed him nothing and had lost 300,000 francs of his private fortune through staying at St. Helena. Napoleon hoped that the Grand Maréchal would draw closer to Montholon.

It was the Emperor's wish to raise Marchand. He thought that all the sovereigns [?] were interested in him. In so much as his former servants Constant and Roustan had been despicable, in so much had Marchand been admirable. In his will Napoleon said that he had treated him royally, and that he had put him in a position to employ more servants than he had himself. Marchand already owned some land in Burgundy. He must not fritter away what he was being given, but with it he should lay the foundations of a solid fortune. His great wealth would bring him consideration. The Emperor hoped that one day the King of France would make Marchand a baron. Gourville[2] was an example of the fact that faithful servants could take their place in the front rank of society; the Abbé de la Rochefoucauld, however, was only a private person. The Emperor hoped that we would all look after Marchand and help him with advice.

HIS SON—The Emperor intrusted to the Grand Maréchal the duty of giving his side arms to his son the King of Rome, when the boy should have reached the age of sixteen. He could leave him nothing more precious. But the arms would have to be kept for him until he was sixteen, because otherwise it would merely mean giving them to Austria.

He said that the dagger had been captured at Malta. It had been given to the Grand Master Lavalette by the Pope, after the defense of Malta. The side arms should be well cared for, especially the pistols, for fear they should grow rusty. The Emperor regretted that he no longer had his carabin, which he had given to the King of Württemberg, since when he had not ordered another to replace it.

Caulaincourt should have in his possession the handsome sabre on which was a portrait of [omission in text]. The Emperor said that he would be very pleased if Caulaincourt would present it to his son the King of Rome. It was his wish that his son should never bear arms against France. He had trusted Montholon to give him his silver, and Marchand was to convey to him his decorations, personal effects and toilet articles, as well as a complete list of every type of costume he had worn, a dozen shirts, and a dozen of every type of underwear the Emperor had used. He asked Ali to convey to his son four hundred books from among those which

---

[2]Gourville, before becoming Collector of Taxes, had started life as a valet de chambre in the household of the Abbé de la Rochefoucauld.

he had most frequently used. Noverraz was to take his fowling pieces to the King of Rome. Pierron, the major-domo, was to convey his china, and Coursot, the butler, was to take him the small pictures that were on the mantelpiece.

The Emperor divided up his various personal possessions among several different people, so as to give proof of his satisfaction to those who had served him well, and so that in the event of the death or any other unforeseen event happening to one of them, all would not be lost. Marshal Turenne should have in his possession Napoleon's grand collars and his collar of the Order of the Legion of Honor and he was to convey them to his son, to whom such relics would be precious.

He left a million francs to the Grand Maréchal and the same amount to General Montholon.

SERVANTS—It was the Emperor's wish to place his servants in such a position that they would never have to serve anyone else. He left 150,000 francs to Ali and 150,000 to Noverraz, who had already received 50,000, making a total of 200,000 francs. No doubt Noverraz would return to Switzerland and settle in the Canton of Vaud, where he would be one of its most wealthy inhabitants. Ali would be well advised to remain near Marchand and to enjoy his protection. It might be a good idea to find him a place near the King of Rome. The Emperor left 150,000 francs to Pierron, and more than 50,000 to Archambault. The cook and Coursot the butler were well provided for. He left 150,000 francs to Monseigneur Vignali, who had earned general respect, who had studied to improve himself, and who had also given lessons to the children of the Grand Maréchal. Who, in other words, had shown himself capable of doing almost anything.

There was only the unfortunate Dr. Antommarchi to whom the Emperor left nothing. He would have liked to have left him 200,000 francs, but he had not done so, owing less to the poor opinion he had of his capabilities, than to the fact that Dr. Antommarchi had shown no devotion to the Emperor, and had not looked after him in a manner to which he had felt that he was entitled. However, there was still time for him to enjoy a share of the benefits, as a codicil could always be made.

BEQUESTS—The Emperor left 100,000 francs to Bignon for the purpose of writing the diplomatic history of Napoleon's reign. He left 100,000 francs to General Marbot with which to refute anti-national military historians. He also asked for his own notes on General Rogniat to be given to Marbot. He left 100,000 to Clauzel and to Lefebvre-Desnouettes, although probably they were above that. The Emperor forgot none of the refugees. He left bequests to Réal and to others, as well as bequests to Drouot and Cambronne. He left 100,000 francs to Corbineau and the same to the wife and children of Letort. His other aides-de-camp, Rapp, Lemarrois, Lobau, and Durosnel were well off, though possibly Dejean was not. The Emperor made bequests to a great many people. He believed that he had forgotten no one.

The Emperor made bequests to the widow of Marshal Duroc and to the widow of the Duke of Istria. It was his wish that the son of the Duke of Istria should marry the Duchess of Frioul; this was, however, no more than an indication of his wishes, and was to remain subject to mutual inclination and to other reasons of propriety.

The Emperor left 100,000 francs to Larrey and named him in his will as the most virtuous of men. He left nothing to General Denon, because he thought him well off; he left 100,000 francs to Arnault and 100,000 francs to Poggi. He provided well for La Valette, and he made his old nurse and her children rich. He left nothing to his family, which enabled him to be generous towards all those who had served him. He treated Las Cases well, appointing him Treasurer to the Commission; in the event of the death of Las Cases, he appointed his son, the King of Rome, and failing him, Marshal Drouot.

The Emperor imposed on all the bequests a tax of 3% for office and traveling expenses.

LAFFITTE [Jacques, banker]—The total amount of the bequests came to 6,100,000 francs. This was composed of an original capital sum of 5,300,000 francs with interest at 5%. The Emperor had torn up the second receipt from Laffitte. He insisted that Laffitte should pay interest at 5% and not at 4%. It was essential to be very strict over the accounts. The Emperor had allocated to

Laffitte only the 100,000 francs he had left for Las Cases; the 12,000 francs per month and the 20,000 francs for Lallemand, the 3,000 francs for Gilly, the 72,000 francs for Balcombe, and possibly the 100,000 francs for O'Meara, and also I think the 24,000 francs for Stokoe. If Laffitte had paid for General Lavalette's trial, it was up to Prince Eugène to see to the matter; he was rich enough. The business with Laffitte was the first that should be attended to, and nothing else was to be undertaken until that had been settled.

PRINCE EUGÈNE—The Emperor claimed two million francs from his Italian estates, and he disposed of this sum accordingly. In the Kingdom of Italy, the Emperor possessed a million francs' worth of china, a considerable amount of furniture and a large stud of horses. For eight months Venice had been swamped with his belongings. Therefore, the Emperor hoped that it would not be necessary to ask Prince Eugène twice. In the basement of Malmaison the Emperor had left 2,000,000 francs of which he had never definitely disposed. The Emperor expressed the wish that, if need be, Prince Eugène would deduct these two millions from the forty millions which he had previously given to him, and for this purpose he had made a separate disposition.

THE EMPRESS—From the Empress the Emperor claimed the 2,000,000 francs belonging to him that he had handed to her at Orleans. He began his codicil to the Empress by asking her to return to the Grand Maréchal the income of 20,000 francs which he had given her on Parma, the 100,000 francs which he had on deposit at the Mont Napoléon de Milan, and finally the sums which he had in Illyria.

The Grand Maréchal observed to the Emperor that he had no possessions in Illyria, but that all his endowments were in Poland, Hanover, and Westphalia. The Emperor intrusted the Grand Maréchal with the duty of officially announcing his death to the Empress. He assumed that she would be remarried to one of the archdukes.

PERSONAL ESTATE—The Emperor added that he had a right to his personal estate, as it consisted of the proceeds from the economies he had been able to make on his Civil List, which the Grand Maréchal knew to have been between twelve and fifteen million francs a year. This had amounted to a total of two hundred millions, of which half had been spent on the Guards and the Army, and half on the towns and provinces which had suffered from foreign invasion. The Court Treasurer La Bouillerie should be asked for a statement, as he had been the chief accountant. They could consult Cambacérès, if he were in Paris, as well as others familiar with the law. This business was to be handled last of all; until the other matters had been settled, this was to remain secret.

The Emperor made a will that pleased everybody. He left great latitude to his testamentary executors, as well as a noble job to be done.

HIS FAMILY—It was the Emperor's wish that the Grand Maréchal should go to Madame Mère, and he requested him to say to her: that Napoleon had considered that her fortune could not be put to better use than by giving gifts of money to her grandsons, and by seeing that they married into Roman families. Her family was to take possession of Rome and to ally itself with all the princely families, that was to say, with all those families in which there had been popes. The marriages which had already taken place with the Hercolani and Gabrielli families were acceptable, but Napoleon had very much disapproved of the Swedish marriage. Nieces of the Emperor might wash the feet of the Pope, but of no one else.

Members of Napoleon's family were to marry into the Colonna, the Orsini, and similar families; they might also intermarry. But they were not to marry in France, unless there were a change of Government. What the Emperor had said was applicable to all his nephews and nieces, as well as to Queen Caroline and King Joseph. His family would probably produce popes, and in any case, it would exercise great influence, even in France. Finally, Rome was the Eternal City, whereas Switzerland was nothing more than a tiny oligarchy.

HIS ILLEGITIMATE CHILDREN—The Emperor acknowledged that he had two illegitimate children. The first, who was the son of

Mme. Walewska, was known. He was to inherit an income of 200,000 francs. But as Mme. Walewska had another son whom she would probably wish to favor, as well as others by her second husband, the Duke of Ornano, the Emperor assumed that his son might receive no more than 120,000 francs a year. His interests must therefore be guarded, even against the Duke of Ornano. For this reason, the Emperor recommended him to the care of Bertrand. A position would have to be found for him in a regiment of French lancers, and he would have to be looked after. It was the Emperor's wish that he should never bear arms against France, and that he should adopt French nationality.

The second child was called Charles, Count Léon. His guardian was the father-in-law of Méneval. As it was Murat who had introduced the mother to him, Napoleon had at first assumed the child to have been his. But upon seeing the child, the Emperor had been so struck by its resemblance to himself, while Queen Hortense, to whom he had shown the child, had found that it bore such a striking resemblance to the Emperor, that he had acknowledged it to be his own son. He had given him 150,000 francs invested in the canals, as he had done for Mme. Béchaud, and he had advised the child's guardian to have the interests placed successively upon the Grand Livre,[3] where he should now possess an income of some 300,000 francs. It would be advisable for Bertrand to buy a small estate for him, if possible near his own in the Berry. Léon could then take the name of the estate. The Emperor also recommended this son to the Grand Maréchal and asked him to watch over his future.

THE GRAND MARÉCHAL—By giving the Grand Maréchal a million francs, the Emperor doubled his fortune. Bertrand would therefore have an income of 100,000 francs a year, and by adding to this a pension of 20,000 francs which the French Government could not well refuse him as a Grand Officer, plus the income of 30,000 francs which the Empress was to return to him, the Grand Maréchal would then possess an income of 150,000 francs a year.

The first thing Bertrand must do was to have his trial annulled.

[3]The Grand Livre, or Great Book of the Public Debt. It consists of a list on which figure all the names of State creditors.—Translator's note.

The Emperor asked the Grand Maréchal if he thought that he would be obliged to appear in person and to give himself up to the authorities? And whether Marshal Clauzel had really been convicted.

The Grand Maréchal was to spend some time in Paris first, winding up the affairs of the Imperial Will. Then for a year he should remain quietly in his own province, and get himself elected a Deputy. This was the best means of reaching the House of Lords, should he fail to get there immediately. Bertrand was not to abandon the Berry, but to buy farms and property in the district fifty miles around Châteauroux, as well as a handsome estate about ten or fifteen miles from that town if possible. But he was not to build a house in Paris, or to live there permanently. Napoleon advised him to have only a small house in Paris, rather like the one which the Emperor had possessed in the rue des Victoires.

In the winter, the Grand Maréchal was to spend only a few months in Paris, without attempting to make a splash. He should model himself on the English, who lived simply when they were in the capital, and kept their luxury for when they were on their country estates. No one thought anything of a man with an income of 80,000 francs a year in Paris; there were so many, no one paid any attention. But in the country, a man with an income of 60,000 francs enjoyed considerable respect. He was someone of importance, one of the leading figures of the county.

If Bertrand were one day in a position to marry his daughter either to one of the sons of Lucien Bonaparte or possibly to the son of Mme. Walewska, the prospect would please the Emperor. The Walewski were Polish princes and young Walewski was not a bastard. The whole affair was the result of gossip, it was the sort of thing to be found in every family. Especially as he was Napoleon's own flesh and blood, which also meant something. Young Walewski would have an income of 120,000 francs, but even if he had no more than 60,000 francs a year, it was still a handsome fortune. The Emperor, however, only intended the Grand Maréchal to bear this suggestion in mind.

LADY HOLLAND—The Emperor left to Lady Holland the snuff-box on which was a satyr. It had been presented by the Pope at the time of the Treaty of Tolentino. He might possibly be mistaken, but the Emperor was under the impression that Lady Holland was the only woman he had mentioned in his will, with the exception of his mother and sisters.

ARRIGHI—Arrighi should have a permanent residence in Corsica and go there to live. He should be told this. He should then get himself elected a Deputy for Corsica so as to enter the House of Lords, and after that return to Corsica every three years.

AJACCIO—In telling the Grand Maréchal to establish himself thoroughly in the Berry, the Emperor added that perhaps he ought to have built himself a palace at Ajaccio, but it had not been part of his policy to remind the French people that he was Corsican by birth; whereas, on the contrary, it had been one of the things which his enemies had striven to underline. Yet he now felt that he should have done so. If he had been born in the province of Berry, like the Grand Maréchal, he would undoubtedly have built a handsome residence there.

JOSEPH—The Emperor thought that his brother Joseph must possess his correspondence with the reigning sovereigns. It ought to be published, either in France, or in America if Joseph had it with him there.

LIBELS—As the Emperor had not read the book by Mme. de Staël, he was unable to reply to it, but it should be possible to find among his correspondence four or five letters Mme. de Staël had written to him while he was in Italy, and which would show her feelings. The Emperor had assumed these letters to be in his red books, but the editors must have suppressed them out of consideration for Mme. de Staël. They ought to be published.

The Emperor repudiated the documents that had been published by his brother Louis. In the position in which the Emperor at present found himself, it had been unworthy as well as clumsy of Louis to attack him in such fashion; and he would be avenged on him through his children. The Emperor requested the Grand Maréchal to tell Louis that their brother Lucien would not have done such a thing. He had not offered him the Throne of Spain, it was true, but he believed that he had offered him the Throne of Naples, which had undoubtedly been a fairly decent crown.

The Emperor also repudiated the authenticity of the letters that Carnot claimed to have written to him. Carnot had never refused the title of Count, on the contrary he had greatly desired the honor and had accepted it with gratitude. He had wanted position and wealth, and he had always treated the Emperor with respect and consideration. Carnot's family were forever urging him to push himself forward, and, on the whole, he had behaved well up to the time of the Provisional Government.

LAFAYETTE—The Emperor stated categorically that he had never proposed making Lafayette a Senator. Far from refusing any such offer, it had been the one thing Lafayette had desired above all others. For this reason he had paid court to Joseph. No one had ever refused him a position, either as Senator or as anything else, with the exception of that odd creature Ducis, who had done so on religious grounds, as Arnault had explained.

When he was First Consul, the Emperor had had a couple of interviews with Lafayette, who had given him a pitiable idea of his political views. Anyway, it was impossible for them to agree, as Lafayette had deserted to the Prussian camp . . . whereas Napoleon had always remained strongly republican.

At that time, Lafayette had not been at all well off. He had claimed estates in Cayenne and had asked for things that the Emperor had been unable to grant because they were illegal. Lafayette had not written the alleged letter when Napoleon was Consul in perpetuity. In those days Lafayette had wished to further the interests of his son, and he had been full of consideration for the Emperor. He may possibly have voted as he claimed to have done, but the Emperor had known nothing about it. It was quite true that Carnot had written to Napoleon to ask for the release of Lafayette, but that had been before the 18th Fructidor. It had been at the request of the Emperor and solely thanks to his influence that Lafayette had been released. Lafayette's wife had joined him while he was still in Italy, and he had not returned to France until after the 18th Brumaire, when he had been busy picking up the pieces of his own fortune, which had amounted to very little. It was not under such circumstances that the Emperor would have refused him a seat in the Senate.

BERNADOTTE—The Emperor also repudiated the letters of Bernadotte. The Emperor had dictated to Bertrand notes on the subject of Bernadotte's *Mémoires* and he had made annotations in the margins of the book. (They were recopied and then rubbed out, I was present when he wrote them and when he checked through the books. BERTRAND.) The Emperor stated that these letters from Bernadotte had been written after the events. Proof of this was self-evident, because at that time Sweden had a consul at Dresden who was engaged in negotiations, and it was not usual to write such letters while negotiations were in progress.

FOUCHÉ AND OTHERS—The Emperor had not mentioned Fouché because he had been unworthy of a reply. Generally speaking, no one had ever refused Napoleon anything. The Emperor could have had all the aristocracy of the Faubourg St. Germain at his court, had he wished. It was wrong to say that d'Argenson had refused to become Court Chamberlain. He would have accepted with alacrity, but the Emperor had preferred to appoint him a Prefect.

The Emperor denounced General Marmont, Marshal Augereau, Talleyrand, and Lafayette to posterity for having caused the rising of the two Chambers. After which the Emperor should have taken over command of the Army.

The Emperor then searched his memory and frequently asked whether he had not forgotten some of his former servants. This bothered him considerably, as he did not want to overlook any of those who had served him well.

"I am searching my conscience, as I wish to pay all my debts, including those of my youth."

He remembered Hubert, who had been his valet in Egypt and who had since become caretaker at the Château de Rambouillet. He made bequests to Lavigne who had been his groom, to another groom from Marseilles(. . .), and to Caesar, his coachman when he was in Egypt, or to his widow.

FISTO (?) must have left money. There were bequests to Paoli, who had been Captain of the Gendarmerie on the Island of Elba; to Mariaggi, the cavalry sergeant at Elba; to a Corsican from Boccognano, who in 1790 or 1792 had rendered the Emperor an outstanding service. He had made Napoleon welcome in his home and had then served him as escort. To a soldier of the Corsican battalion of the Island of Elba, quartered at Bastelica, whose name he had forgotten, but whom Costa would know. To the son of the widow Matra who had been at Elba. To young Vantini, his aide-de-camp at Elba. To the Captain of the Island Port, by name of Philidor. To the Lieutenant Commander of the Imperial Navy in command of the brig *Inconstant*. To the little Corsican who had been a lieutenant on that brig, and whom he had had educated in France. The Emperor bequeathed 100,000 francs to the widow of Representative de Gasparin of the town of Orange, and 100,000 francs to the children of General Dugommier, as well as 100,000 francs to the children of Muiron (although the Emperor was not sure that he had left any children).

The Emperor hesitated before deciding to make a bequest to the man who had attempted to assassinate Wellington, were he guilty or not, and with it a note explaining his motives: for his having violated the surrender, having allowed Ney and Labédoyère to be murdered, for having stripped the museum, etc.

The arrival has been announced of a storeship which left England before the *Repulse*.

April 23—The Emperor had something to eat in the morning. At half-past eleven he took the dose of gentian. The doctors were announced. The Emperor said that he had not smelt the mixture, but that the taste was not unpleasant and that he was willing to take more of it. He inquired as to whether it had been known "during the age of Hippocratus."

"Oh yes," replied the doctors.

"Where was it to be found?" the Emperor asked.

"Everywhere in Europe, in England and in Italy where it was a root with which everyone was familiar. The people especially used it a great deal. It was an *anti-fébrile*, and the people used it because it was much cheaper than quinine."

Napoleon asked the doctors whether we had acquired from America any other form of medicinal plant besides quinine, which had been unknown before the discovery of America. He also asked whether the Chinese had made any contributions to the pharmacopoeia. Dr. Arnott replied in the negative. Most of the opium used in America came from China. He said, however, that the principal cargo of Chinese ships consisted in tea. These ships, one helping the other, paid a Government tax of up to 20,000 pounds sterling, or 5,000,000 francs. Every year twenty to twenty-one ships were chartered, which amounted to 100,000,000 francs a year.

Napoleon remarked that England was badly governed. Given her commercial resources, had he been governing England the people would not have had a farthing of tax to pay, whereas actually taxation was breaking them. They were the most miserable of people. The best resource of an oligarchy lay in moderation, but the ruling classes had lost sight of this and in consequence would perish. William Pitt had carried his policy abroad and he mainly would be to blame for the ruin of England. The English Government was spending money like water, as was obvious on this very Island of St. Helena; yet the people of England were poverty-stricken and weighed down by taxation. The English Government was therefore all the more to blame.

The Emperor talked about Lord Chatham's expedition to the island of Walcheren, which had been very badly led. On the second day the English had taken possession of the fortress of Batz, which had been abandoned by a Dutch general. The fortress had had one hundred and fifty guns which, if they had been used to cover the river, would have prevented the fleet from coming up and reaching Antwerp; this would have meant the capture of the fleet and would also have saved Antwerp. But as the fleet had been able to come up the river and reach Antwerp, it had then been safely under cover. And what finer garrison could be wished for than 6,000 sailors? Antwerp should have been taken by surprise on the second or third day, as the town was impregnable against a normally conducted siege because it had the whole of France behind it and French troops must not be given time to arrive there. The right plan would have been to have disembarked on the Meuse at Willemstad, and to have reached Middleburgh opposite Antwerp on the same day, and then to have tried a *coup de main*. The whole thing would not have taken more than 6,000 men, whereas the English had used 40,000.

Dr. Arnott said the 40,000 had been considerably reduced through sickness.

"At Mantua," Napoleon said, "I saw poor fevered wretches who, after they had been attacked by the fever, were dragging themselves from hospital to hospital and yet ended by dying. To try and help them, I had them spend the night, even when it was very hot, beside the great fires we lit. Then I ordered quinine to be put in their wine. They roared like devils. However, it didn't have much effect; I had a great many sick."

The Emperor drank a little coffee.

"You don't drink this in England, do you?" he asked Dr. Arnott.

"A great deal, nowadays," Arnott replied. "A lot of it comes from the West Indies. It is cheaper than tea, hence the increase in consumption."

The doctors took their leave. The Emperor then spent three or four hours writing out a new codicil to his will, in which he made bequests to the people who had been with him at Elba. To the widows of Representative de Gasparin and of General Dugommier, or to their children. The Emperor said:

"I don't think Muiron left any children. I saw his father several times at the Tuileries, and he would have told me about them."

At a quarter to six the doctors arrived. The Emperor took a second dose of gentian. In an hour he was to have his meal. He told the doctors that he had been writing for four hours.

"You dictated, of course?" Arnott asked.

"No, no," the Emperor replied, "I wrote entirely in my own hand. I write very badly, very rapidly, and no one can read what I have written. On the whole you English write much better than we do. In my youth I despised such things, but I have since come to regret it. Moreover, in those days my mind worked too swiftly for my pen to keep up with my thoughts. In my prime I was able to dictate to four secretaries at once and to keep them exceedingly busy. I am a glutton for work.

"But you have murdered me. I came in all good faith to give myself up to you, you the people of England, not to the Prince

Regent whom I despised, nor to your ruling classes whom I knew too well, for I believed that the English people would not hear of my being treated in such a fashion. But your governing class was too powerful for them.

"Therefore, there is nothing left for me now but to go to London. But, should your ruling classes place my body in Westminster, I predict that on my tomb the English people will swear to destroy the power of the House of Brunswick and of the governing Classes of England. Such a thing would be a shameful monument and not a thing of glory for your country, and ignominy would be its sole reward.

"I have been murdered by their English *sicaire*." ("You won't translate that word," Napoleon said to the Grand Maréchal, "but put it in nevertheless. He will understand.")⁴

"And," the Emperor continued, "I sincerely hope that John Bull will see him hanged. We shall soon receive news from England. I would like to learn that *they* have lost Lord Castlereagh."

Napoleon said all this pleasantly and in a good-humored tone of voice. The doctors left at a quarter past six, and then Napoleon talked with the Grand Maréchal. He told him that Las Cases was well provided for. He had appointed him Treasurer to the Commissions. In the event of the death of Las Cases, he had appointed the King of Rome, and failing him, Marshal Drouot.

The Grand Maréchal spoke to the Emperor about Tallien, whom Napoleon would have liked to have created Duke of Thermidor, and also about Dumouriez.

"But," Napoleon replied, "Tallien is dead and Dumouriez is an intriguer. Moreover, I didn't know him and under the circumstances there is no place for Dumouriez."

The Grand Maréchal told the Emperor that in the dispositions with which he had intrusted him on board the *Bellerophone*, and again in August 1819, the Emperor had not made any that were more favorable than those he had already mentioned, but that at that time Napoleon had given him far greater proof of his confidence. In August he had confided his manuscripts to Bertrand and had intrusted him with the responsibility of seeing that they were published. He had also entrusted him with distributing the money

⁴Sicaire: hired assassin.

from his own coffers. The Emperor had divided his diamonds equally between Mme. Bertrand and Mme. de Montholon, whereas this time he had not even remembered Mme. Bertrand in his will. The Emperor had refused to see her during his illness, which had lent color to the slanderous gossip of which she had been the victim, some of which was so terrible that it was hardly possible to mention the accusations most frequently made. Bertrand reproached the Emperor with the fact that he had not been given the opportunity to justify either his wife or himself, which was a misfortune for him, and Bertrand believed, it would not bring anyone happiness. Bertrand admitted that there had been several brushes between Montholon and himself in the early days, but that as soon as Montholon had been alone and ill, he had hastened to give him what comfort he could, though this had appeared to displease Montholon at the time. Bertrand had acted thus out of friendliness as much as from his belief that in so doing he was carrying out the Emperor's wishes; however, Montholon at the request of the Emperor had ceased to visit him, and to please the Emperor Dr. Antommarchi was also to avoid him, while all visitors to the island were to avoid his home as much as they did Plantation House. How far he had been from foreseeing such an outcome!

The Emperor replied that no women were mentioned in his will, neither Mme. de Montholon nor any other, with the exception of his mother and sisters. He had reached no decision on the subject of his manuscripts. If he were in danger of dying, very probably he would burn all his papers and preserve only the works on the Italian and Egyptian campaigns, as well as those on the campaigns of Caesar, and a few books with which he was familiar.

"I have given my diamonds to Marchand," Napoleon said. "One day I put them around his neck, saying that were I to die, they were to be his. I wanted to give them to the Duchess of Frioul.

"Mme. Bertrand grew away from me; she neither wished to dine nor to spend her evenings in my company. Of course, it was true that she had four children and no maid, and therefore it would have been difficult for her to do so. The first and most essential thing is to have a good manservant and a good maid, and after that, a good surgeon, if she were wealthy enough to attach one to her service. I did not do this in my youth, because I enjoyed very good health. Also I have always been much more fond of crowds than of individuals. I certainly felt the difference between having Marchand for a servant and that rascal Constant. That is something to which I am indebted to Montesquiou, who created my household of interesting young people like Marchand."

Possibly the Grand Maréchal has forfeited some of the Emperor's confidence and affection; but he nonetheless has certain claims on him. Bertrand has a reserved nature which has become greatly accentuated through his natural seriousness of mind.

Montholon, who has no claims upon the Emperor, has very probably sought to create them. He felt that the Emperor would indemnify him for whatever Semonville might have caused him to lose. Mme. de Montholon is very different from Mme. Bertrand; a scheming woman, who has known where her best interests lie. When pensions which she believed could never be paid were mentioned to her, she wouldn't listen. She only gave her heart for value received. Montholon has been the dupe of that woman, but he loves her and will hear nothing against her. They both know where their interests lie, far better than we do. Mme. Bertrand, on the contrary, does not.

"Mme. Montholon was right," Bertrand said bitterly. "At the first sign of unpleasantness, she left. I should have done likewise, a year ago."

But on the whole, the Emperor has been kind. He has spoken quietly, without wishing to wound Bertrand. If he were really ill, he said, he would see Mme. Bertrand two or three times. If he recovered, he would receive her again. (At seven o'clock he had supper, and then at eight o'clock he brought up all his soup.)

"Mme. Bertrand wants to rule despotically [. . .]," the Emperor said. "Montholon, who is an easy-going chap, was on the verge of allowing himself to be dominated by her, but it was I who restrained him and prevented this from happening. The unfortunate Dr. Antommarchi is in a similar position at the moment. He wants to be told everything that I do. But I don't want him told anything. Very soon I shan't even be able to piss without the doctor telling everyone. . . .

"Independence is a fine thing, but it has cost the doctor 200,000 francs, so he may well boast of his independence . . . As for you,

Bertrand," the Emperor continued, "with a wife and four children and no manservant or any domestics other than that slut of a peasant girl from the Berry, you have been unable to do anything else, and I give you full credit.

"But I can't enter into all these details. I have neither wife nor child, and someone must be fond of me. I am well aware that Montholon pays court to me for the sake of what he may inherit. But if one wants people's money, it is best not to belabor them."

April 24—In the morning Napoleon had something to eat. He had passed a fairly good night, despite a temperature. At half-past eleven he took a dose of gentian, then the doctors were announced. Napoleon told them that he felt weak, but that he had had no pain, the only thing being that he had run a temperature during the night.

He again had a long talk with Dr. Arnott, and asked him what pay he received.

"More than a captain," Arnott replied.

"How much does a captain get?"

"Thirty-eight pounds sterling a month."

"Have you the rank of captain?"

"Yes."

"Do you come after them in rank, or do you retain your seniority of appointment among the other officers?"

"My seniority. At the moment I am the senior captain."

"Does your principal assistant hold the rank of lieutenant?"

"Yes."

"Could you be placed under arrest by a captain or a lieutenant in the event of either of them being in command of a battalion?"

"In such case, yes."

"Do the officers pay you when you have attended them?"

"No."

"Do they send you a present?"

"Sometimes, but not very often."

"Do you accept them?"

"Yes."

"Do you attend the people on the island or elsewhere, and do you charge for such services?"

"The local people have their own surgeon, and so I have attended none of them. Occasionally I have been called in on consultation."

"Were you paid?"

"No."

"If you happened to be called in to attend a high-ranking officer, such as Reade or Gorrequer, would they not send you a present?"

"Possibly."

"Would you not accept it?"

"Oh yes."

"Would it not be an insult for you to refuse it? Are you paid by the Government alone or by the Government and the officers together?"

"By the Government alone. In the surgeon's service, he is paid by the Government as well as by the officers. When an officer has been attended by a surgeon he always makes him a present, a watch or some such thing. We think very highly of our surgeons."

"Do many people ask you for news of me?"

"No, although everyone knows that I am seeing you."

There was a pause.

"Where did you study medicine?" Napoleon asked.

"At Edinburgh."

"Isn't London the leading university?"

"For surgery, yes; but for practical medicine Edinburgh is better."

"Which is the third in importance?"

"Dublin."

"You must have a lot of money?"

"Very little."

"Is it invested in property or in Government securities?"

"I have some real estate and some investments."

"What do you do with your money? You are well paid."

"It goes very quickly. Everything here is so dear."

"Where do you come from?"

"From Edinburgh."

"Oh, all Scotsmen are misers!" (The doctor laughed. He has the reputation of being very careful with his money.)

"How much do you spend in your canteen?"

"About a dollar a day, I believe, including wine."

"How much wine do the general officers drink in a day?"

"Half a bottle."

"Oh! For Englishmen that is impossible."

"I never drink any more."

"Whereas I," said Napoleon, "drink almost a whole bottle with my dinner . . . mixed with water, of course."

"We always drink it unadulterated."

"But you drink beer."

"A glass now and then, three or four times a week, perhaps.

"Which wine do you drink?"

"That depends. Sometimes claret, sometimes Madeira."

"Does the Government give you any rations?"

"Yes. The ration consists of a pound of bread, a pound of salt beef, and a quart of beer, or half a bottle of wine. For that we pay next to nothing; a mere six shillings a month."

"What kind of wine?"

"Wine from the Cape."

"Is that what you drink with your meals?"

"No, we don't care for it much. We have a military mess. We give it our wine ration and then we buy something else."

"When you were in France your soldiers must have had a fine time. You must have had trouble keeping them in order."

"Very true."

"What did you do?"

"They were frequently drunk."

"When our fleet from Brest visited Toulon, our sailors were always drunk. They had to be picked off the streets. What do your sailors drink?"

"Beer."

"But when they get their pay, surely they drink wine?"

"No, they drink spirits or beer."

"What kind of spirits?"

"English spirits usually, made from grain."

"Is there much difference in taste?"

"A very great difference."

"Have you been to Paris?"

"Yes."

"When?"

"After the Peace of Amiens."

"How long were you there?"

"For five weeks. I would have stayed longer, but the rupture was near, and I hastened to make my departure."

"Oh, ho, so you were afraid that I would have had you arrested?"

"Ten days later, it would have been too late."

"Did you call on Lord Whitworth?"

"Yes."

"Did you see Lady Dorset?"

"Yes."

"Did you dine with them?"

"No."

"Where did you stay?"

"At the Hôtel St. Thomas."

"Where did you eat?"

"In different restaurants. I had friends and I dined here and there, wherever they happened to be. In the Palais Royal there were two restaurants which the English favored particularly."

"How much did it cost you?"

"One or two dollars a day, which included board and lodging."

"Would it have cost you twice as much in London to live as well?"

"Yes."

"Do you think that, proportionately, things cost twice as much in London as they do in Paris?"

"Yes. Nevertheless, I think that it would be nearer the truth to say that the sort of life one can lead on three dollars in Paris would cost four dollars in London. But not if one leaves either of the two capitals. In England the cost of living is double that of France."

"Ah, that varies according to the state of the stock market. In England there are outlets everywhere, but in France, as soon as one leaves the big towns, consumption diminishes. How much does a dinner cost in London?"

"In the taverns two dollars, or one louis, including wine."

"But say one doesn't drink wine?"

"In the taverns you have to take wine, otherwise they won't serve dinner. Their main profit comes from wine."

"What sort of wines do they drink there? Claret?"

"No, only wealthy people can afford claret."

"What do claret or sherry cost?"

"Fifteen shillings a bottle."

"Your soldiers must have regaled themselves when they were in France, where wine costs only two sous a bottle—or in Sicily."

"Yes, they were all dead drunk."

"What interest does real estate pay in England?"

"Three to four per cent."

"I would never have believed it."

"Land is increasing in value. In wartime it didn't bring in so much, when there was the Income Tax. But since that has been done away with, those are the usual rates of interest."

"Oh, I would not have believed it. Does one find much business at such a price?"

"Yes, a lease is usually for a period of from seven to fifteen years. Without that, farmers could not produce decent crops."

"Do they pay regularly?"

"Yes."

"Can they be forced to pay?"

"No doubt the law courts make that possible. During the war, there were frequent failures. But since the peace, order had been re-established."

"Since the war there should be grapes in England."

"Possibly."

"Have you any in England?"

"Very little, and then only in certain selected places, usually in hothouses. Every day ships from France bring eggs, chickens and fruit, etc. In the port markets there is as much French as English spoken."

"Apparently the English Government has passed stringent measures against such imports, otherwise all the food produce of France would go to England, and your farmers would be ruined. The necessities of life are comparatively cheap in England. It is the luxury articles which are very expensive. Are your surgeons better than ours?"

"On the whole, about the same. To make a comparison, I would say that ours amputate better than yours do."

"Why?"

"We dress the amputations better. We cover up the wound better."

"Are French surgeons also of this opinion?"

"I have met some who were."

"Which of the two nations dressed the wounded better on the field of battle?"

"I think that the French got them off the field, evacuated their wounded, far better than we did."

"Oh, that is merely a question of practice. Which of the two nations lost the most wounded?"

"France, or so I believe."

"Why?"

"Because I think that we performed better amputations."

"Therefore your surgery is superior to ours?"

"I did not say that. There are certain types of operations in which the French may possibly surpass us. For example, the operation for gallstones."

"Is your medical science better than ours?"

"I think that they are about equal."

"Are the Spanish surgeons better?"

"No, they are ignoramuses."

"The Portuguese? Sicilians? Neapolitans?"

"No. At Naples and in Sicily, generally speaking, the surgeons and physicians belong to a very different category, in so far as I could judge."

"Who screamed loudest on the battlefields? The English or the French?"

"About the same, I think."

"Did the English cry out much during an operation?"

"Some did terribly, while others made not a sound."

"On the battlefield, was it possible to distinguish between a Frenchman and an Italian, for example, from the courage they displayed in standing an operation?"

"No. I am not sufficiently familiar with the two nations to be able to judge."

"Were you satisfied with the way in which our ambulances were organized, and with our army medical corps?"

"Very satisfied."

"Were they as good as yours?"

"I believe them to have been so."

"Were you satisfied with our hospitals?"

"Yes."

"Did you find them well cared for?"

"Yes."

"Are your own hospitals better?"

"No."

"Did your wounded complain of the treatment they received and of the way in which they were cared for?"

"No."

"Have you seen the École de Médecine at Paris?"

"Yes."

"Is it better or less good than yours?"

"I attended none of the classes and heard none of the professors lecture."

"Did you see the Botanical Gardens?"

"Yes."

"Is the one in England finer?"

"No."

"Did you visit any of the Paris hospitals?"

"Yes."

"Were you pleased with the Hôtel Dieu?"

"Yes."

"Is it as well kept as the one in London? Is it finer? What did you most admire in Paris?"

"The view of the Tuileries, the gardens."

"Is London more beautiful than Paris?"

"It is much bigger," replied Dr. Arnott, "and, on the whole, I think more beautiful. Although, with the exception of Somerset House, we have not such fine buildings. But generally speaking the streets are more beautiful and the city is much larger."

"Oh, you have lakes and rivers; and the splendid sight of your ships. Does the tide rise as far up as London?"

"Yes."

"Is the water from the Thames good?"

"Excellent."

"But how can that be, with the tides? Where is it taken from?"

"At about two miles beyond the city, at low tide."

That was an hour's conversation, in so far as I can remember.

In the evening at five o'clock, there was a further conversation. . . . The Emperor questioned Dr. Arnott as closely as he had done during the morning visit. Then he had another talk about his personal affairs with the Grand Maréchal.

Conversation of the evening of April 24, 1821 [at the bedside of the Emperor in the sitting room at Longwood].

TURENNE—The Emperor said that he had examined the condition of the things which Turenne had preserved. There were a great many of them, among others a sword, a sabre, and his collar of the Legion of Honor as well as that of the Golden Fleece. Turenne was to convey them all to his son.

DENON—Denon had had views made of the Italian battlefields. He had been paid yearly to do this, and a great many of them had been engraved. These were to be collected and used to decorate Napoleon's book on the Italian Campaigns, and for the production of a sumptuous volume.

LETTERS WHICH NAPOLEON HAD EXCHANGED WITH OTHER RULING SOVEREIGNS—The Emperor repeated his instructions to Bertrand that his correspondence with other sovereigns should be published. It would be an historical monument. If the correspondence were in Joseph's possession, it should be printed in America. If it were in the National Archives, efforts should be made to obtain it. That might, however, prove to be difficult, because there might be someone at the National Archives who would be strongly opposed to any such thing.

THE EMPRESS—The Emperor wished the Grand Maréchal to go and see the Empress. The easiest thing would be to ask the permission of the King of France. A necklet of Napoleon's hair would be a sufficient pretext; moreover it would be an obvious thing for the Emperor during his last moments to have intrusted Bertrand with a confidential message for the Empress. And if, on the Austrian side, it should prove difficult to approach the Empress, it would be quite sufficient for Bertrand to say that he had a diamond or some such precious object to give to the Empress personally, and they would immediately assume there were millions involved, which would open all doors to him. The Austrians were greedy and impecunious. The Empress would in all probability be married off to one of her uncles or cousins.

HIS SON—His son was settled quite naturally in Austria, and it appeared that he had been granted an income of 500,000 francs.

It might be wise to put someone like Méneval in his entourage, someone who could talk to him about his father, which would enable him to see things in their true light, should he have been misinformed. But possibly Austria would not permit this.

If his son were forced to leave Austria, Switzerland would appear to be the most suitable country for him to settle in. He should have his name entered in the Golden Book of the Berne nobility; that would be better than America. It was always a tremendous thing to change from one climate and hemisphere to another.

HIS FAMILY—The Emperor repeated that his family was to take possession of Rome, through allying itself with the princely families of Rome. By which the Emperor meant all those families in which there had been popes, and which had therefore ordered the conscience of the Universe. It would not be long before his family would have a pope, cardinals, and papal legates. This only, would give his family influence in every court in Europe, and, which was important, it would involve a considerable number of powerful families in preserving and perpetuating the memory of his fame. It would mean attaching a powerful theocracy to the interests of his own family and to the greater honor of his memory.

Such families existed everywhere, not only in Rome. They were to be found at Bologna, Rimini, and Reggio. As a matter of fact, the Bonapartes had originally come from Rome. There had been Bonapartes there in the year 1000. It had been a Bonaparte who in

1500 had written *The Sacking of Rome by the Connétable de Bourbon*, and who had cursed him roundly for it.

The Emperor said that his name would always be popular in Italy. The Italians would always look upon the period in which the Emperor had tried to establish their independence as a lost opportunity. He had appealed to the Italian imagination by reviving the name and memory of their native land. And for this his memory would be forever cherished by the Italians.

Prince Lucien, Felix Baciocchi, and the children of his wife Princess Elisa, were already settled in Rome. Prince Joseph and Queen Caroline of Naples could also marry their daughters to Roman families, provided that they each had a dowry of three hundred thousand francs and Madame could make no better investment with her money. She must be made to grasp the fact that this would be a means of assuring the fame and preserving the illustriousness of her House. She should promise a dowry of three hundred thousand francs to each of her grandchildren, girls as well as boys, who would settle in Rome. Napoleon said that his mother ought to have about six or seven million francs, and Princess Pauline had at least three million francs as well as the diamonds. Cardinal Fesch should have as much again, even if he only had his collection of pictures. They could use their wealth to no better purpose.

SWITZERLAND—Jérôme, whose wife was a Protestant, Caroline who was unable to live in Rome on account of its proximity to Naples, and Joseph who was also unable to go there either for the same reason or because of the way in which he had behaved at the time of the assassination of Duphot, should settle in Switzerland: one in Berne, another in Zurich, and the third in Fribourg. They should see that their names were entered in the Golden Book at Berne. They would be welcome everywhere, and especially in Switzerland, bringing as they would millions of francs with them. And, furthermore, imagination would set no limit on what they might bring. Therefore, there were certain to be popes and *Landammans* among his descendants.

Possibly Joseph would prefer to remain in America, to see his daughters settled over there, and to marry them into the Washington and Jefferson families and have future Presidents of the United States among his relations.

But his family could only live in a dignified manner under a theocracy such as existed in Rome, or in a Republic possessing genuine stability and independence, like Switzerland, for example. By becoming members of the Swiss governing class, they would be independent, under no obligations to anyone else, and they would preserve their dignity.

Only under such circumstances would his family be respected. The Emperor said that his family might kiss the Pope's rump, which amounted to kissing the rump of no one in particular, or of a member of no particular family. But it could not kiss the backside of the Kings of England, Naples, or Sweden.

Madame must be made to realize this, and to give three hundred thousand francs to each of her grandchildren who settled in Rome or in Switzerland. Prince Jérôme could settle in Switzerland should his wife prefer not to live in Rome, as she was a Protestant. Trieste was a one-eyed hole, but everyone would be pleased and flattered to see him arrive in Berne. He could bring five or six million francs with him, but who was to know that he had not brought forty million . . . He could live there independently. He would have to have his name entered in the Golden Book, but he should arrange for this before he reached Berne, and he was not to waste the opportunity. He should then ally himself with all the leading Swiss families, and his or Joseph's daughter might marry young De Watteville, Napoleon's former aide-de-camp. Berne was to be preferred to any of the other Swiss cantons as it was the most important. Napoleon did not know whether the fact that Jérôme's children had been brought up in the Catholic Faith might constitute an obstacle to their living in Berne. . . . Jérôme might acquire a country place on either the Lake of Geneva, the Lake of Neufchâtel, the Lake of Zurich, or perhaps in the canton of Vaud, where everyone spoke French and which would be about thirty-six miles from his permanent residence. There were some very agreeable sites to be found, with houses already built, which had been owned by people with an income of sixty thousand francs a year. Geneva itself was a pleasant town where everyone spoke

French. Jérôme could live in magnificent style in Geneva. It was a great thing to be independent of everybody, and to have no obligations towards anyone; this was the only tenable position for members of the Emperor's family.

QUEEN CAROLINE—If Queen Caroline could not settle in Rome, because her safety might be endangered there, she also should settle in Switzerland, though in a different canton from Jérôme; possibly at Zurich. Everything that Napoleon had just said about Jérôme applied equally well to Queen Caroline; as much to the manner in which her children were to be settled in life, as to the subject of her country house. In this way they would conquer the leading Swiss families.

JOSEPH— . . . All that which had been said about Jérôme and Queen Caroline, applied equally well to him. They would then be the masters of Switzerland and would be certain to have a *Landamman* among their descendants. Thus his family would be settled in two or three different places:

First of all there were the three families in Rome: Lucien, Louis, and the children of Princess Elisa. Second, the three families in Switzerland; Joseph, Jérôme and Caroline. Third, there remained only Pauline and the Emperor himself, which made a total of eight brothers and sisters. Madame Mère must understand this situation thoroughly. Possibly Joseph and Lucien might have a code by means of which these views of the Emperor could be transmitted to her, as well as to Jérôme and to Queen Caroline.

Lucien would have no difficulty in understanding what the Emperor had said about Rome. . . . He should see that one of his sons became a cardinal without delay. Bertrand was to tell him that the Emperor had disapproved of the publication of his poems; he had talent and was a worker, but he could not employ his talent and his time to better purpose than by writing a history of the Emperor. Lucien had, after all, seen a great many things, and he was in a better position than anyone to collect material; anyway, it was the best and surest means of achieving immortality. There remained, of course, the military aspect of the Emperor's career, which Lucien was certainly not in a position to handle.

PRIVATE ESTATE—In his will the Emperor had given detailed instructions regarding everything that concerned his private property. Three periods could be distinguished.

First, Rambouillet, which had been furnished with the furniture that he had possessed as a General, and which had belonged to him at that time, as well as the furnishings from the house in the rue Chantereine and from Malmaison. Second, most of the furniture in the Tuileries and at St. Cloud, had been bought during the time he was First Consul, out of his salary as a temporary magistrate of the Republic, and he therefore had as much right as any other public servant, to dispose of what he had bought. Then had come the Empire and the Civil List, which was a third question and a third state of affairs. Among the crown diamonds were some five to six hundred thousand francs' worth of diamonds that he had bought out of his own funds. If need be, the jeweler could furnish a statement.

The Emperor asked the Grand Maréchal several times if he had quite understood this matter as well as everything else appertaining to his family, and he impressed on him the need to make a note of this conversation.

April 25—On the morning of April 25, the Emperor asked the Grand Maréchal whether he had made a note of his conversation of the previous evening. The Grand Maréchal replied in the affirmative. The Emperor then said that all the scenes of the battlefields by Denon and the plans of the battlefields made by D'Albe, should be used to make a handsome atlas for the two books on Egypt and Italy. Both books were to be dedicated to his son. Arnault should be entrusted with correcting the style in which he had written up the Italian and Egyptian Campaigns, as well as with correcting any small errors in his French. The other works on Caesar, Turenne, and Frederick the Great, were of less importance.

Antommarchi could be sent back to Italy from England by sea. He could land at Civita Vecchia and convey to the Emperor's family news of his death and of the final proceedings. Coursot might also be sent to Italy and he could be intrusted with letters to Rome. The Bourbons would probably be quite pleasant, as they would be so pleased to hear of Napoleon's death.

The Emperor told the Grand Maréchal to find out for certain whether Cardinal Caselli were still alive.

"His name appeared in the Imperial Almanach for 1812. He would be a means of approaching the Empress. Furthermore, the Austrians are so poor and so greedy that by telling them that you have some important things to give to the Empress—where I am concerned, imagination knows no bounds—they will probably expect at least three hundred millions!"

The Emperor added that the testamentary executors could read what was written in that part of the will on which they had set their personal seal. As this was on the exterior of the will, they could take cognizance of it.

The Emperor was very sick during the night; he vomited more than he had ever done. It was a residue of the old digestive trouble. He then passed a movement black with bile. . . . As it was the day of the races, Dr. Arnott paid his morning visit at ten o'clock. The Emperor dismissed him at half past eleven and only asked him a few questions. The Emperor was weak and fairly quiet. He persuaded General Montholon and Mme. Bertrand to go to the races. Then at half-past four he vomited a great deal of very black matter.

The doctors arrived at half-past five. The Emperor talked to them and asked Dr. Arnott whether many people had asked for news of him. Dr. Arnott replied that no one had done so.

"Doubtless the Governor expects me to die shortly," the Emperor remarked. He then inquired whether one could get bitter almonds at Longwood. They were seldom seen here. Only once, three years before had any one been able to get some. The Emperor told the Grand Maréchal that his books on the Italian and Egyptian Campaigns were to be dedicated to the King of Rome; but that the commentaries on Caesar, Turenne, and Frederick were of no great importance. Cardinal Caselli would be the best means of putting the Grand Maréchal in touch with the Empress. Napoleon thought that Bertrand would find the Bourbons well disposed towards him, because they would be so pleased at the death of the Emperor.

Napoleon ate a few leaves of gentian and in the course of the day he had some soup. In the evening he sent for Pierron. Between ten and eleven o'clock in the evening, he ate a *galette*, a plum, two grapes and drank a spoonful of champagne and a spoonful of Malaga, which made him slightly tipsy.

The Emperor talked a great deal about food, such as pork and ham and above all bitter almonds. He told Pierron that he had made his will, and that in it he had made them all rich. He then told the Grand Maréchal that he might familiarize himself with what had been written on the subject of the bequests in the will.

The Emperor questioned Dr. Arnott about licorice, and asked him whether licorice roots were superior to licorice juice. Dr. Arnott replied that the juice was to be preferred, as it was more refined.

"Where does licorice come from?"

"From Europe. Very little of it is to be found in England," Dr. Arnott said, "but there is a great deal in France and Italy. The Italian licorice is the finer."

"Is any to be found in Malta or in Sicily?" Napoleon asked.

Arnott replied that he had never seen any there. The Emperor then asked Dr. Antommarchi whether there were any in Corsica. Antommarchi replied that he thought there was.

Mr. Ward has left Longwood and gone to sleep in town. He is not to return to Longwood.

The Emperor was extremely restless, especially between eleven o'clock and midnight. He had a temperature until three o'clock in the morning. He was sick during the night and then slept for three hours. He talked with Dr. Antommarchi from about eight in the morning until eleven o'clock. He told him that he would give him 100,000 francs and also a letter to the Empress so that he could become her doctor.

When the Grand Maréchal entered the room, Napoleon told him that he had spoken to the doctor in the morning. He discussed Ward's departure, and spoke about Major Harrison. He wished to send General Montholon to see Montchenu and to try and obtain some news. The doctors arrived and the Emperor asked a lot of questions relative to the functioning of the stomach.

"How many openings are there to the stomach, through which pass the food one has eaten?" he inquired.

"There are two," the doctor replied, "the throat, by means of which one is able to vomit; and the pylorus, through which food passes into the intestines. There are no others."

"How is the pylorus closed? By a spreading of its inner lining?"

"No, by a kind of sponge, which opens and closes."

"So everything passes through there and into the bowels?"

"Yes."

"How does the liver communicate with the stomach? Through a kind of tube?"

"No, only through the bile ducts."

"What goes into the liver?"

"The digestive juices and bile, in fact whatever is absorbed into the body to maintain it."

"Then everything that enters the bowels is turned into matter there?"

"Yes."

"Is there a return passage back through the belly?"

"No, matter remains generally in the bowels, and it is principally enclosed in the large intestine."

"And how does urine leave the stomach?"

"Through two lateral tubes which communicate with the bladder."

"And the sperm?"

"Passes through two tubes communicating with the testicles."

"So that if the first two tubes and the last two were tied up, one could no longer pass either water or sperm?"

"Quite so. The same thing arises in the female ovary. If the tubes leading to it are tied up, women are no longer able to conceive. This is, in fact, done, so as to prevent a woman from having children."

"And how does blood reach the heart?"

"Through a multitude of small veins spread over the stomach. They absorb what blood is required and send it to the heart."

"My father had a tumor of the pylorus. Can it be cured after it has formed?"

"No. It cannot be cured even if it is formed in the breast."

(The Emperor asked the doctor several times to feel his right side, where he felt a pain.)

"Is that the pylorus?" he asked.

"No, it is the liver."

"Can you tell whether there is anything wrong with the pylorus?"

"No, that is impossible, because it is underneath the liver. It is cut off from the outside of the body by the whole of the liver."

The doctor said that the long conversation in the morning had been for the purpose of turning him inside out and of finding out whether the Emperor's illness were located in the pylorus; the doctors of the Montpellier Faculty had claimed that such things were hereditary; and the Emperor had wished to have the doctor's opinion on his illness and general condition. The Emperor asked Dr. Arnott what he thought about his illness. The doctor replied that it was obviously located in the stomach and in the digestive organs. Their art would consist in building up his strength, which they would strive to do, if it were humanly possible.

The Emperor said that he had never treated his stomach carelessly. In his whole life it had never worried him for a single day, and therefore it was rather extraordinary for it to have gone back on him now. Dr. Arnott replied that there were many instances of men who had led a most regular life being smitten with this illness, and that the stomach was a very sensitive organ.

At eleven o'clock the Emperor drank a cup of chocolate and ate a biscuit, which he promptly threw up. Then without having had anything to eat, he again vomited at half-past five, and brought up something which the doctors said was phlegm. At six o'clock he had a little soup and some floating island and drank one spoonful of wine to two of water. He told the doctors that he felt no desire to eat, and that it would be better for him not to eat anything. They replied that it would be wiser for him to have something in his stomach. At half-past six the doctors took their leave. The Emperor talked to the Grand Maréchal for a while; then at seven o'clock he left the sitting room and retired to bed, as he had done on the two preceding days, supported on either side by Bertrand and Marchand. The Emperor discovered that he was much weaker, and in the course of the evening he said that he was far weaker than he had been on the morning of the previous day. Marchand dressed his blister, which had not been done the night before.

The Emperor instructed the Grand Maréchal to set his seal on those codicils to his will which had not yet been sealed, and to make a copy of what was written on the back of the codicils, which would constitute an official report. After that had been done, Marchand would make them into packets, and when the Emperor was at the point of death, they were to be handed to him. The Grand Maréchal, Monseigneur Vignali, General Montholon, and Marchand set their seals on the six packets and signed them, as well as the packets which had not yet been sealed, which made *nine packets* in all.

The Governor sent a box of bitter almonds to Napoleon, and Arthur Bertrand brought some peach kernels. Captain Crockatt has been installed at Longwood and is to sleep there. Captain Lutyens has left Longwood, and the Governor has officially informed the Grand Maréchal of his departure.

April 26—Up until noon, the Emperor repeatedly asked for something to drink. Then he asked for nothing more until five o'clock, but he moved about in bed a great deal and was very restless. He had been sick early in the morning and again at half-past eight, bringing up phlegm and mucus as before. There has been an increasing return of this type of sickness for the past three days, whereas previously his vomit has been small in amount and of a whitish substance. The Emperor kept saying that he felt pains in his pylorus. In the evening he asked for some orangeade, saying that he found it refreshing to his pylorus and that it did him good. At eight o'clock he ate some vermicelli soup. At eleven he was exceedingly sick again.

He had pains in the stomach, and it seemed to him that everything he took came up instead of going down. The doctors told him that was imagination, that such a thing was impossible.

He was sick once again, and then he asked for some wine and water. When soup was brought to him, he said he preferred soup made with wine and two-thirds water. This was prepared for him from Madeira wine. The Emperor took a little of it and then asked for a spoonful of semolina. Four or five times he asked for some coffee, even just a spoonful, if the doctors would let him have it. They refused, but said that they would see on the morrow.

The vomiting recommenced, and up until half-past two the Emperor again vomited four or five times, bringing up phlegm and mucus tinted red by the wine. It appeared that what the Emperor had eaten during the morning had been digested, and that he had not been sick.

At three o'clock, the Emperor moved into the room "with the clock." After taking a spoonful of orange-flower water, his stomach calmed down, he was quieter, and the vomiting had ceased. The doctors advised him to have a plaster put on his chest. It would not cause a sore, but it would warm and strengthen the stomach. They sent into Jamestown for one.

Dr. Arnott went to the Camp and announced that a mail bag and a storeship had arrived from England. It was learned that this news transport had been sent to announce a change in the Government in England. This revived the spirits and strength of the Emperor for a short time. At half-past five the news was denied! It appears that the schooner has come from the Cape and not from England, as had been said, and it has only brought letters from the Cape. Lady Lowe has sent Mme. Bertrand a fine Chinese pheasant. The feathers are superb and measure about five feet in length.

The doctors went in to the Emperor. He was much quieter, and he asked whether the ship had come from England. Napoleon wanted some soup, but the doctors said that he must wait until eight o'clock in the evening. They advised him to have an enema, as he had not had one the evening before. They also wished him to take two doses of gentian a day, in the morning and in the evening. They were of the opinion that this would do him a great deal of good.

At seven o'clock Dr. Arnott took his leave. Between eight and nine o'clock the Emperor was given an enema. He was so weak that he could not evacuate properly. The enema had no result. The Emperor changed beds, and went into the sitting room, walking with great difficulty. He has never been so weak. Antommarchi thinks that he will be unable to change rooms on the morrow.

Today he frequently appeared to have lost his memory. For the past ten days, sometimes on two or three occasions, he has asked the same question and forgotten that it had been answered. Occasionally his mind wanders, although rarely.

The Grand Maréchal wrote out the text of the official report on the wills, the codicils, and the boxes. Mme. Bertrand, worried at her husband's failure to return home, came to the Emperor's apartments at two o'clock in the afternoon, and remained there for an hour. Montholon told the Emperor that she was there, and the Emperor replied (according to what Montholon later told Mme. Bertrand): "I did not see her, as I feared to be upset. I resented her refusal to become my mistress, and also I wanted to teach her a lesson.

"Had you been her lover," he said to Montholon, "I would have treated you like an outcast, instead of heaping kindnesses upon you as I have done. However, I never thought any such thing.

"As for Antommarchi, I shall never forgive him for having attended a woman who refused to become my mistress, and for having encouraged her not to do so. If I recover I shall see her without fail, and in any case I will do so before I die."

"Well, now you see that you should have thanked me for not having mopped up your tears . . . ," Mme. Bertrand said to Montholon.

In the evening the Emperor said five or six times to Marchand: "How is Mme. la Maréchale? Tell me, how is she?" Perhaps he wanted to make it up with her, and to be nice to her. It would upset him if he were to hurt Mme. Bertrand and her husband. He has told Montholon that whatever remains of his estate once the bequests have been paid, are to be shared with Bertrand.

Conversation of April 26, at seven o'clock—The Emperor moved into the sitting room, leaning on the arms of Bertrand and Marchand. After getting in bed, he said to the Grand Maréchal:

That it was his wish that the Empress should not remarry, but that nevertheless she would probably be married to some minor archduke among her cousins. She was to watch over the education of his son and over his safety. She was to be suspicious of the Bourbons, who would certainly try and take the King of Rome away from her. An attempt would probably be made to force his son to become a cardinal. The most important thing for him was never to take orders. He was always to be proud of his French birth. There was no means of knowing what his destiny would be; he might one day reign over France. Therefore, it was essential for him to avoid doing anything that would alienate the French or that would set them against him.

It was essential for him to be well brought up. He was to learn Latin, mathematics, geography, and history. Efforts should be made to give him a true idea of his father and related events, for, very probably attempts would be made to distort his ideas on that subject. When he reached the age of sixteen, men like Méneval, Fain, and D'Albe, who had traveled widely, should be sent to him, so that they might talk to him naturally and easily of all that they had seen and learned. It was desirable that he should see Lucien Bonaparte and his family, so that he might become attached to them. He must become fond of them.

Under the circumstances it was fortunate for him that he was the son of a mother able to place him under the natural protection of a powerful State. He was the son of a mother whose marriage had been a powerful alliance.

If he were to die before he was sixteen, the Grand Maréchal was to keep the Emperor's side arms.

The Emperor desired to be buried in the cemetery of Père Lachaise. There the Grand Maréchal was to have a small monument erected to him. If the Bourbons had him buried at St. Denis, so much the better! Otherwise let him be buried at Rueil, where the Empress Josephine reposed. Or finally, let him be buried on an island in the Rhône, near Lyons.

As heir the Bourbons had at present the son of the Duke of Berry and after him all the House of Orléans, which was numerous and well thought of by the French nation.

Madame should leave more to his son the King of Rome than to any of the other grandchildren. Such small attentions would attach people, and Pauline and Cardinal Fesch were to do likewise. His family were to neglect nothing that would attach the Emperor's son to them.

We had learned that the Patriarch of Venice had made the Emperor his heir. Bertrand was to see what it amounted to.

Antommarchi was to be sent back to Italy by sea from England, to his own family and to the Empress. Coursot was also to be sent to Italy, and letters were to be intrusted to him. Antommarchi was to embalm his heart and to convey it to the Empress. The Emperor's heart was to be placed in a silver vessel.

All the maps made by D'Albe and the battle scenes by Denon

were to be collected and they were to be used to decorate his Egyptian and Italian Campaigns. Arnault was to be intrusted with correcting the errors in his *Mémoires*.

Lucien was to cease writing poetry and to busy himself with writing a history of the Revolution and of the Emperor's reign. As he was a worker, he could easily write some fifteen or twenty volumes on the subject. But who could handle the military history of his reign? Up to the present, Jomini had been the only one to show any ability, but he was now in the pay of Russia.

The Emperor asked whether Regnault de Saint-Jean-d'Angély were dead? The Grand Maréchal said that the Duke of Bassano should know a great deal and that he was in a position to write.

"Yes," replied Napoleon, "but he is lazy, and also he will want to write his own memoirs."

For a long time Daru had been a Secretary of State and he wrote easily. Ségur was probably the one to write the most, while Bignon was at present interested in writing the diplomatic history of Napoleon's reign.

"Yes."

"D'Hauterive also has ability, he might be able to write."

"Yes, but he is so very much a creature of Talleyrand's."

The Emperor added that Bourrienne, who had been his secretary under the Consulate, must have a great many letters in his possession, and that they could be procured if a high enough price were paid for them. Méneval also should have a considerable number of letters. He had frequently been in such a hurry that he had not had the time to copy out the minutes that were to be sent off. In any case, everyone had a private reason for keeping something. The Emperor repeated that efforts must be made to obtain possession of the volume containing his correspondence with the other sovereigns and to have it published. Also an attempt must be made to obtain access to the Archives.

"What line do you want your friends to take? What rules of conduct are they to follow, and what is to be their goal?" Bertrand inquired.

"To place the interests of France, and the honor and glory of their country above all. I can think of nothing else," replied the Emperor.

He advised the Grand Maréchal to write down the conversation which he had just had with him at his bedside.

April 28—The Emperor's conversation with Pierron: "How many oxen, sheep, goats, etc? . . ."

(Note to serve as a reminder of this visit.)

Lady Lowe, on her way back from shopping, called on Mme. Bertrand. She said that she had been consistently kept in the dark about everything that happened on the island, and that she knew nothing about any matters relating to Longwood. When anything was being discussed, she was asked to leave the room, or else Reade and the Governor would go into another room. She very much regretted not having left the island, if anything disastrous were to happen. It was painful to see such a great man die under such miserable conditions. She spoke with tears in her eyes.

She said that she had much admired the courage and patience of Mme. Bertrand for enduring such a painful position; unable to see anyone and overwhelmed by all kinds of privations. She would be glad to come and see Mme. Bertrand. She would have come before, but she had been ill. She was not one to stand on ceremony. . . .

She was sorry that the Emperor was not seeing Mr. Shortt. He was much the most capable man to have reached the island since she herself had arrived on it, not excepting Mr. Baxter who had saved the life of M. de Montchenu, and who was excellent, especially with children.

Mme. Bertrand was in the Emperor's apartments when the visit of Lady Lowe was announced. She went to receive her, and afterwards returned to the Emperor's apartments and remained there until half-past six. The Emperor was asked if he would see her and was told of the pheasant Lady Lowe had sent Mme. Bertrand the day before. The Emperor replied, "This is not the moment."

April 29—During the night of 28 and 29 the Emperor had Montholon and Marchand write on cards in the dark. In the morning he asked for a fire to be lit. He then said "drink, drink." [English in the text.]

The Emperor passed a disturbed night. Between one and two

o'clock he was sick several times, then he talked from three to four o'clock. Montholon said that during the night he spoke sadly of depressing things, like the death of all the men he had known, such as Lannes and Crétin. At half-past six he was sick. Then at eight o'clock he had some soup and was sick again at ten o'clock.

The doctors arrived and advised the Emperor to have an enema. This was the third day the Emperor had gone without one. The day before he had been too weak to stand it. The doctors advised him to take the dose of gentian. The Emperor said that he would take it, then later, after the doctors had left, he refused to do so.

The plaster that the doctors had prescribed the day before was placed on his abdomen. Then Dr. Antommarchi shaved him. The Emperor asked him whether he was to keep the plaster on for long. Antommarchi replied that it would not cause him any pain or discomfort.

For the first time that morning the Grand Maréchal found the Emperor's will power very weak and thought that he had altered very much for the worse. The Emperor sent for Pierron, to ask him whether he had been into Jamestown the day before and whether the schooner which had put in the previous day had brought any oranges. Pierron replied that it had. The oranges were brought to the Emperor, who found that they were bitter without sugar, and ever more bitter with sugar.

After having sucked a little of the juice of an orange, the Emperor complained of pains in the region of the pylorus. He stopped eating the oranges and asked whether they would become any sweeter if they were kept. Pierron replied that they would if they were kept for two weeks or a month.

"Very well then, keep some of them for me, or else make me some marmalade and orangeade; then put the rest aside. Did this boat bring any limes?"

"No."

"Any almonds?"

"No."

"Pomegranates?"

"No."

"Grapes?"

"No."

"Wine?"

"No, at least not in bottles, but in casks."

"It brought nothing then?"

"It brought cattle."

"How many oxen?"

"Forty."

"How many sheep?"

"Two hundred."

"How many goats?"

"None."

"How many chickens?"

"None."

"On the whole, one could say that it brought nothing. Did it bring any walnuts?"

"No."

"Walnuts come, so I understand, from cold climates and almonds from hot ones. Are the limes good here?"

"Yes."

"And the pomegranates?"

"I have never seen any good ones."

"Did it bring any limes, pomegranates, almonds?"

Three times the Emperor called Pierron in and made him go over the same things, like a man who had completely lost his memory. The Emperor could only be recognized by the multitude of incessant questions which he asked. Dr. Arnott noticed the change in his voice and the fact that he repeated questions to which the doctor had already replied. He had never before noticed this lack of memory. Arnott even had to repeat that he had passed through Paris.

"I told you yesterday," he said to the Emperor, "that I wasn't afraid that you were in any immediate danger. But today I must tell you that the illness has altered and that it has become much more serious. I am now very much concerned, although I cannot say that there is as yet any indication of an approaching dissolution, or of an immediate death. Nevertheless, I feel that it is my duty to warn you, so that if you have any arrangements which you wish to make you can do so now."

The Emperor had lain down on his right side, something he had rarely done since he had been ill. Usually he has lain on his left side, with his face to the wall. In this new position, his face was lit up by the light filtering through the shutters, which revealed a profile more emaciated and altered than any I had ever seen.

Since the previous day, his deafness had increased to an amazing degree. It was necessary to speak to him very loudly and to shout at him as though he were deaf. Which was something I had never seen before, although I had always known him to be, at least for a great many years, more or less hard of hearing.

After having eaten the oranges, the Emperor was sick.

"I am paying for the oranges I have eaten," he remarked.

He sent for Pierron and again asked him the same questions, but in a more animated fashion and with a somewhat stronger voice. He made a list of everything a ship could bring, and of everything which this ship had not brought. He asked again whether the oranges were sweet and juicy, and said that they were to be kept and to be allowed to ripen.

At noon Dr. Arnott went to the Camp, returning at two o'clock. At noon the Emperor was given some soup, an egg, a biscuit, and a spoonful of wine. Antommarchi also gave him three spoonfuls of coffee. It seemed that General Montholon had said to him:

"Cram some food into the Emperor and try and give him some strength. I have something for him to sign." It was the letter to the Empress in which Dr. Antommarchi was recommended to her.

At one o'clock the Grand Maréchal went out to get a meal. . . . At half-past two Antommarchi told Montholon that if he had something for the Emperor to sign, it would be advisable to take advantage of that moment, because his end was near and his consciousness was beginning to fade.

Mme. Bertrand, who had just arrived at Longwood, shed a few tears. Through the intermediary of Montholon she had brought the superb pheasant Lady Lowe had sent to her, as a gift for the Emperor. Montholon told the Emperor that Mme. Bertrand had brought him a fine bird, and that she had asked whether she might be allowed to present it to him herself.

"This is not the moment," the Emperor said, and then was sick. He added: "You see, I cannot receive her at present."

Then he said: "I didn't go for a walk in the garden this morning, did I?"

"No, Sire."

"What! I didn't go for a walk in the garden this morning?"

"No."

"Antommarchi, didn't I speak to you about the garden?"

"No."

"That's strange. Were the oranges from the Cape, sweet?"

"Yes," replied Montholon, unaware that the Emperor had already tasted them.

"Tell them to bring me some."

The oranges were brought. The Grand Maréchal said: "But Your Majesty tasted them this morning. He found them bitter, and they made him sick."

"No, no, I haven't eaten any of them." Then he tasted them. "How very sour they are. They are more like limes than oranges. They should be made into marmalade and the remainder left to ripen. Tell Pierron."

"Yes, Sire."

The Emperor sat in his chair for a short while, and the opportunity was taken to make his bed. He returned to bed and it was then that Dr. Antommarchi advised Montholon to take advantage of the moment to make the Emperor do what he wanted. He and Montholon then shut themselves in with the Emperor.

The Governor sent for Dr. Arnott. Lady Lowe came to see Mme. Bertrand, who left the Emperor's apartments. Lady Lowe told her that she was sorry that she had not left the island as she would now be a witness to what was about to happen. She had had nothing to do with the treatment that we had had to endure, and I believe she shed a few tears and expressed admirable sentiments.

Montholon left the Emperor, and the doctors went in to him. They insisted—it was five o'clock—that the Emperor should have an enema.

"Very well," Napoleon replied, "I shall have one this evening. Marchand, you can prepare it. Marchand bring the syringe. But I can't have it in front of all these gentlemen."

The Grand Maréchal escorted Dr. Arnott out of the room. Antommarchi remained behind with General Montholon and

Marchand. The Emperor sat on the syringe, but he was overcome with dizziness and fell back onto his bed. They proposed to give the enema to him. "What do you take me for," he protested, "a coglione or a woman?"

However, as they insisted, the Emperor decided to try again. He sat up in his open-seated chair and took some of the enema. He had pulled off the plaster that had been placed on his belly. The doctors found that he had evacuated very little. They advised him to take his medicine.

"Very well, I will take it, if you insist. But I feel like doing something."

He again sat on his chair [. . .] (It was then nearly half-past six.)

At about two o'clock, although the Grand Maréchal was standing in front of him, the Emperor had asked General Montholon: "Do you know whether Bertrand has signed the codicils?"

"Yes, Sire," Montholon replied. The Emperor did not see the Grand Maréchal, although his eyes were fixed upon him.

In the morning the Emperor had asked at least twenty times whether he might be allowed to have some coffee. But every time the answer had been: "No, Sire."

"Won't the doctors allow me just a spoonful?"

"No, Sire. Not at present. Your stomach is over-irritated, and it might cause you to be sick a little sooner." He had been sick perhaps eight or nine times in the course of the day.

What thoughts spring to mind at the sight of so great a change! Tears came to my eyes, as I looked at this man, formerly so terrifying, who had commanded so proudly and in a manner so absolute, now reduced to begging for a spoonful of coffee, asking permission, obedient as a child, asking permission again and again without obtaining it. Repeatedly asking permission, and always unsuccessfully, yet without any signs of bad temper. At other periods of his illness he had sent his doctors to the devil and had done as he pleased. But at present he was as docile as a child. That was what the Great Napoleon had become, a humble and an unhappy man.

Montholon told Mme. Bertrand that the Emperor had not referred to her in his will, but that he had treated the Grand Maréchal very well. She was not to let this upset her as the contents of the will would only be known to the testamentary executors. Montholon told the Grand Maréchal that he had been unable to get the Emperor to sign anything.

He showed the Grand Maréchal the eight codicils which the Emperor had begun and had been unable to finish, in which he had said that being ill of body, yet in full possession of his faculties, he had made the following dispositions.

He requested the Empress to take Dr. Antommarchi into her service and to pay him a salary of six thousand francs, and to install Abbé Vignali in the entourage of her son. He left his house in Corsica to Madame Mère. It had been his intention to leave Princess Pauline his estates on the Island of Elba, and to Cardinal Fesch everything which he possessed in common with the aforesaid cardinal.

Montholon said that the Emperor was no longer in his right mind, and that it might be said that the Emperor had not made his will, but that he, Montholon, had dictated it to him . . . The Emperor had said, although with exaggeration, that he wanted to leave ten million francs to the French Army and two hundred millions out of the *Domaine extraordinaire* to some one or other. And yet he had asked whether he had left anything to Montholon, Marchand, Bertrand, and Pierron, etc.

Montholon handed to the Grand Maréchal the manuscript of the Egyptian Campaign, as well as divers papers in the handwriting of the Grand Maréchal that had been in the possession of the Emperor. In the evening, at nine o'clock, the Emperor had sent for Montholon to do some work for him, but had then done nothing. The Emperor had been fairly quiet by eleven o'clock but was not asleep.

At half-past eleven he made Marchand write down on a card that he left his house and estate at Salines in Corsica to his son, with an income of fifty thousand francs. During the night, from one o'clock until three, the Emperor had dictated to General Montholon and had made him write on cards in the dark. He no longer appeared to be quite lucid. He said that he would give to his son the four hundred millions of the *Domaine extraordinaire*.

"I leave to him my crowns of both France and Italy. Generally speaking I have left everything to him, nevertheless it is a good thing for him to have an income of fifty thousand francs in Austria, for after all, he is a *tudesque*."

From three to four o'clock, he slept. At four o'clock he was sick. Between four and seven o'clock he had an attack of hiccups and was sick again. At eight o'clock he had an enema, and then ate several spoonfuls of soup. From six till eight o'clock he said at least twenty times: "Tell them to light a fire, it's cold. A fire, a fire!" From eight until a quarter to eleven he slept. At eleven o'clock the doctors arrived, accompanied by the Grand Maréchal. When he woke up, the Emperor said to him:

"How is your wife?"

"Well, Sire."

"And how are you?"

"Well. Did Your Majesty use the syringe this morning?"

"No. Did I have it, Marchand?"

"Yes, Sire."

"Oh! Did the doctors think my movement was good? Oh! Is the weather fine?"

"Very fine."

"A fire, it is so cold!"

The doctors urged him to eat. The Emperor had a couple of spoonfuls of soup, a biscuit, a glass of wine, an egg. He said three or four different times in English, "Drink, drink, drink." He ate his egg and then said again, "Drink, drink." He drank. His eyes appeared to be slightly out of focus. Up until noon he drank wine mixed with water four times. At eleven o'clock, the doctors advised him to have a blister placed on his stomach. "Very well, do it," the Emperor replied. They went out of the room and the Emperor asked: "But Bertrand, why the blister?"

"To strengthen the stomach and to draw out the irritation."

"Some good wine would be much better."

The blister was applied at noon. Between noon and one o'clock the Emperor asked three times: "Have the doctors left?"

"No, Sire, they are there in the next room."

He called several times for wine mixed with water. He was given some. Then he was told that the doctors had advised him to drink preferably lemonade, barley syrup, or any of the fruit syrups. Between one o'clock and three, he ceased to repeat the same things but asked a different question every minute.

"Which is the best fruit syrup? Lemonade or barley?"

"Barley is heavier and less refreshing."

"Which do the doctors advise?"

"Whichever you like best."

"Then all that can be replaced by lemonade?"

"Yes, Sire."

"Is barley syrup made from barley?"

"No, Sire. It is made from the milk of almonds."

"Do they make fruit syrups out of cherries?"

"Yes."

"From apples?"

"Yes."

"From pears?"

"No."

"From almonds? Oh yes, of course, barley syrup. From walnuts?"

"No."

"Walnuts come from countries where the climate is colder, and almonds grow in countries where the climate is warmer."

"Yes, Sire."

Then he would begin again. "Do they make fruit syrup from cherries?" etc. "Which is more refreshing, almonds or lemonade?" etc. He asked all this literally dozens of times.

At half-past two he was sick. At three o'clock his questions ceased, and he slept fairly soundly until half-past six. He was awakened by a kind of hiccup, but he said nothing and remained quiet until eight o'clock. Dr. Antommarchi found that for the past eight hours the blister had had no effect. The Emperor's temperature was normal, and his pulse was irregular. He decided to apply two new blisters to the Emperor's thighs. He suggested this to the Emperor who said, "Do it." Dr. Antommarchi applied the blisters.

The Grand Maréchal sent for Dr. Arnott, who found the patient's pulse very regular and good. His sleep during the day had been very quiet. The vomiting had stopped entirely between eight in the morning and ten o'clock. On the whole, the doctors thought that the Emperor's condition was better than it had been on the previous day. At ten o'clock, Dr. Arnott returned to Camp. At noon mass was said in the Emperor's apartments. Mme. Bertrand and all her children were present. Mme. Bertrand remained at Longwood until seven o'clock in the evening, only going out for a breath of fresh air. The Emperor asked Montholon whether Mme. Bertrand had found him much changed [. . .].

April 30—The night was fairly quiet. The Emperor rested more than he had slept. He did not rub his thighs as on the preceding night. At seven o'clock he had a temperature, and asked for a fire to be lit. He was quite lucid. At half-past seven the Grand Maréchal came in.

"How is all your family?" Napoleon asked him.

"Very well, Sire."

"What is the weather like?"

"Very fine."

"Is there any sun?"

"Yes."

"What time is it?"

"Eight o'clock."

Half an hour later the Emperor asked, "Where is Gourgaud?"

"In Paris."

"Why did he leave?"

"Because he was ill."

"With my permission?"

"Yes, Sire. You even wrote a letter for him."

"Have I just been given a drink?"

"Yes, Sire."

"Was it water mixed with wine?"

"No, it was some lemonade."

"Bring me some champagne and water."

In the morning the Emperor told Montholon that he was near his end. Some vermicelli was brought to him. At first he refused to eat any, and then he took ten minutes to eat three spoonfuls. He swallowed the yolk of a fresh egg, without being able to chew a piece of bread that he had just put in his mouth. He drank some wine and water.

"Is there any water in it?"

"Yes, Sire."

His blister was dressed. It was then nine o'clock and the blister had been in place since noon of the day before.

"So I have a blister?" he remarked.

"Yes, Sire."

He gave a cry when it was taken off. The blister had barely taken. Antommarchi then removed the two blisters on the thighs and treated them before replacing them.

"What are you doing?" the Emperor asked him.

"I am applying two blisters to the thighs."

"So I have three blisters in all?"

"Yes, Sire."

"Bagatelle."

Ten minutes later he said to the Grand Maréchal, "Do I have three blisters?"

"Yes, Sire."

"Aren't there any on my arms?"

Later an attempt was made to change the bed linen. On the day before, his little bit of china had upset twice. For the first ten days of his illness, the Emperor had used a china milk jug when he had wanted to pass water while in bed. Before that he had always got up and stood over his pot, leaning his head against the wall. This had been his custom for a very long time, even when he had been in good health; possibly for the greater part of his life. He was like that, having for years experienced difficulty in passing water. I have often heard him say that he would die of bladder trouble.

This time when it was suggested that the sheets should be changed the Emperor asked to be left in peace. A moment later he was sick, although he didn't bring up anything he had eaten. It was a quarter past nine. During the night the Emperor remained quite lucid. He woke up crying:

"Oh! Oh! Death!" He told Montholon, "I am dead, my friend."

The Emperor talked to Montholon a great deal about his death, and dictated several things which Montholon took down. At ten o'clock the Emperor was quite clear-headed. Antommarchi reminded him that he had promised him a letter to the Empress. "I will do it. I will make you independent. I often think of you," the Emperor replied.

Then Antommarchi added: "Mme. Bertrand is most unhappy that she no longer sees you. It upsets everyone."

"But I would see her with pleasure if she were here. Bring her to me yourself at a time when you think that I am in a fit state to receive her."

The Grand Maréchal arrived at half-past ten. The Emperor was sick.

"Well, Grand Maréchal," he said, "what have you to say?"

"The doctors think you are very strong considering the small amount of food you eat."

A quarter of an hour later, the Grand Maréchal said: "There are some things I have to say that can only be said to you, if Your Majesty is able to hear me."

"Very well, tell me."

"Sire, I have made a note of your conversations as Your Majesty appeared to wish me to do. I have kept a diary of these past five or six years, and they consist of notes which will be of great interest to posterity. Notes on your conversations, and comments on events, men, on books which you have read, on the French nation, and on a great many other subjects."

It was necessary to shout very loudly. The Emperor said "Oh!" and looked at Bertrand vacantly. He then closed his eyes and said nothing further.

At half-past eleven the doctors were shown in. The Emperor was advised to take a vomit preventive, but he refused to do so. He had an enema and said that he felt like having one. They tried to sit him on the syringe, but he hadn't the strength. He looked as though he would faint. He threw himself down on his bed without wanting to change to the other one. The doctors came back into the room. The Grand Maréchal besought the Emperor to allow an enema to be given to him. "It is absolutely necessary," he said. "It will do you good."

"Fine."

Marchand administered the enema to the Emperor, who lost some of it and evacuated nothing. His temperature, which had gone down, rose a little. The Emperor was depressed. He was sick again at half-past one and then lay until three o'clock with closed eyes and without speaking; only occasionally glancing around the room to see who was present.

In the morning he had asked Marchand what people were saying about his health. Marchand replied that they thought it to be improving. Between three o'clock and half-past four he was quiet and said almost nothing, but looked around a little and spat. At half-past four, the Grand Maréchal arrived.

"Is that you, Montholon?"

"No, it's Bertrand. Montholon is ill."

Bertrand remained by the Emperor's bedside until half-past five. Napoleon looked at him frequently but said nothing. Antommarchi came and urged the Emperor to have something to eat. But he didn't feel like it. He offered the Emperor some soup, but it was refused. As well as a glass of wine and water. It was then five o'clock. At half-past five the doctors arrived and were announced by Marchand.

"Very well. Have they been here long?"

"Yes, Sire. Shall I show them in?"

The doctors came into the room. Napoleon didn't open his eyes, and after a quarter of an hour the doctors retired into the next room to consult. They could be heard talking. The Emperor opened his eyes at once.

"Have they gone?" he asked.

"No, Sire. They are in the next room."

"Oh! So they are in consultation."

A quarter of an hour later:

"Have they gone?"

"No, Sire. The doctors are still there. They are deliberating."

The doctors re-entered the room.

"Sire," they said, "it is four days since your arm was dressed. That is very dangerous, it should be dressed."

"Very well, don't make a fuss. The bed can be pushed back."

The arm was dressed. The wound stank. Fifteen minutes later the Emperor was told: "The doctors think that it would be advisable for Your Majesty to have an enema. I beg you to authorize Marchand to administer it."

Marchand prepared the enema. Dr. Arnott and General Bertrand left the room, but as the Emperor said nothing and did not move, the Grand Maréchal was recalled. He said to the Emperor:

"The doctors beg Your Majesty to have an enema. It is absolutely necessary."

"Very well," replied the Emperor, "I will sit up."

"Your Majesty is too weak. Let him permit Marchand to administer the enema. He is so capable, and he did it so very well this morning."

"I quite agree with you."

The Grand Maréchal retired. The Emperor prepared himself, but said: "Someone must help me turn over."

"I will do so, Sire," replied Marchand. The Emperor retained the enema, and then sat on his chair for twenty minutes.

"Is that you, Antommarchi?" he asked as he returned to bed. During this time it had been moved, and the Emperor found himself in a clean, freshly made bed; it was then a quarter to seven.

Arnott returned to the Camp. Dr. Antommarchi went to have his dinner, and so did Marchand and Ali. At half-past seven Marchand returned. The Grand Maréchal went out for his dinner. At half-past five the Emperor's temperature was higher than Antommarchi had ever known it to be. His pulse was ninety, whereas Antommarchi had never known it to be more than eighty-four during the first days of his attendance upon him.

From half-past seven until nine o'clock, the Emperor remained quiet, though he refused to eat anything. At nine o'clock the Grand Maréchal returned and then remained with the Emperor. From nine until ten o'clock, the Emperor suffered from hiccups. He heaved a deep sigh, as he had difficulty in breathing. He told Marchand to remove the blister. After fifteen hours, the two blisters on the thighs had shown no result. Marchand took them off. The one on the stomach also amounted to very little. The skin was white, and Marchand dressed it. The Emperor breathed with considerable difficulty and emitted "ah's" such as I had never heard before. The doctor urged him to eat something, either some soup or an egg, but the only thing the Emperor would say was:

"Leave me alone, no more questions, yes, later on, keep quiet."

"Is Your Majesty in pain?"

"No."

"Yet Your Majesty would appear to suffer."

"No."

The soup was taken away. The Grand Maréchal sent for Dr. Arnott at eleven o'clock. At half-past eleven the Emperor threw up a great deal of mucus and felt relieved. His breathing was easier and his pulse quieter. At a quarter to twelve Dr. Arnott arrived and he left again half an hour later, as the Emperor was better.

There was no longer any immediate danger. But Antommarchi had thought that between ten and eleven o'clock the Emperor was going to die.

CHAPTER FIVE

May 1821

May 1—Half an hour after midnight Marchand went to lie down while the Grand Maréchal remained with the Emperor. At two o'clock it seemed to him that the Emperor barely breathed; previously he had been asleep. The Grand Maréchal roused Dr. Antommarchi, who found the Emperor's pulse reasonably good, and his respiration easy. At half-past two in the morning the Emperor asked to pass water. He rested for an hour and then began to breathe with increasing difficulty and frequently spat. At half-past four he sat upright and remained in that position for a moment, as his breathing was more difficult. He hiccuped several times.

At five o'clock he was somewhat calmer, and his head was higher on the pillow. The Grand Maréchal went to bed and Marchand replaced him.

At half-past five the Emperor was sick, half over his sheet, half in the basin. He was then somewhat quieter, and up until seven o'clock and then till nine o'clock this condition was maintained. He spoke of the water from the fountain near Dr. Kay's house as being the best. The Grand Maréchal entered the room.

"What is the weather like?"

"Fine."

"Give me something to drink."

"Some orangeade?"

"No, some brandy and water," replied Napoleon. He drank some of it and said: "Oh, that was good." Then he asked for some water. "It hasn't been blest, has it?" he inquired.

There were further questions about the water, but less often than on the previous day. The Emperor spoke of the races, of Montchenu, of the Governor and his cottage. He had hiccups and was given orange-flower water and sweetened water.

Dr. Antommarchi came at ten o'clock and Mme. Bertrand at a quarter past.

"Good morning, Madame la Maréchale," said Napoleon.

"Your Majesty appears to be fairly well," replied Mme. Bertrand. Then there were further questions about the water.

"Which is better? That from the Pic de Diane, or that from the Falls? Have you got a fountain? There is one here, etc." At a quarter to eleven the Emperor said: "Go, Madame la Maréchale."

"Very well, Sire," and Mme. Bertrand took her leave.

At a quarter to twelve the doctors arrived. Arnott found the Emperor's pulse rapid, though weaker. The Emperor said nothing. Arnott was also of the opinion that he was in danger, and said that he must not be worried or upset. They advised the Emperor to have his back and buttocks washed with eau de Cologne. "Very well," he said. Then later he asked: "Was that all the result of their consultation? It didn't amount to much . . . did it? Well, what do you think . . . ?" Preparations were made to wash him.

Napoleon raised the supreme question. He would seem to say that there was no *afterwards*.

The Grand Maréchal went out for an hour and a half and returned at half-past two. The Emperor asked where he had been. In his absence Monseigneur Vignali had an altar set up, and he spent some time alone with the Emperor and administered extreme unction.

There was a conversation on this subject between General de Montholon and Abbé Vignali. The Grand Maréchal was of the opinion that it should not be said that the Emperor had taken communion, as it was untrue and possibly not a wise thing to say. It would be better to state that: "The Emperor expressed the wish to receive communion, but he was overtaken by delirium sooner than was expected."

Dr. Arnott returned. It was impossible to get the Emperor to take anything, not even soup or an egg. Some gentian was offered to him, but he refused it. For the remainder of the day, it was only with difficulty that he was persuaded to drink some water and orange-flower water, or a little wine and water to stop the hiccups. Almost the entire afternoon and evening he had frequent hiccups and difficulty in breathing. He showed the greatest repugnance to eating anything. He spoke to the Grand Maréchal about Balmain and asked perhaps thirty times, between three o'clock and half-past six:

"Is he here?"

"No."

"Has he left?"

"Yes."

"For England?"

"Yes."

"Why?"

"Because he had been recalled by his government."

"Oh, so he isn't coming back?"

"No."

"So we shan't have anything more to do with him?"

"No."

Sometimes the Emperor would say: "He was the cleverest man on the island. So the amiable Balmain has gone? I thought that he was still feeling Mme. Bertrand's pulse." (Here he made the gesture of feeling a pulse with two of his fingers.) "And O'Meara, is he here?"

"He has left."

"Oh! I didn't see him, did you?"

"Yes."

"Did he take leave of you?"

"Yes."

"Who sent him away?"

"The Governor."

"Why? Because he was too fond of us?"

"Yes."

"So he won't be coming back?"

"No."

"Has anyone had any news of him? Does **anyone** know what he is doing in London?"

"No."

"Is Montchenu still here?"

"Yes. He has quite recovered."

"And the very tall aide-de-camp."

"He is here."

"And Mr. Balcombe, where is he?"

"He has left."

"What! He has left? When was that?"

"Several months ago."

"And his wife as well? Oh! How very odd. She really has gone." The Emperor repeated this at least ten times.

"And Mr. Sturmer?"

"He has gone."

"Gone? But how very peculiar. And what about Mme. Sturmer?"

"She went as well."

"Then only Montchenu is still here?"

"Yes."

"And his tall aide-de-camp."

"Yes."

"Oh! How very odd." This at least ten times.

These questions followed uninterruptedly upon each other from three o'clock until half-past six. Montholon went to bed. Pierron went to have his dinner and returned at half-past six. The Emperor spoke to him about his mother. At eight o'clock the Grand Maréchal returned, at the very moment the Emperor was asking whether he were present. Napoleon had fallen into a kind of revery or slightly wandering state, and thought that he was at table. He asked Marchand what wines remained. "Some Cape wine, or some Bordeaux or Champagne?"

"Sire, do you wish something to drink?"

"What?"

"Some wine and water?"

"Some wine if you like," Napoleon replied, "but no water. I shall take nothing. . . . Serve the wine."

Then after a pause: "Wake these gentlemen."

"We are here, Sire."

"Who?"

"The Grand Maréchal."

"Oh, very good. Serve the wine."

The hiccups continued. Until half-past eleven he had difficulty in breathing. At midnight Dr. Arnott thought that the rest of the night would be quiet, and he and Marchand went to bed. Mme. Bertrand returned home. The Grand Maréchal, Monseigneur Vignali, and Ali remained with the Emperor.

May 2—From midnight until half-past two the Emperor slept, sometimes peacefully sometimes restlessly. At half-past two he hiccuped. Montholon went to the side of the bed.

"Who is there?" asked the Emperor.

"Montholon."

"What do you want?"

"I thought Your Majesty called me."

"No."

A quarter of an hour later Napoleon said that he wanted to get up. He threw off the bedclothes and said that he wanted to go for a walk. Montholon told him that he must wait until it was day.

"No," replied the Emperor.

Bertrand went for the doctor. The Emperor tried to walk. Montholon and Vignali held his arms on either side.

"Don't maul me!" he said.

Vignali left him and knelt down and prayed. The Emperor fell back on his bed. Ali woke up and came running in, followed by the doctor. The Emperor was put back into his bed. He had a very severe spasm of the stomach, and everyone thought that it was the end. However, his pulse grew steadier, although the agitation continued until four o'clock. Mme. Bertrand arrived. With a great effort the Emperor gave a loud sigh and said: "Oh, my God, my God, my God."

Marchand, who had been waked asked him what was wrong. The Emperor replied that he wanted his blister loosened; it was suffocating him. Marchand untied it. "But you are making it tighter," cried the Emperor.

Bertrand woke Dr. Antommarchi, who found the Emperor's condition very bad and asked them to send for Dr. Arnott. At five o'clock a horse was sent for him. Arnott arrived at six. The Emperor hardly breathed. At seven he was offered some sweetened orange-flower water.

"My troops! . . . What is that?"

"Some orange-flower water."

"Oh! I understand." Then he said: "Six of one, half a dozen of the other." Then a little later, "It's a lost cause."

There were alternate periods of calm sleep and hiccups, which started in the lower abdomen and which seemed to cause him considerable pain.

At half-past two the Grand Maréchal had a talk with Marchand. The Emperor had told Marchand to hand everything over to Montholon. First of all the three first wills; then, when the others had been sealed, Marchand had asked the Emperor if he was to hand them as well to General Montholon. The Emperor had replied, "Undoubtedly." In any case this was quite in accordance with the will and everything else. General Montholon was the testamentary executor.

"But there are three of us," protested Bertrand.

"Yes."

Since when the Emperor had said that this had been purely a matter of form; the will and the letter to M. de la Bouillerie had mentioned only Montholon. It was he who had written them, as well as the Instructions to the Executors, and also, I believe, the letter to Laffitte. The Emperor had asked Monseigneur Vignali to tell his mother that Montholon was the executor of the will.

"Yes, those were the first arrangements made, but since the twenty-sixth, when the Emperor said [to the Grand Maréchal] to make out the official report on the will, he must have altered them."

"No."

At three o'clock the doctor went over to the Emperor. Bertrand was deep in thought when the Emperor said: "Well, Bertrand, what have you to say?" "Sire, the doctors find that your pulse is better." A further question, then Arnott took his leave and the Emperor said: "Go away, Bertrand."

The Grand Maréchal walked up and down under the covered way; Montholon went out to join him and then Marchand arrived. Marchand had told Montholon that the Grand Maréchal would walk there if he didn't go to him. He had prevented the doctors from entering. Ali told the Grand Maréchal to return.

At about four or five o'clock the doctors urged the Emperor to have an enema. He did not answer. At six o'clock he was quiet, and this condition was maintained until ten o'clock at night. The previous evening his pulse was 90. This morning it was 98, at three o'clock it was 102, and at four and five o'clock it was 108. This evening it was quite as rapid, but stronger.

Dr. Arnott considered that there are signs today of approaching death, and a greater probability of the Emperor being near his end than of a recovery. Arnott says that he is suffering from an insidious disease and that the break-up will follow rapidly upon his present comfortable state.

Montholon took Vignali aside while the doctors were in the room with the Grand Maréchal and Marchand. There was the question of the night vigil to settle. The doctors ordered an enema. The Grand Maréchal told the Emperor three times, but he did not reply. They did not bother him any more around five o'clock in the afternoon.

May 3—Marchand sat up until three in the morning. Dr. Arnott spent the night with the Captain, Antommarchi in the Library, and Montholon, Marchand, Ali, Vignali and the Grand Maréchal in the Emperor's room. The Emperor was quiet, his breathing normal, and he slept.

At three o'clock Montholon relieved Marchand. The Emperor uttered a few disjointed words. At five o'clock he said: "Marchand, how much did you take in all? Fourteen ounces?"

This was followed by hiccups, which returned again for about five minutes. Towards half-past six the doctors had the Emperor drink a little sweetened wine, rather like a syrup. After each mouthful the Emperor said half in English: "Good, bon, very well," and again, "good, bon." He repeated this two or three times and on almost every occasion during the day when he was given wine, or sweetened orange-flower water.

Just before ten o'clock in the evening, Antommarchi gave him a biscuit dipped in wine. "Good, bon." Then his flannel vest was changed, the blister on his abdomen was dressed, and the Emperor nearly fainted. He was very weak; with the eyes of a dying man, he looked at Montholon with an expression that inspired pity and that seemed to say: "How can you torment me so cruelly?"

All day he had no strength to refuse what was brought him. He took everything he was given, did everything he was asked to do, without saying anything. He only spoke with his eyes, except on two occasions. As the hiccups were becoming frequent, he was given a teaspoonful of ether, which calmed him and enabled him to have a few minutes sleep. The second time he said, "That rascal Marchand!" At half-past eleven when his top sheet was changed, he said to the perspiring Grand Maréchal who had taken his hand, "You are very hot." And on another occasion: "Chase away the flies, my friend."

Between noon and one-thirty, there were alternative periods of hiccuping and of calm. Dr. Arnott found him weaker than in the morning. At half-past seven Arnott insisted on his taking some medicine, and then on his having an enema.

About giving the medicine, Arnott remarked that it is no longer possible to get the Emperor to swallow anything, not even the things he likes best, except drop by drop. All day a glass had to be held to his lips; he never raised his hand to hold it. Once, by a sign of the hand, he indicated that he had swallowed what was given to him. He frequently changed color, that is to say he became more and more pale and white.

On the subject of the enema, Arnott said that professional men would be unable to understand his having left the Emperor for three days without a movement. It was therefore absolutely necessary to obtain one, either by means of medicine or by means of an enema. He did not think that this would save the Emperor, as he was certainly in the greatest danger, with almost everything against him, but that nevertheless as a professional man and for the sake of his own reputation, he had to induce a movement. It was absolutely necessary, and it was possible, without moving the Emperor and by leaving him on his back, to lift his legs and to put a sheet folded in four or in eight under him to receive [. . .]

Antommarchi refused to hear of this and said that the activity which the giving of the enema would entail and which would follow its administration would expose the patient; that he was too weak, and that he, Antommarchi, would take the responsibility for opposing it. The Grand Maréchal asked both the doctors to think it over for half an hour and to try and come to an agreement, if that were possible.

He spoke about it to Montholon who told him that when the doctors disagreed, we could not take a decision, especially when one doctor declared that there was danger of the patient dying under the application of the remedy.

Arnott persisted in his idea. After having talked it over with Mme. Bertrand, the Grand Maréchal had a further talk with Antommarchi, who persisted in his view. There was a conference with Arnott, as a result of which nothing was proposed.

Furthermore Montholon had told Antommarchi that as he was the Emperor's own doctor, and Arnott the consultant, in the event of any difference of opinion arising between them, his would be followed. Antommarchi went back to saying that for the moment it was indispensable to build up the Emperor's strength, but that as soon as it was feasible, he would advise the enema.

Towards half-past two, the Governor came to see Montholon. He said that he had been ordered by his Government, in the event of the Emperor being in immediate danger of his life, to send the chief doctor on the island, as well as the Admiral's own surgeon, to attend the Emperor. He now knew beyond any possible doubt that the Emperor was very dangerously ill. It had been rumored for some time, but he had not believed it. Dr. Arnott had told him that considering the Emperor's character and what he himself had seen, to send unfamiliar doctors to attend him would be to kill him. The slightest unfamiliar thing upset him. The presence of Dr. Arnott had, in the beginning, greatly distressed him. During his first visits the doctor had observed that the Emperor's pulse always quickened upon his arrival and that it grew calmer afterwards. Therefore, the Governor was taking the responsibility upon himself of not sending another doctor, but he nevertheless offered the services of Mr. Shortt and of the naval surgeon Mitchell, who was the Admiral's medical attendant, in case they were desired for a consultation on the Emperor's condition. He added that if some of the responsibility lay with him, we also had our share of it. He was willing to assume his and it was up to us to realize what we were responsible for. Anyway the doctors he had mentioned would hold themselves at our disposal in the Alarm House.

The Governor added that he had learned that the two doctors were in disagreement, and that in such a case it seemed normal to have a consultation. Sir Hudson Lowe said further, that some papers had been brought by the *Wellington*. In the House of Commons, the name of Queen Caroline had been deleted from the Prayer Book, but she retained her title of Queen and fifty thousand pounds sterling. Nothing was known about affairs in France. The Austrian Army had crossed the Po, but it had then stopped as a result of an agreement with the Neapolitans, who were to receive a constitution similar to that of France.

Montholon and Bertrand agreed that there should be a consultation with the other doctors. Antommarchi was also of this opinion, and went to see the Captain to ask him to send for the doctors. When they arrived and were assembled in Antommarchi's room, he returned to Montholon and Bertrand to say that after hearing a description of the Emperor's illness, they had declared themselves unable to give an opinion without having examined the patient. Montholon told Antommarchi to tell them that they were to give their opinion for what it was worth; and if that were the result of the consultation, well and good; they could take their leave.

The doctors asked to speak to General Montholon, who received them. Mr. Shortt said that although these gentlemen well understood the position of the patient, they were nevertheless unable to give a very definite opinion. In such cases they had seen doctors be seriously mistaken and completely alter their opinion upon seeing the patient. It was their belief that the Emperor would not live much longer; they did not think therefore that they could save him; but in this situation they suggested he be given ten grains of calomel to be taken in a biscuit which should be dipped in wine, since it appeared that the patient liked this type of food. They had known this treatment to give amazing results. As the three English doctors were all of this opinion, Antommarchi said that, although he would not have suggested such a thing, he nevertheless agreed to it, in view of the unanimity of the three opinions.

May 3 (continued)—It was five o'clock. At half-past five the calomel was administered and afterwards some sabayon and wine. It was necessary to give alternate spoonfuls of food and drink.

Count Bertrand's three children came to see the Emperor and stood at the foot of the bed. Hortense and Henri did not recognize him.

Bertrand spoke to Monseigneur Vignali to tell him to come and see the Emperor when he liked, but not to remain with him constantly, and even to make a point of showing himself to the English so that the ill-wishers, slanderers, and enemies of the Emperor should not be able to say—as he knew it had already been said on the island—that the Emperor, that strong man, was dying like a monk with a priest always in attendance—all of which Vignali quite understood.

Between six o'clock in the evening and eleven o'clock, the Emperor was at times fairly quiet and could breathe easily, while at other times he had hiccups, sighed heavily, and had the eyes of a dying man. He could barely articulate his words, saying nevertheless, "Let me piss." Between half-past six and seven o'clock when the Grand Maréchal went to remove his little piece of china, the Emperor said: "Leave it there, my friend."

At eleven, as the calomel had not acted, Dr. Arnott spoke of giving the Emperor another ten grains at midnight as had been agreed, because he must have a movement, otherwise nothing would have been achieved. Dr. Antommarchi replied that he had not been told that such had been the treatment agreed upon. He had consented to ten grains of calomel being administered, but not to twenty; and he would not hear of it. This provoked further disagreement. Montholon and Bertrand decided to call in the other doctors who were at the Alarm House. They arrived before midnight.

Both Dr. Arnott and Dr. Antommarchi were thoroughly aroused over their respective opinions when, at half-past eleven, the Emperor passed a large black stool, in quantity bigger than anything he had evacuated for the past month. Perhaps this stool would save the Emperor, who had been weak after passing it and had given rise to a moment of anxiety. The Emperor then ate a few spoonfuls of sabayon. By one o'clock he was out of danger. . . .

Then he asked the name of his son. Twice his voice recovered its clearness. Since eight o'clock he gave the appearance of having recovered his lucidity of mind, but he ceased to speak. He could no longer move his hand, but frequently opened eyes that had become dull, dying, and painful to see. I did not dare to meet his gaze, as I feared that he would see the disquiet in my eyes.

May 4—Another stool at half-past eleven. Between midnight and three in the morning, the Emperor slept peacefully. Between three and five o'clock he hiccuped. At half-past six he passed another stool, and his clothes were changed. His voice was clearer and his pulse stronger and less rapid. At eight o'clock he was again very weak. . . . One should not delude oneself. At a quarter to eleven he said: "Well, Bertrand, my friend."

At noon another stool. After he had been changed, he revived somewhat and ate some jelly. At a quarter to seven he looked around at everybody. From seven to eight o'clock he had a series of fainting fits, accompanied by an increasing number of stools. But he recovered immediately.

At two o'clock his eyes swept around the room several times. At half-past two he said, "Madame Bertrand, Oh!" His expressions were full of pity. At a quarter to three he had two fainting fits at five-minute intervals. Then another movement. That day, as well as on the previous day, the Emperor frequently crossed his hands on his breast, locking his fingers together. . . . At three o'clock he said: "Give me my piece of china." At a quarter past three he had some cold beef tea. Dr. Arnott had hopes, as the pulse was stronger, but Dr. Antommarchi had none. Until four o'clock the Emperor took cold beef tea and orange-flower water at five- and ten-minute intervals; then he slept for a quarter of an hour. At four o'clock he gave a deep sigh and then hiccuped until half-past four. He then heaved another sigh, though less deeply, and took some more beef tea and orange-flower water. The expression of his eyes was very significant.

At about half-past four the Governor told Montholon that he had to go to Plantation House, but that he wished to know how the Emperor was. General Montholon told him that his condition was very grave and that there was little hope. "Nevertheless, Dr. Arnott told me that the Emperor is still conscious," replied the Governor. He had installed the two doctors Shortt and Mitchell in the servants' quarters of the New House.

Until five o'clock more hiccups, with orange-flower water and beef tea. The Emperor's pulse was still rapid, but much weaker. Dr. Arnott and Antommarchi came to see him at about half-past five. Montholon and Bertrand received the doctors Shortt and Mitchell, who told them that the Governor insisted that they were to see the Emperor that same evening, as soon as it had grown dark enough for them to approach the patient, to take his pulse and feel the abdomen, etc.

Until six o'clock there were hiccups, and orange-flower water was given. The Emperor took eight or ten spoonfuls of beef tea. Until half-past six he slept, or at least was quiet.

The Emperor took nothing. Until seven o'clock he breathed with more difficulty though with less hiccuping. He took nothing. At seven o'clock he said [omission in text]. Between seven o'clock and half-past eight, he was fairly quiet with little hiccuping. He drank some orange-flower water. At eight o'clock he passed a fairly large movement. . . . When he was changed he said "Ah!" several times. Arnott found his pulse steady. It was 102. In the morning it had been 100. The Emperor said to Marchand: "What do you want?" and gave him a pat without appearing aware of what he was doing. He looked as though he were far away.

Until nine o'clock he was fairly quiet. No hiccups although he was weak. At nine he hiccuped. At a quarter past nine he had a demi-tasse of beef tea. At half-past nine Antommarchi thought he would not survive the night. Arnott said that for the past few nights he, too, had been afraid. The Emperor appeared to be in pain.

From half-past nine until a quarter to eleven, he hiccuped weakly, though persistently. He twice had a sip of orange-flower water and wanted to spit but hadn't sufficient strength. From half-past ten to a quarter past eleven he slept fairly peacefully. From half-past eleven until midnight he hiccuped weakly and was in pain. His pulse was weak, his skin chill to the touch, and his eyes only half open.

On the third and fourth of May, the Emperor frequently crossed his hands on his stomach with fingers interlocked, or else held his hands straight out, sometimes moving his right hand and putting it outside the bed. Frequently he would pick up his handkerchief with his left hand to wipe his mouth after he had expectorated. He would uncover himself as a sign that he wanted to pass water and, generally speaking, he liked to push back the covers as far down as his knees, as had frequently been his custom. . . . Until the last moment, that is up until the day on which he became motionless, he was very sensitive to flies. They caused him to moan twice on the last day.

May 5 (day of the Emperor's death)—From midnight to one o'clock there were persistent hiccups, but the Emperor was much stronger. Between one o'clock and three in the morning he drank more often. At first he would lift his hand, then later he would turn aside his head to signify that he had had enough. At three o'clock he gave quite a loud hiccup and a groan which seemed to come from deep down inside him.

From three o'clock until half-past four there were hiccups and stifled groans. Then afterwards he moaned and yawned. He appeared to be in great pain. He uttered several words which could not be distinguished and then said "Who retreats" or definitely: "At the head of the Army."

From half-past four to five o'clock the Emperor was terribly weak and moaned. The doctor ordered him to be raised up on his pillows. The Emperor no longer opened his eyes. He seemed to be much weaker than on the previous day. He was no more than a corpse. His vest was covered with red spital that hadn't been able to roll any farther. The curtains were pulled back and the windows of the billiard room were opened. Throughout the entire night the Emperor had hiccups that were more like deep or shallow groans, sometimes sufficiently loud to wake those who dozed in the room with him; these were General Montholon, the Grand Maréchal, Vignali, and Ali.

From five o'clock in the morning until six o'clock he breathed more easily, which was attributed to the raised position of the upper part of the body.

At six o'clock Dr. Antommarchi tapped with his finger on the Emperor's stomach, which vibrated like a drum. The stomach looked swollen and already lifeless. The doctor told the others that the last moments of the Emperor were near. The Grand Maréchal and Mme. Bertrand were informed.

From six o'clock until a quarter past the Emperor hiccuped and moaned painfully. From six until half-past there was a period of great calm, while he breathed easily. During this half hour, with his head slightly turned to the left and his eyes fixed on the waist-coat of Count Bertrand, owing more to his position than to any especial interest, the Emperor appeared to see nothing, as though his eyes were veiled.

At half-past six he straightened his head and gazed at the foot of the bed. His eyes were open, set, and veiled. Until eight o'clock he had a little quiet sleep, giving now and then a sigh every quarter of an hour or so.

At eight o'clock there were several moans or rather dull sounds, which seemed to have their beginning in the lower abdomen and to whistle as they passed through his windpipe. They seemed to issue from an instrument rather than to be a moan. A tear slid from the Emperor's left eye into the corner of his ear. Bertrand wiped it away. Dr. Arnott was amazed that the Emperor held on to life for so long.

Until half-past ten or eleven o'clock his condition was generally quiet. He breathed softly. The whole body was quite motionless now, only an occasional flicker in the pupil of the eye, although these were rare. The eyes, which were glazed and veiled, were three-quarters closed. Every half hour there were sighs or sounds. A second tear appeared in the same place as the first. The Emperor's right hand lay on the coverlet, his left under his buttock. Since six o'clock in the morning he had lain quiet and motionless.

Sixteen people were present, twelve of them French. They included Mme. Bertrand and two other women, Ali, Noverraz, and Napoleon Bertrand, who was there at seven o'clock; but at half-past seven he felt sick.

From eleven o'clock until noon, Dr. Arnott placed mustard plasters on the Emperor's feet, while Dr. Antommarchi applied two blisters, one on the chest, the other on the calf of the leg. The Emperor sighed several times. Once or twice the doctor felt for the pulse of the neck.

At half-past two Dr. Arnott had a bottle filled with boiling water placed on the Emperor's stomach. At five o'clock and forty-nine minutes the Emperor breathed his last. During the last three minutes he sighed three times. . . .

At the moment of crisis there was a flicker of movement in the pupils of his eyes. Then there was a regular movement of the mouth, and of the chin to the forehead, of clockwork regularity. During the night the Emperor had spoken the name of his son before saying "A la tête de l'Armée." The day before he had twice asked, "Comment s'appelle mon fils?" and Marchand had replied, "Napoléon."

Count Montholon immediately wrote to the Governor to inform him of the death of the Emperor. Captain [Crockatt] came into the room. He had left the sitting room. He was to be sent to London with the news. The Governor wanted to send his own doctor [Mr. Shortt] and that of the Admiral [Mr. Mitchell] to guard the body of the Emperor, or otherwise the orderly officer. It was pointed out that there was no objection to Dr. Arnott, who had attended the Emperor during his lifetime, guarding the body after death. The Governor then made Dr. Arnott responsible for the body.

At ten o'clock Abbé Vignali said some prayers. Marchand started his vigil, while Archambault stood in the shadows by the door. At half-past eleven, the Emperor was shaved. Six hours after his death the body was washed and the linen changed.

May 6—At six o'clock the Governor, accompanied by his Staff and the island officials, with M. de Montchenu the French Commissioner, entered the Emperor's room.

At eight o'clock the plaster cast of the Emperor's head was to have been made, but the necessary material was lacking. At that moment the Emperor's face made him look younger than he really was; he looked about forty. By four o'clock he looked older than he really was.

At ten o'clock Mr. Ibbetson and Commander Hariette [read Marryat] came to draw the Emperor on his death bed. Mr. Marryat would appear to have made a fairly good likeness of the profile.

At half-past two the post-mortem examination began. Seventeen people were present: Bertrand, Montholon, Vignali, Antommarchi, Marchand, Ali, and Pierron (seven Frenchmen); Arnott, Shortt, Mitchell, Livingstone, Burton, Rutledge, and Henry (seven English surgeons), Reade, Major Harrison, Captain Crockatt. Total: seventeen persons.

The Emperor's bladder was found to be small, which had caused him to urinate frequently, and there was something wrong with the heart which had slowed down the circulation. There was a malformation of the left kidney; and finally the most remarkable thing of all was the stomach, seat of all the trouble. Tumors on the pylorus had produced various ulcers all around it, in the parts nearest to the stomach. One of these ulcers had become cancerous and had made a hole in the wall of the stomach the size of a little finger. On this side the stomach adhered to the liver, which had become somewhat enlarged and was rather congested, although the official English report omitted any mention of this.

At four o'clock the Emperor was dressed in the uniform of the Chasseurs de la Guarde with his boots, spurs, orders, medals, decorations, and his hat. The body was laid on the cloak that he had worn at Marengo, and which had been spread over the camp bed on which he died. White curtains had been twisted around the four pillars, in front of the altar. The walls of the room had been draped with black, as well as the floor and the ceiling. The bed was surrounded by candelabra and torches, with a chandelier in the middle. The Grand Maréchal stood at the head of the bed, General de Montholon at the foot, with Marchand behind him. Also at the head of the bed were Mme. Bertrand and her children, and behind her Monseigneur the Abbé Vignali knelt before the altar.

The public entered through the door of the former chapel and went out through the glass doors of the bedroom. They came in groups of four, six, or ten persons at a time, and left after a few minutes. The majority touched the Emperor's hand. Several women or officers were unable to restrain their tears. By half-past five everyone had been through. Between half-past five and six o'clock, several of the officers came for a second time. Between six and eight o'clock, when it was known that there was no difficulty about viewing the body of the Emperor, the entire 20th Regiment put on full dress; then between seven and nine o'clock, first the senior officers and then a considerable number of the men, filed past the body.

During the vigil of May 6, the Governor had several conversations with Montholon, in the course of which he said that all correspondence should be looked upon as having been political issues that were now closed. This was because Montholon had said that he would communicate the contents of the Emperor's will to him. The Governor had replied that he had no need to know it.

He informed Montholon that according to the instructions which he had received from his Government, the Emperor was to be buried at St. Helena. He asked where they wished him to be buried. General Montholon replied that he did not know the Emperor's wishes on the subject. After having discussed the matter with the Grand Maréchal, Montholon told the Governor that it had been the Emperor's wish to be buried beside the fountain that had provided him with drinking water for six years. Montholon remained with the Governor, who was to give the necessary orders.

The Governor read out the instructions that he had received from his Government and said that he would send General Montholon a copy of them. Then later, he said that he would not do this, as the verbal report he had given was sufficient. General Montholon replied that he would lodge a protest. The Governor enjoined him to see that all the entrances to Longwood were closed.

May 7—At eight o'clock it was signaled that the Governor's child was ill. At half-past seven the Grand Maréchal and Montholon went to visit the site of the grave, near Torbett's fountain. Men were working on the road. The grave was being dug. It was to be paved and would measure three feet by seven, and was to be lined with large stones to be taken from the New House. It was thought that this work could not be finished before Wednesday and that the funeral would take place on Thursday.

Mass was at ten o'clock. Several civic personalities as well as officers and men came to view the body during the morning; some of them remained for the mass.

The Governor came to see General Montholon and asked to be shown the will. Count Bertrand, Vignali, and Marchand met in General Montholon's house, where he opened and read the will. The Governor reread it several times and said that according to English law it was not a legal document, as it had not been signed in the presence of witnesses.

He was told that according to French law it was a very legal document, because it had been written and signed in the handwriting of the testator. In France such wills were preferred to those made before a notary in the presence of witnesses, and that as this will was to be executed in France it was necessary for it to have been made in accordance with French laws.

The Governor said that he had no intention of opposing it. He seemed surprised that the Emperor had not left any diamonds. But the diamonds were of two kinds. There were those which had belonged to the Crown and which had been left in Paris, and the others which had been Napoleon's own property and which "were captured at Waterloo, as you know."

"I was unaware of that," the Governor replied. (Reade added that it was true.)

"And the manuscripts?"

"Those written prior to August 1819 were sent to Europe, since when the Emperor has done no more work."

"Did the Emperor possess any furniture?"

"Of course. There are the two beds on which he slept, the brass bedstead, the screens, and several other pieces which he had bought."

"We will set up an inventory of all that."

"Very well, but only after final respects have been paid to the Emperor."

Antommarchi had preserved the Emperor's stomach. He was asked to place it in the coffin. The Governor said that he could not allow anything to be removed, and that everything must be placed in the coffin. It was only a temporary resting place, and the English Government would decide what was to be done later.

"I assume that you will not wish to place an inscription upon the tombstone, because it would be necessary to use titles and that I cannot allow."

"No, we only want to put, Napoleon, born in—— died in——"

"I cannot allow you to put Napoleon alone. You must put Napoleon Bonaparte."

At four o'clock a plaster cast of the Emperor's face was made. He was already disfigured, and the body emitted an extremely bad odor.

At five o'clock they sealed with lead the silver vessel, surmounted by an eagle and filled with spirits of wine, in which was Napoleon's heart. At seven o'clock the body was laid in the coffin, which was a little too narrow; especially with the hat on his head, and so it had to be placed on his knees.

The description of the contents of the coffin was as follows: "The heart and the stomach were placed in a silver vessel, without any spirits of wine. Also placed in the coffin were [the rest of the sentence is missing]."

The tin envelope was sealed and then the lead one. It is said that with the air excluded, the body will be preserved for centuries.

May 8—The mass was at eleven o'clock. The 66th Regiment, aware that the 20th had been to pay its respects, wished to do likewise, but as the body was already in the coffin they did not come. A statement was made concerning the sum in the Imperial coffers, which amounted to 300,162 francs. The bequests were distributed, as well as the reserve [the amount is blank]. So much remained for the doctors.

The Governor arrived, but seeing that General Montholon was busy he withdrew. M. de Montchenu came as well. He will not leave until after we do. We shall be sent to England. Montholon can go directly to France, and Count Bertrand probably shortly afterwards.

Sir Thomas Reade went to see Countess Bertrand to offer his services in preparing her passage to England. The departure of her servants and of all the women she desires to take with her presents no difficulty. She can take all the furniture and everything else she requires, such as the sofa and the piano, etc.

The Lyster affair was nothing. It was that rascal O'Meara, of whom Reade spoke disparagingly, who was at the bottom of it. The Governor will never forgive him and will catch up with him sometime. Today O'Meara is physician to the Queen, but it is assumed that he hasn't a large clientele. It is the Governor's wish that the past should be buried at Longwood.

Reade said that Montholon and his wife were the slyest and most artful couple they, the English, had ever known. Both of them were exceedingly clever. Jackson had not been the lover of Mme. de Montholon. He had been an English spy. For six months they had known everything that happened at Longwood; the most minute details as well as what books were published. It had not been for nothing that Jackson had been allowed to remain at Longwood until four in the morning. No matter how late it was, they always had Jackson's report on whom had gone home.

It was not he who had wished to follow Mme. de Montholon, but it was they who had sent him to Brussels so that he could win over Mme. de Montholon at his ease. Moreover no one made much ado about Mme. de Montholon. Reade added: "The Emperor's affairs were very badly administered in England. He was in the hands of people who swallowed up all his money."

The carriages have all been draped and have gone.

May 9—Mass and the service for the dead at ten o'clock. In the morning the lead coffin was placed inside a walnut one. It was then draped with a blue velvet pall on which was laid the cloak that He had worn at Marengo, a crucifix, and a white satin cushion on which reposed his sword, forming a cross with the scabbard. Then the body was carried out to the hearse.

The funeral procession set off in the following order. First Monseigneur Vignali wearing his canonicals. Beside him walked Henri Bertrand carrying the basin of holy water. Behind them walked Dr. Antommarchi and Dr. Arnott. Then came the body of the Emperor on a basket-shaped dais that had been erected on his old carriage, which was draped in black and drawn by his four horses, with two postilions in livery. Marchand and Napoleon Bertrand held the two front tassels of the pall, and Montholon and Bertrand the two back ones. The Emperor's state horse followed, led by Archambault. Then came Ali, Noverraz, Pierron, Coursot, and the cook. In the Emperor's carriage, also draped in black and drawn by two horses with one postilion, were Mme. Bertrand with Hortense and Arthur. They were followed by the Governor and his retinue.

At the entrance to Longwood and on the bank to the left of the road were drawn up the 20th and the 66th Regiments; the Company regiment; the artillery of the Company, and the Chasseur volunteers. Groups of onlookers were gathered on the slight rise in front of Hutt's Gate. On the eminence leading up towards Plantation House, opposite Major Harrison, the artillery company was drawn up with ten or eleven pieces of field artillery.

The funeral procession left the main road. As the track leading to the grave was not wide enough, grenadiers of the 20th Regiment carried the body, relayed in turn by men of the 66th Regiment, the Artillery, and the Navy. They set the coffin down by the side of the grave. The troops followed the procession from Longwood as far as to where the road branched off. Three salvos of fifteen shots were fired by the artillery from the main road as the body was lowered from the hearse. A salvo was fired every minute by the naval and coastal artillery.

The Governor's procession rode from the gardens of Longwood to the fork in the road, where it dismounted and went on foot. Monseigneur Vignali, alone, blessed the grave. The body was lowered into it by means of pulleys, and the opening of the vault was closed by a large stone. Monseigneur Vignali blessed the coffin and repeated some prayers.

The stone which covered the entrance to the vault was bricked up, and then the whole surface was covered with a layer of cement. The top of the grave, which was seven feet long by four feet wide, was closed, and the opening covered over by a wooden plank to which black drapery had been attached.

The whole ceremony lasted one to two hours. Lady Lowe and her daughter were present with the Governor. There was a great concourse of people; the whole island was present.

That evening M. de Montchenu and his aide-de-camp dined at Longwood. Later he had a talk with Montholon. He said that the Governor was aware that papers have been destroyed. Montchenu gave a frank account of his conversations with the Governor. He would like to feel as certain as Bertrand and Montholon of being admitted to the House of Lords. In the morning Montholon had spoken to Montchenu about Bertrand's affair with the Governor. The only thing he learned was that the Governor feared Bertrand's uncompromising attitude. . . . Admiral Lambert said that upon our arrival we would find everything settled. It is generally believed that we will leave on a "Chinaman."

May 10—The Governor arrived accompanied by Mr. Gorrequer. He carefully examined all the portraits, the Emperor's clothes, his toilet articles, the snuffbox for Lady Holland and the one for Dr. Arnott. He expressed the wish that Lady Lowe might also see them. She had asked to see the Emperor's room just as it had been during his lifetime. The Governor was told that if Lady Lowe would come on the following Monday, Mme. Bertrand would show her everything and that all the china would be displayed so that she could see the different pieces.

The Governor again said that the will could not be considered valid because it had not been made according to English law. . . . He wished all the Emperor's effects to be placed under his seal as well as ours and to be sent with us to England, so that the English Government could settle the matter.

He referred to the manuscripts again. General de Montholon repeated that everything that had been written before last August had been sent back to Europe, and that the Emperor had done no work since then. There remained only two manuscripts, both of which he had shown to the Governor. One, on the Bourbons, had been published; the other, *Remarks on the Concordats*, had been announced in Europe, but it had not been published. O'Meara had been the editor of the first manuscript. The Governor had seen that several other installments had also been announced for September and October.

Bertrand said that, properly speaking, the only manuscript which he had in his possession was *Letters from the Cape*, which was a reply to Warden. It had been published under this title so that it should be attributed to Las Cases. In any case the manuscript amounted to no more than a first draft and was very different from the published text. He had kept several other things which had been dictated by the Emperor; also some writings which he considered to be more his own work than that of the Emperor, but on which were notes in the Emperor's hand, which rendered them valuable as souvenirs to his family and children.

Admiral Lambert visited Mme. Bertrand and afterwards went to see the Emperor's effects. The Governor has read the list of everything contained in the three boxes. All the lists of contents will be handed over to him.

May 11—In accordance with the wishes expressed by the Governor on behalf of Lady Lowe, a start was made in the morning on returning the bedroom to the condition which it was in during the Emperor's lifetime. Everything was in its usual place. Beds, settee, chairs, boxes, the two writing desks, the two snuffboxes (with the exception of the jewels and snuffboxes that were placed in the three sealed boxes), the blankets on the two beds and settee, the big armchair, the footstools, the flannel bag by the foot of the armchair to cover the Emperor's legs, the handkerchiefs on the settee and armchairs, the head kerchiefs and the flannel vest on a chair, the two chamber pots, the portraits on the mantelpiece, the bust of the King of Rome, the two flasks, and a variety of useful objects.

In the sitting room were displayed the toilet articles; the Emperor's uniform of a Grenadier, of a Chasseur, and of the National Guard; the civilian clothes for St. Helena; the gray frock coat, the Marengo cloak. On a table were the Emperor's field glasses, silver brandy flasks, the two St. Helena spyglasses; buttonhooks, garter buckles, and shoe buckles. Shirts and handkerchiefs were on a table in the middle of the room. Boots, shoes, and slippers on the floor. The three boxes with a list of their contents were on one window sill, and cases containing the Emperor's pistols were on the other.

In the billiard room were fifty-three china plates stacked on two tables. Coffee cups; silver-gilt forks and spoons. Two trays with antique milk jugs and sugar basins. Two coffeepots. On the third table in the center were plates, fruit dishes, and dessert baskets with handles, and the stands for the fruit dishes in their cases. Silver and silver-gilt on the remaining tables, as well as bells, candelabra, dishes, plates, knives and forks, etc., soup plates, etc., etc.

From five until six o'clock, Lady Lowe, the Governor, and his staff looked at everything. On her arrival Lady Lowe kissed Mme. Bertrand when she went forward to greet her and to show her over the Emperor's apartments. Lady Lowe came back that way upon her return, but without her husband.

Admiral Lambert went to see Mme. Bertrand at ten o'clock. He said that the Governor looked upon everything that was past as political matters to be entirely forgotten; that he had had absolutely nothing to do with Lieutenant Colonel Lyster's challenge to Count Bertrand, and even less to do with the second, rude and uncalled-for letter which Lyster had written to Bertrand. He had strongly disapproved of Lyster's action, and would have sent him away from the island if he had not been a member of his staff. As to what concerned him personally, it was he, the Governor, who had been provoked by Count Bertrand. His position as Governor made it impossible for him to accept the challenge. It was he who was the offended party as well as the challenged, and therefore, in view of recent events, and through the intervention of the Admiral, he was prepared to consider the matter closed. As for etiquette, he as Governor owed no one any explanation, not even Lord Moyra should he visit the island. He realized that Count Bertrand was of superior rank to himself, but that the Governor owed no one a visit. And he paid none except on official occasions, such as the dinners of the diplomatic corps, etc. He was aware that Count Bertrand was independent of him, owed him nothing, and did not expect anything, especially when he was about to leave St. Helena. But that if Count Bertrand were to call on him, the Governor would immediately return his call. Everyone called on him; and if he had been Sir Thomas Reade or any one else except the Governor, he would have paid the first call.

Lady Lowe told Mme. Bertrand and the Grand Maréchal that she hoped to receive them at Plantation House, as well as their children.

May 12—The Governor arrived at eleven o'clock. He let it be known that, in accordance with his instructions, he could not let anything leave Longwood without having inspected it himself. It was also his wish that the three sealed boxes should be opened. He said that unless this were done, he would not affix a seal on any packing case. He also wished to glance through the manuscripts which were in the possession of Counts Montholon and Bertrand. As a result of this the three boxes were opened in the library, in the presence of Counts Bertrand and Montholon, Marchand, the Governor, Sir Thomas Reade, and Mr. Gorrequer. In them were found the objects which figured on the lists that had already been handed to the Governor. Sir Hudson Lowe then went with Counts Montholon and Bertrand and glanced through the papers in their possession.

The Governor informed us that we would leave on the *Camel*, a troopship attached to the cruise, a former frigate of 44, on which Admiral Lambert would place one of his most experienced naval officers as well as the necessary crew. Arrangements would be made to accommodate the different members of the Emperor's suite, and Mr. Darling would see to the furnishings. The Governor would have the ship stocked with provisions; and should the Government refuse to allow us to land in England, the *Camel* would take us immediately to Ostend. The Governor added that forty packing cases would be sent to Longwood the following day.

The army corps came to visit the Emperor's apartments and effects. The officers of the 20th of the Line between noon and one o'clock. The officers of the 66th Regiment between one and two o'clock. Officers of the Company came between two o'clock and three. The sailors from three o'clock to four, and the inhabitants of St. Helena from four to five o'clock.

Mme. Bertrand and the doctor visited the Emperor's grave. The opening was being filled in with bricks, stones, and slaked lime. A military post of twelve men, a sergeant, and an officer had been set up. A guardhouse was being built for one officer and another for the men.

They say that the body of the Emperor will not remain there for long.

NOTES TO CHAPTER ONE—JANUARY 1821

Many pages of Bertrand's journal require a certain number of notes of explanation or notes giving secondary references; the reader is given these here at the end of the volume rather than an index that would have been a useless addition.

January 1821

BERTRAND, HENRI-GATIEN or GRATIEN (Count)—Born at Châteauroux, in the Department of the Indre, March 28, 1773; he was forty-eight years old in 1821. Of all who accompanied the Emperor to St. Helena, Bertrand was the Emperor's Nestor. He was the first enrolled in the engineering school at Mézières, in the Ardennes, and he spent all his military career as a sapper. Gazetted a captain in 1795, the following year he accompanied General Aubert-Dubayet to Constantinople. He joined the Army of Italy in 1797 and met Bonaparte for the first time at Passeriano. He was sent to join the Army of the East and was present on July 21, 1789, at the Battle of the Pyramids (with the Bon Division). At this time he was given command of a battalion, and on August 7 he assisted at the revolt in Cairo; unaware that years later at St. Helena he would take down an account of the Egyptian campaign dictated by Napoleon. He was wounded at Abukir and captured a Turkish flag. (This relic is carefully preserved by the Olphe-Galliard family.) Bertrand was made a Colonel and Director of Engineers at Alexandria, August 4, 1799, and Brigadier General, at the age of twenty-seven, September 6, 1800. He left Egypt and in September 1803 commanded the Corps of Engineers at the camp of Saint-Omer. On March 7, 1805, he was promoted to aide-de-camp to the Emperor. In September he was sent on a mission to the Court of the Elector of Bavaria, at Munich, and participated actively in the preparations for the Austrian campaign. He gave proof of his courage during the crossing of the bridges at Vienna. He took part in the German campaign, fought at Jena and at the successful attack on Spandau, and entered Berlin with the Emperor. At the Siege of

Danzig he was seconded to Marshal Lefebvre, Duke of Danzig. For this he was promoted to Divisional General in May 1807. He followed the Emperor to Spain and in forty-eight hours crossed from Valladolid to Bayonne—"The fastest march I have ever made." As Commander in chief of the Engineers attached to the Army of Germany, he took part in the bombardment of Vienna, and was in charge of the building of bridges across the Danube, "the finest piece of work since the Romans," according to Napoleon, who mentioned him in the 24th Dispatch. Made a Count of the Empire March 19, 1808, he was at the battle of Essling, and in Paris for the celebration of Napoleon's marriage. He then left to replace Marmont as Governor General of the Illyrian Provinces: March 1811–December 1812. He was then given command of the Fourth Army Corps and was present at the Saxon campaign, Lützen, Bautzen, Leipzig. He was created Grand Marshal of the Palace, in place of Michel Duroc, on November 18, 1813; after the French campaign and the Abdication at Fontainebleau, he filled this post at Elba, and after Waterloo, at the Island of Aix, from where he embarked with the deposed Emperor first on the *Saal*, then on the *Bellerophon* en route for St. Helena. Condemned to death in his absence May 9, 1816, the Grand Maréchal, a model of fidelity, shared the captivity of his chief during the whole five years and ten months that it lasted. Upon his return to France, he was re-instated in his rank in October 1821, and called upon to take command of the Ecole Polytechnique in 1830. In 1831 he was elected Deputy for Châteauroux, and the next year was placed on the retired list at his own request. In 1840 he accompanied the Prince de Joinville to St. Helena and brought back the ashes of the Emperor. He presided over the ceremony in the Invalides. He died at his home at Châteauroux, rue Descente-des-Cordeliers, which has since become the municipal museum. On May 5, 1847, the twenty-sixth anniversary of the Emperor's death, his body was transferred to the Invalides and buried beside the Tomb of Napoleon. At his funeral, General Fabvier recalled Napoleon's words: "The name of Bertrand is linked with mine; for as long as I live, he will live"; for the memory of the Grand Maréchal, this amounts to a certificate of immortality. See G. Six, *Sayings of the Generals*, and J. de Vasson, *Bertrand, The Grand Maréchal of St. Helena*, 1935, which contains a bibliography.

BERTRAND, FRANÇOISE-ELIZABETH (Countess, Née Fanny Dillon) —Daughter of Arthur Dillon, proprietary Colonel of the Dillon Regiment, future Commander in chief of the Army of the Ardennes, "who, though English by birth and French by adoption, had halted the Prussian invasion at the Hill of Biesme, had recaptured Verdun without firing a shot and had died the victim of intrigues," in 1794. See F. Masson, *At St. Helena*, 3rd series: *The Father of Countess Bertrand*. Left a widower by the death of his first wife, Mlle. de Rothe (their daughter Henriette later became Marquise de la Tour du Pin-Gouvernet), Arthur Dillon married, in February 1785, Mme. le Vassor de la Touche, widow of a lieutenant commander in the Royal Navy, by whom he had Fanny, born July 25, 1785, at the Château de Gontreil, in the parish of Quévy-le-Grand. Concerning Fanny's marriage to Bertrand, see *Mémoires of Mme. de Boigne*, Vol. I, pp. 233 and 271, who sees it as a "prank" of the Emperor, who had been mortified when Mlle. Dillon spurned the suggestion with the laughing remark: "But Sire, Bertrand! A jester's monkey, to the life!" Fanny would have preferred to have married Prince Alphonse Pignatelli, who died of tuberculosis; see Mme. de la Tour du Pin, *Diary of a Woman of Fifty*, p. 268. Fanny's marriage to Bertrand took place at St.-Leu, September 14, 1808, at the house of Queen Hortense; see J. de Vasson, *Bertrand*, p. 62, who wrote in her *Mémoires* (ed. J. Hanoteau, Vol. II, p. 172): "Mlle. Dillon was spirited, high minded and of a noble character, yet inclined to be extreme in her devotion to anyone of whom she was fond. She showed her liveliness in the excessive attachment she had for her husband. Their example proves that difference of character is no obstacle to happiness."

Graceful and attractive, more than pretty—see Haller's miniature of her, reproduced in J. de Vasson—she possessed a charm combining Créole languor (she was related to Josephine) with English indolence, to which the prisoner of Longwood did not remain indifferent, especially after the departure of "la Montholon," as General Gourgaud called her.

DEPARTURE OF THE BERTRAND FAMILY FROM ST. HELENA—On the subject of the impending departure of the Bertrands from St. Helena, see F. Masson, *At St. Helena*, ed. in-8vo. pp. 415-19. According to Thiers, *History of the Consulate and the Empire*, Vol. XX, p. 698, talk of their departure started as early as 1820. There is evidence that the idea lasted until much later. Mention of it is to be found in a letter from General Montholon to his wife, January 19, 1821, published by Ph. Gonnard, p. 68: "Lovely Fanny doesn't want to spend another year of her youth upon our dismal rock, 'for anything in the world' . . . Up till now, Bertrand's requests have got no further than Longwood, but you may be certain . . . that in three months' time, they will no longer be at St. Helena."

MONTHOLON, CHARLES-TRISTAN (General, Count of)—Born and died in Paris; July 21, 1783–August 20, 1853. His principal claim to glory is the fact that he was the Emperor's companion at St. Helena, and the author of *Tales of the Captivity*, 2 vols., 1847. He volunteered at sixteen and fought at the battle of Novi. He served under General Campionnet, and then under Marshal Augereau, to whom he later became aide-de-camp. He was gazetted a captain in 1801, and became a major in 1807. He was created a chamberlain and Count of the Empire in 1809. Then he was made Minister Plenipotentiary to the Court of Ferdinand, Grand Duke of Würtzburg, in 1812. Placed on half-pay, he was made Commandant of the Department of the Loire in 1814. He was made a lieutenant general before the battle of Ligny, but was not confirmed in this last promotion. He was crossed off the Army list after leaving for St. Helena. His service record is in no way comparable to that of Bertrand, with whom he was named co-executor of Napoleon's last wishes, in the Imperial will.

In 1840, having been implicated in the attempted landing of Prince Louis-Napoleon, he was imprisoned at Ham and sentenced to twenty years' detention; he was pardoned before having served full sentence. Elected a Deputy of the Department of Charente-Inférieure after the Revolution of 1848, and after having held this electoral mandate until the Coup d'Etat of December 2, he died in Paris in 1853, at the age of seventy. See the biographical note at the beginning of his *Tales of the Captivity*, the Appendix to the *Mémoires of the Countess Montholon*, published by Couédic and Fleury, 1901, and F. Masson's "Montholon, Prior to St. Helena," in the *Review of Napoleonic Studies*, 1912. His first wife, whom he married in 1812, was a Parisian named Albine-Hélène de Vassal (1780–1848), by whom he had four children: Tristan (1813–31); Charles (1814–?); Napoléone, born at Longwood, June 18, 1816, and died at Marseilles June 29, 1895; and Josephine, born at Longwood, January 26, 1818, died at Brussels in 1820.

Mme. Montholon left Longwood on July 2, 1819, to the great regret of the Emperor, who openly showed his sorrow. "He wept real tears for you, possibly for the first time in his life," says a letter from Montholon to his wife on July 2, published by Ph. Gonnard. Concerning the possibility of an intimate relationship between Napoleon and Mme. Montholon, see the entry for October 31, 1818; in the *Diary of Verling*, also a hint from Baron Stürmer, Austrian Commissioner at

St. Helena, made on March 31, 1818 (reports published by Hans Schlitter): "Mme. Montholon was able to triumph over her rivals and to climb into the Imperial bed." An allusion by Mme. Bertrand to Montholon will necessitate a further reference on this point.

ANTOMMARCHI, FRANÇOIS—Born at Moriglia, Corsica, in 1789. This adventurer had a very murky background. He claimed to be the son of a notary; a Doctor of Philosophy and of Medicine—University of Pisa; a professor of that university, posted at Florence; and a disciple of the celebrated master, Mascagni. These were just so many fictitious titles to flatter his personal vanity. In reality he was nothing more than a dissecting-theater employee at Florence, a type of "barber" surgeon. Fesch had chosen him in preference to Dr. Foureau de Beauregard, and he was sent to St. Helena together with two priests and a servant, and landed at Jamestown on September 18, 1819. He lost no time in making himself unpopular with Napoleon and his suite on account of his bumptiousness, overweening conceit, and impudence. It was not long before his professional incompetence had produced the most dire effects upon the Emperor's weak state of health. As a record, his *Mémoires* are quite worthless. They are "paved with lies," according to Octave Aubry.

Napoleon's death mask, which made his reputation, would now appear to have been a fraud, even before becoming a profitable speculation. See F. Masson, *At St. Helena*, 1st series: *Antommarchi, Napoleon's Doctor*, and idem, 3rd series; and the *Souvenirs of the Mameluke Ali*, pp. 264–66. On the subject of the death mask, see ibid, and the letters of Dr. Francis Burton in the Appendix of this book.

SALICETI, CHRISTOPHER—This lawyer from Bastia, Deputy for Corsica to the Convention, had strongly supported the Bonaparte family before the 18th Brumaire. Rousselin de St. Albin made use of him when he desired information about Bonaparte's rôle at the siege of Toulon. See Catalogue Émile Brouwet, 1935, Part 2, No. 137. Placed at the head of a mission to Italy, he later became Minister of Police and Minister for War, under Joseph and Murat, at Naples. He died in 1809.

THE FIRST CONSUL AT TARARE—This anecdote, which takes place during the trip Napoleon made, as Consul, to Lyons in January 1802, when he was to preside over the Consulta of the Italian Republic, pleased him so much that he repeated it to several of the inmates of

Longwood. Especially to Las Cases; see his *Memorial*, ed. 1823, Vol. II, p. 331. See also O'Meara, *Napoleon in Exile*, ed. 1823, Vol. I, p. 96, who enlarged on it; and Gourgaud's *Diary*, December 16, 1816.

THE SIEGE OF DANZIG—This is the siege of 1813, bravely sustained by General Rapp, who was born at Colmar, April 27, 1771, and died at Rheinwiller in the Grand Duchy of Baden, November 8, 1821. He was forced to capitulate November 29, 1813. In 1814 Marchangy published a study of the siege. In 1820 D'Artois published an *Account of the Defense of Danzig*; on page 142, this author brings the number of the besiegers up to 55,000. In his *Mémoires*, p. 303, Rapp puts the number at 60,000; concerning the question of making a sortie on the Nehrung, see Rapp, ibid, p. 292, the *General Correspondence of Napoleon*, Vol. I, No. 19, p. 649, and D'Artois, op. cit., p. 112.

ARCHDUKE CHARLES—Born 1771; died 1847. Son of Emperor Leopold II and younger brother of Franz II, he was a famous Austrian general and strategist. He commanded the Imperial Armies in 1796 against Marshal Jourdan and General Moreau and forced them back across the Rhine. For further information about the Archduke, see Marcel Dunan, *Napoleon and Germany*, p. 603.

GUYOT, CLAUDE-ÉTIENNE (Baron)—A cavalry general (1768–1837). He was formerly a captain in the Light Cavalry of the Consular Guards, and was promoted after Austerlitz and Eylau to the rank of colonel; when in command of a detachment of the Light Cavalry of the Guards, he followed Napoleon to Spain. He then became Colonel (Second) of the Guards' Light Cavalry, and was made a brigadier general in 1809 and a lieutenant general in 1811. He took part, still with the Light Cavalry, in the Russian campaign, and led the Heavy Cavalry of the Guards in Belgium, receiving two bullet wounds at Waterloo.

JOMINI, ANTOINE-HENRI (Baron of)—Born in the Canton of Vaud in Switzerland in 1779; died at Pau in 1869. He started life as a stockbroker. After leaving the army with the rank of battalion commander, in 1803, he wrote a *Treatise upon Outstanding Military Operations* that had the honor of being commented upon by Napoleon. This commentary, found by General Montholon among Napoleon's papers, was published by the Commission charged with the publication of the Emperor's writings, at the end of the *General Correspondence*,

Vol. XXIV. See Xavier de Courville's biography; *Jomini or Napoleon's Soothsayer*, 1935; also F. Masson, *Yesterday and To-day*, 1908, pp. 28ff.

RIVOLI—What Napoleon says here about the battle of Rivoli, he said elsewhere about Austerlitz. "In war, success is so very much a question of a glance and of instant decision that the battle of Austerlitz, which was such a complete victory, would have been lost, had I attacked six hours earlier." Las Cases, *Memorial*, Vol. II, p. 179.

January 7

BROUGHAM AND THE TRIAL OF THE QUEEN OF ENGLAND—Born in 1760 and married in 1795 to the future George IV, Caroline of Brunswick, mistress of the adventurer Pergamini, was publicly accused of adultery. See Maurice Soulié, *The Scandalous Queen*. Public opinion was much shaken by the lawsuit. All the English and French papers of the time were filled with accounts of the matter. The *Journal des Débats* of July 16, 1820, reproduced the bill for the deposition of Caroline; of July 18, published her letter protesting against the bill; of July 28 printed the act of accusation; and of October 4 and 8 reported the speech of Lord Brougham, who defended her. At the end of the trial, public disorder and demonstrations almost brought about the fall of the Cabinet.

LABAUME, EUGÈNE—In 1820 his *History of the Fall of the Empire*, 2 vols. in-8vo., was published by Asselin in Paris. From this it will be seen that the "latest" books occasionally reached St. Helena.

HARDENBERG, CHARLES-AUGUSTUS (Baron, later Prince of)—A Hanoverian statesman who in 1806 became Prussia's Foreign Minister. In 1811, he sought an alliance with France. See his letter to Baron Krusemark, of August 30, 1811, quoted by Koch and Schoelle in *A Short History of Peace Treaties*, 1818, Vol. X, pp. 112ff.: "It is on behalf of France that we are re-arming, should she need a faithful ally . . . Count de St. Marsan seemed filled with a sense of the sincerity of our declarations and esteemed them to be of a kind likely to have an effect upon the magnanimous spirit of the Emperor Napoleon." A treaty of alliance was, in fact, signed, on February 24, 1812, between General von Krusemark and the Duke of Bassano: ibid, p. 116. On the "tribulations of Prussia," and the waverings of Hardenberg between a French or a Russian alliance, see Vandal, *Napoleon and Alexander*,

Vol. III, Chapter VIII. The question had already arisen for him in 1806. See the *Mémoires of Metternich*, Vol. II, pp. 114–16. Hardenberg's *Mémoires* were published by Ranke at Leipzig, in 1877.

COLE, JOSEPH—Postmaster at St. Helena, and a partner in Balcombe, Fowler & Co. See Arnold Chaplin, *A St. Helena's Who's Who*, 1914.

January 10

READING MATTER, ETC.—The *Mémoires of Bernadotte* is the abridged title of *Mémoires to Be Used for a History of Charles XIV, King of Sweden*, published in 1820 by Coupé de St. Donnat and Roquefort. Coupé de St. Donnat had stayed in Stockholm in 1818. The volume of scandalous chronicles of the court of King Jerome must be the one published in 1820, by an "eyewitness" (Lombard de Langres) under the title: *The Kingdom of Westphalia, Jerome Bonaparte, His Favorites, and His Court.*

BERNADOTTE—Examples of Bernadotte's boastfulness are not lacking, apart from the order of the day given out at Léopoldau, July 7, 1809, and amended by the Emperor. See Vox, *Six Hundred Letters about Work*, pp. 63 and 432. Count de Rochechouart in his *Mémoires*, p. 293, states that after Leipzig, Bernadotte said: "Who would suit the French better than I?" for the throne of France; and the *Journal* of Baron Mounier, p. 212, quotes him as saying: "But why has France put herself in the hands of a Corsican? Were there no generals famous for their victories who were born in France, born in the country of Henri IV?"

DEBTS OF BERNADOTTE TO THE EMPEROR—The most typical of these debts is the one mentioned by Baron Fain, *Mémoires*, p. 299 and note, which was contracted by the Prince of Ponte-Corvo, when, in September 1810, he announced to the Emperor the election of Bernadotte as Hereditary Crown Prince of Sweden. Napoleon signed a voucher for a million francs for traveling expenses.

BERNADOTTE'S ELECTION—See Christian Shefer, *Bernadotte as King*, 1899, p. 16, who quotes Fersen: "Sweden is lost if we fail to choose one of the French marshals." This remark gave impetus to Mörner's canvassing in favor of Bernadotte's candidature, seconded by

Baron Wrede. Albert Vandal, author of *Nap. and Alexander*, Vol. II, Chapter XII, has told this story in full, and before him Méneval, in *Mémoires*, Vol. II, p. 374, who based his information upon the testimony of Ségur. Bertrand gives here interesting confirmation on the subject.

DÉSIRÉE CLARY (EUGÉNIE-BERNARDINE-DÉSIRÉE)—Born November 9, 1777, at Marseilles; married Bernadotte at Sceaux, August 17, 1798; died at Stockholm, December 17, 1860. About the love affair of Désirée and the Emperor, see Emile Dard, *Among the Entourage of the Emperor*, 1940; and *Bernadotte, Marshal of France*, by T. T. Höjer, translated into French in 1943, pp. 140ff. "Bonaparte," wrote Mme. de Rémusat, "did not much like Marshal Bernadotte; but it is possible that he felt obliged to raise him to power because he had married the sister of his brother Joseph's wife, and it was only suitable that the sister of a queen should, at the very least, be a princess." As to the "suitability," it is obvious in this context that the speaker has not hesitated to express himself very crudely indeed. Speaking to Las Cases (*Memorial*, Vol. V, p. 202) upon the same subject, Napoleon expressed himself more obliquely. It is possible, of course, that Las Cases watered down the story. By the rudeness of the expressions used here, Bertrand, in noting them down, competes with several indelicate passages in the *Diary* of Gourgaud, who is by no means chary of reporting them.

VICEROY, PRINCE EUGÈNE—Napoleon's stepson, and Viceroy of Italy after the decree of June 7, 1805. He married Augusta-Amelia, daughter of Maximilian-Joseph, King of Bavaria, at Munich on January 14, 1806, and was, in fact, considered as a possible candidate for the Swedish throne. It appears that the proposal was made at the Elysée Palace at the time of the festivities in honor of the Emperor's marriage. The offer was transmitted by Michel Duroc, Grand Marshal of the Palace. This was contested by du Casse, but later affirmed to be so, by Baron Darnay, a friend of the Prince. The fact is here confirmed; see Fourmestraux, *Prince Eugène*, 1867, p. 214. The question of professing the Protestant faith, which would have required a dispensation for Eugène and Augusta-Amelia, did not arise for Bernadotte who, upon mounting the throne declared that "he belonged to the Lutheran faith to which, in his heart, he had long been attached": Ch. Schefer, *Bernadotte*, p. 62. This whole passage has been commented upon by Napoleon in *Mémoires for Use in Writing a History of France*, 2nd ed. Bossange, 1830, Vol. IV, p. 294.

OSCAR (Bernadotte's son)—Born July 4, 1799, he ascended the Swedish throne in 1844, upon the death of Charles XIV. His Christian name—a national one in Scandinavia—had been given him by Napoleon, his godfather, in memory of the poet Ossian, about whose poems Napoleon "was crazy." See Las Cases, Vol. V, p. 205. Concerning Bonaparte's passion for the poems of Ossian, see Van Tieghem's article in the *Review of Napoleonic Studies*, 1918, pp. 44-64.

BUONAVITA, ABBÉ ANTONIO—He was sixty-five or sixty-seven years of age when he was sent to St. Helena by Fesch, along with the abbé Vignali and "Dr." Antommarchi. This elderly Corsican priest had been a civil servant in Mexico, then in 1814 he had come from Corsica to the island of Elba as chaplain to Madame Mère. Apoplectic and a cripple, he was unable to carry out his duties for the Emperor, who felt very sorry for him. On the departure and replacement of Buonavita, see Forsyth, *History of the Captivity*, French trans., Vol. III, p. 259, and Ali, *Souvenirs*, p. 261.

VIGNALI, ABBÉ ANGELO—Buonavita's deputy. He remained at St. Helena after the departure of his colleague. He administered extreme unction to the Emperor (see below), and figured as one of Napoleon's legatees. He was given the special mission of delivering the Emperor's will. Several papers, when announcing his departure for St. Helena, had conferred on him medical qualifications that he didn't possess.

HUME, CROMWELL, AND NAPOLEON—David Hume wrote a *History of England*, which appeared in 1754-61 and was published in a translation in Paris from 1819 onwards. In all probability it is from this work that the chapter on Cromwell mentioned here was taken. Under the Consulate, a pamphlet appeared entitled *Parallels between Caesar, Cromwell, Monk, and Bonaparte*; regarding this tract, see the *Diary of Roederer*, published by M. Vitrac, p. 37 and note. The pamphlet, attributed by some to Fontanès, by others to Lacretelle the younger, but in any case, inspired by Lucien Bonaparte, develops the comparison of Bonaparte with Cromwell and then strongly refutes it; see *Mémoires of Lucien Bonaparte*, Vol. I, pp. 421ff., and Roederer, *Complete Works*, Vol. III, pp. 342f. At St. Helena, the Emperor had already told Las Cases (*Memorial*, Vol. III, p. 249) that he and Cromwell had nothing in common. Metternich, *Mémoires*, Vol. I, p. 290, had already disposed of this mania for comparisons: "It is useless to attempt to compare Napoleon to . . . etc." Bignon, *Hist. France*, Vol. I, p. 11, had in the same way refuted Sir Walter Scott's remark, when he wrote that instead of playing the part of a Washington, Bonaparte preferred "to play that of Cromwell."

SIEYÈS—This former abbé suffered from "Constitutional" mania. The opinion expressed here by Napoleon may be compared with those of Las Cases in July 1816, *Memorial*, Vol. IV, pp. 400f., and of Montholon, in 1820, *Tales of the Captivity*, Vol. II, p. 375. On the subject of the Constitution of the Year VIII, consult Jean Thiry, *Napoleon's Senate*, Chapter II, who quotes Boulay de la Meurthe's *Constitutional Theories of Sieyès*.

VILLEMAIN, ABEL-FRANÇOIS—This protégé of Fontanès, Grand Master of the University in 1808, became a lecturer at the Ecole Normale, and in 1816 was appointed Professor of Oratory by Royer-Collard. *Cromwell*, which he wrote at the age of twenty-seven in 1819, is considered to be very indifferent. His *Contemporary Souvenirs*, which appeared in 1854, contains a vivid portrait of the very endearing character of the Count de Narbonne.

NARBONNE, LOUIS (Count of)—Born at Colorno, Parma, in 1755. This former Minister of War under Louis XVI was supposed to be the illegitimate son of Louis XV. A friend of Talleyrand, he entered Napoleon's service in 1809, became an aide-de-camp, and was sent on a confidential mission to Berlin before becoming French Ambassador in Vienna. On the subject of his ambassadorship in Vienna, consult Emile Dard's monograph, *A Confidant of the Emperor*, Chapter XII; on his confidential mission to Berlin, ibid, pp. 240ff. While he was at Berlin, Narbonne learned of the defection of General York who, at the head of the Prussian Auxiliary Corps, instead of following Marshal Macdonald on the road to Tilsit, deliberately allowed himself to be surrounded by the Russian Army and then signed with Russia the Tauroggen Agreement. On the subject of this desertion, which, according to Narbonne "overwhelmed" Hardenberg, see *Mémoires of Caulaincourt*, published by J. Hanoteau, Vol. II, pp. 45, 394, and the note. Narbonne accompanied Caulaincourt to the Congress of Prague. "He is a man of considerable wit, who also possesses sound judgment," Napoleon said of him to General Gourgaud at St. Helena. "I should have posted him to the Ministry of Public Relations, in place of Caulaincourt." On the subject of the Congress of Prague, July 1813, qualified by Bausset as a "diplomatic phantasmagoria," consult Caulaincourt's *Mémoires*, Vol. I, pp. 152ff.; also Koch and Schoelle, *Short Hist. Peace Treaties*, Vol. X, pp. 247ff.

VANDAMME, DOMINIQUE-JOSEPH-RENÉ (General, Count d'Unsburg)—Born at Cassel on November 5, 1770. Commander in chief of the 1st Corps of the Grand Army in Saxony, he underwent the "event" of Kulm, where he capitulated on August 30, 1813. On the subject of that unfortunate incident, see Koch and Schoelle, *Short Hist. Peace Treaties*, Vol. X, p. 274, and Bignon, *Hist. France*, Vol. III, p. 215. During this time, Marshal Macdonald was defeated by Blücher, August 26, on the Katzbach and lost more than a hundred guns. Concerning this painful event, see Fain, *Manuscript of 1813*, Vol. II, p. 304, or Odeleben, *The Campaign of 1813*, translated into French by Aubert de Vitry, Vol. I, p. 267. The battle of Vittoria, fought and lost on June 21, 1813, preceded these disasters. See Bignon, op. cit., Vol. III, p. 173, and *Victories and Conquests*, Vol. XXII, pp. 246ff. It is possible, as Napoleon says to Bertrand, that Fouché had already begun to betray him at this period. In this regard, consult Louis Madelin, *Fouché*, 1901, pp. 244, 275, and 277.

NARBONNE AS A DIPLOMAT—Whenever the Emperor spoke of Narbonne at St. Helena, he always made a great fuss about him. All those at Longwood agree when mentioning this in their various memoirs. For example, see Las Cases, *Memorial*, Vol. III, pp. 93f.; O'Meara, *Nap. in Exile*, Vol. II, p. 153; and Montholon *Tales of the Captivity*, Vol. I, p. 278. Narbonne arrived at Vienna, March 17, 1813, to replace Otto (see below). On the subject of Narbonne as Ambassador in Vienna, consult Villemain, *Souvenirs*, Vol. I, p. 294. Bignon, *Hist. France*, Vol. III, p. 246, and Bausset's *Mémoires*, Vol. II, p. 166, which sums up Narbonne as follows: "The wit and personality of Louis, Count de Narbonne were more suitable than Otto's, for negotiations with Metternich, Austria's supreme minister." "Narbonne combined the most exquisite courtesy and French charm with a subtle mind and a nimble wit."

OTTO, LOUIS-GUILLAUME (Count de Moslay after 1811)—Born at Kork, in the Grand Duchy of Baden, August 7, 1754. He was attached to the service of the Count de la Luzerne and became French by naturalization. Ambassador at Vienna from 1809, he died in Paris on November 9, 1817.

BAGRATION (Princess)—Her famous political salon in Vienna in 1813 was visited by, among others, the Count de Nesselrode. See *Letters and Papers of the Chancellor, Count de Nesselrode*, published by his grandson, Vol. IV, p. 132.

CHILDREN OF THE GRAND MARÉCHAL—The Bertrands had five children: Napoleon, born in 1808; Hortense, born in 1810; Henry, born December 6, 1811, at Trieste, when the Grand Maréchal was Governor General of Illyria; Arthur, born at Longwood in January 1817, and wittily presented to Napoleon as "the first Frenchman to reach Longwood without the permission of Lord Bathurst"; and Alphonse-Charles-Henri-François, who was born in 1824. Therefore at St. Helena Arthur was a child of four and Hortense a little girl of eleven. They were very mischievous; the two children entertained the Emperor, who in turn used to amuse himself by teasing them. Arthur Bertrand in his *Letters on the Expedition to St. Helena in 1840*, pp. 110–13, Ali, *Souvenirs*, p. 242, and Marchand, *Souvenirs inédits*, took pleasure in recalling instances of the familiarity that the Grand Maréchal's children enjoyed with the Emperor. Particularly the presents which they received: the gift to Hortense of the First Consul's coat, as well as some earrings (see the anecdote of the ears that were pierced with the help of a kitchen skewer); and the present of a gold watch to Napoleon Bertrand; and of a Javanese pony to Arthur who, unable to speak anything except a kind of English jargon, took this present to be for "when gon fair" (when the gun on High Knoll fired at noon). See O. Aubry, *St. Helena*, Vol. II, p. 169, which follows Marchand's version without acknowledging it and J. de Vasson, *Bertrand*, p. 221, who names its source.

COMPLAINTS OF THE EMPEROR AGAINST HIS FAMILY—"It was sufficient for me to make one of my brothers a king for him to believe at once that it was *by the grace of God* . . . He became not a lieutenant on whom I could lean, but another enemy that I had to watch out for."—Las Cases, *Memorial*, Vol. VI, p. 258. In his *Diary*, January 30, 1817, Gourgaud reports reproaches that are similar to those Napoleon makes here against Joseph. "My family has never upheld me. My brothers have as many pretentions as if they could say: 'The King, our Father.' ": Caulaincourt, *Mémoires*, Vol. II, p. 228. In 1809, Napoleon expressed himself to Roederer, *Diary*, p. 237, on the subject of Jerome, as he does here to Bertrand.

CZAR ALEXANDER AND LANNES—The incident retailed here, took place at the Meeting at Erfurt, when Marshal Lannes, who had gone to receive the Czar at Friedberg, had ridden in his coach. See Bittard des Portes, "The Preliminaries to the Meeting at Erfurt," in *Review of Diplomatic History*, Year IV, No. 1.

SAINT-DIZIER—"Instead of marching on Paris as I had expected," Caulaincourt says in his *Mémoires*, Vol. II, p. 51, "which would probably have saved everything, the Emperor, betrayed by sight of a Russian Corps in the neighborhood of Saint-Dizier, thought it was the Allied Army and changed all his plans in the night." Napoleon throws all the blame for this false maneuver upon Marmont and Sebastiani.

MEERFELDT AND MURAT AT LEIPZIG—Taken prisoner near Doelitz, this Austrian general commanded a Corps of 10,000 men in the Schwarzenberg Army from the day of October 16, 1813. He had been one of the generals who negotiated the Peace of Leoben and the Peace of Campo-Formio, and on the night of the Battle of Austerlitz, it was he who was sent to ask for an armistice. On the interview between Napoleon and General Meerfeldt after his capture, see Fain's *Manuscript of 1813*, Vol. II, p. 409. The more than ambiguous attitude of Murat at Leipzig has been admirably analyzed by F. Masson in *Napoleon and His Family*, Vol. IX, p. 77: "Austria is in agreement with England on the subject of offering the Kingdom of Naples to Murat, in return for his joining the coalition. Murat has agreed. Will he maintain his attitude of faithful lieutenant towards the Emperor, or will he adopt the attitude of a hidden enemy?" At St. Helena the Emperor settled the argument and inclined towards the second assumption, which has since been confirmed by Bausset, *Mémoires*, Vol. IV, pp. 265 and 284: "Murat was unruly," the Emperor said, "but I thought that he was attached to me. It was his wife who was the cause of his defection. Caroline! my sister! to betray me!"

BERWICK, JACQUES FITZ-JAMES (Duke of)—A Marshal of France and the illegitimate son of James II and Arabella Churchill. A naturalized Frenchman, he fought under Marshals Luxembourg and Villeroi, and in 1704 he commanded the French troops in Spain. As for General Louis Joseph, Duke of Vendôme (1654–1712), he was used by Louis XIV in the war in Flanders in 1708, date of the loss of Lille, which had been captured from the Spaniards in 1667.

WREDE, CHARLES-PHILIPPE (Prince of)—Born at Heidelberg in 1767. Field marshal of the Bavarian troops, he fought in Russia under

General Gouvion-Saint-Cyr, Commander of the 6th Corps. Then, after the defection of Bavaria, he turned against the French. He was beaten at Hanau, on October 30, 1813. See Bignon, *Hist. France*, Vol. III, p. 240. He represented Bavaria at the Congress of Vienna in 1815.

CONGRESS OF PRAGUE—See reference at end of note on Narbonne, above.

CONGRESS OF CHÂTILLON—This Congress took place in February– March 1814, in the native district of General Marmont—which was not a propitious sign. Caulaincourt had a difficult not to say a crushing rôle to play, as may be seen from his *Mémoires*, Vol. III, Chapter I, and in the preface written by the editor, J. Hanoteau—see especially p. 174. At the meetings of February 7, the allied plenipotentiaries suggested the frontiers that had existed before the Revolution, and the evacuation of the conquered provinces, including Antwerp. On March 15, Caulaincourt agreed to abandon all the French gains save at Lucca and at Neufchâtel, and did not breathe a word about Belgium, which was the crucial point. Negotiations were broken off on March 20. Count de Rumigny, who made a note of Napoleon's criticism against Caulaincourt ("He grasps none of the subtleties"), added that the Duke of Vicenza was "too upright and loyal," which is an honorable rectification. The truth is that the "Congress had no hope of survival," (E. Driault, *The Fall of the Empire*, p. 26), and no one, either on the side of the allies nor on the side of Napoleon, cared to reach a conclusion. Pons, in his *Congress of Châtillon*, which appeared in 1828 as a pendant to *The Battle and Capitulation of Paris*, analyzes the eight conferences that stretched from February 5 to March 19.

January 21

NAPOLEON'S SEESAW—Antommarchi refers to this seesaw in his *Mémoires*, January 28, 1821, about which contrivance Ali, *Souvenirs*, p. 253, gives, as is his wont, the most minute details. Mme. Bertrand is the only one who adds to this information a familiar and intimate flavor, reporting the heart-rending jokes with which the Emperor enlivened his exercise upon the contraption. Arthur Bertrand recalled this strange cavalcade in *Letters . . . St. Helena*, p. 115.

NOVERRAZ—Swiss by origin, from the Vaud, he was admitted to the Emperor's household in 1809. Promoted to the Light Infantry, he fought the campaigns of 1813 and 1814, "on the seat of the Imperial coaches." He accompanied his imperial master on the trip from Fontainebleau to Fréjus, and made a point of defending him at Orgon. At Longwood, he was third footman, and together with Marchand and Ali-Saint-Denis was responsible for the indoor service. In July 1819, he married Josephine Schouter, Countess Montholon's personal maid. He was with Napoleon during the entire Captivity. In 1840 he witnessed the exhumation. He died in 1849.

January 22

ABO—The Meeting at Abo, Finland, took place during August 27–31 between Bernadotte (Charles-Jean), the Prince Royal of Sweden, and Emperor Alexander of Russia, in the presence of Lord Cathcart: see Koch and Schoelle, *Short Hist. Peace Treaties*, Vol. X, p. 154. Russia had undertaken to provide the Prince Royal with 35,000 men for an operation against Norway. When this undertaking was canceled at Abo, Russia was able to dispose of these effectives and to use them to increase the army of Count Wittgenstein. "These troops saved St. Petersburg from General Oudinot, when they had joined up with the troops of Count Wittgenstein. It is reported that at this conference, Emperor Alexander bought the co-operation of Bernadotte by promising him the French throne": these lines were written by General Count de Langeron, a Frenchman in the service of Russia, who is dubious about this information. See his *Mémoires* published in 1902 by the Society of Contemporary History, p. 454. See also L. Madelin, *Fouché's Mémoires*, published by Flammarion, pp. 366–400 and notes.

GUSTAVE IV OF SWEDEN—Las Cases has recorded (*Memorial*, Vol. V, p. 198) Napoleon's opinion on the subject of the madness of Gustave IV. Bernadotte was worried by the existence of a son of Gustave IV whose claims were used by both the English and the Russians to contest the legitimacy of Bernadotte's right to the throne. See Bignon, *Hist. France*, Vol. III, p. 104.

DUPHOT—Assassinated by the Roman populace on December 27, 1797. For an account of this murder see Gaffarel, *Bonaparte and the Italian Republics*, pp. 229–35. For the proposed marriage between Duphot and Désirée Clary, see T. T. Höjer, *Bernadotte*, p. 142.

SCENE OVER ANTOMMARCHI—No mention of this scene appears in the writings of the interested party, no more than in the *Mémoires* of General Montholon; the only echoes of this affair, faint ones, are found in Forsyth, *Hist. Captivity*, Vol. III, p. 258. ("Napoleon had no confidence in Dr. Antommarchi, etc.") In his unpublished recollections, Marchand glosses over this incident. "On several occasions Dr. Antommarchi deservedly got called down by the Emperor, irritated at not finding him immediately available when he wanted him . . ." Ali says almost the same thing, *Souvenirs*, pp. 264–65. It required the objectivity of Bertrand to make such a fuss about an escapade which not only compromised his conjugal pride, but seems to have involved his wife's reputation.

January 24

MONTCHENU (Marquis de)—This former émigré, who returned to France after Brumaire, had lived for eight years in Westphalia. He was not only a gossip but also a figure of fun. Talleyrand, thinking to be unpleasant to Napoleon, suggested that Montchenu be appointed Louis XVIII's commissioner at St. Helena. His niggardliness and his gift for sponging, soon earned him the name, in Jamestown, of Marquis de *Mont-chez-nous*. His Russian and Austrian colleagues, Count Balmain and Baron von Stürmer, openly made fun of him. "M. de Montchenu has none of the qualities necessary to fill the position entrusted to him . . . he has little ability, no education, and is completely devoid of tact": Stürmer's report to Metternich, published by H. Schlitter, September 2, 1816. In 1894, G. Firmin-Didot published *History of the Captivity*, based on the reports of the ineffable Marquis; and J. de Maupéou, one of his descendants, published a study entitled "A Royalist at St. Helena," in *Rev. des Deux Mondes*, June 15, 1933.

DECAZES, ÉLIE, (Count, later Duke)—Born 1780; died 1860. After having been a member of the household of Louis, then of that of Madame Mère, he fell out with the Imperial Family. Devoted to the Bourbons, he was made Minister of the Interior in 1818, replacing the Duke de Richelieu. He became President of the *Conseil* on November 19, 1819, a position which he resigned on February 18, 1820, for that of French Ambassador in London. In *Recollections of a Paris Doctor*, p. 177, Dr. Poumiès de la Siboutie says: "It was by flattering the King's pretentions to a brilliant mind that Decazes opened up for himself the way to favor and fortune." On the subject of their relationship, see E. Daudet, *Louis XVIII and the Duke Decazes*, 1899, and *Decazes as Ambassador in London*, 1910.

CONGRESS OF AIX-LA-CHAPELLE—This Congress was held by the Holy Alliance in 1818. It appears that Metternich would have preferred the title of Diplomatic Conference to the overly ambitious name of Congress. In fact, the Congress was solely occupied with the questions of the liberation of France and of its re-integration into the European concert of nations. The activity of the Bourbons amounted to the evacuation of the territories demanded and obtained by the Duke de Richelieu. The result was that from a distance this achievement gave the prisoner at Longwood some anxiety, and also a certain amount of hope. On several occasions, the papers had mentioned the possibility of Napoleon's being transferred to Malta or even to Belle Isle; but as always these were only journalistic rumors.

INCIDENTS OF THE FRENCH CAMPAIGN: VITRY—Napoleon passed through Vitry for the first time on January 27, 1814, while en route to Saint-Dizier, and the second time on March 27; see A. Houssaye, *1814*, p. 401. Berthier, Ney, and Sebastiani tried to dissuade him from attacking. "Vitry, which was well fortified, had been repaired and put in a state of defense on the orders of Marshal Blücher. On March 23, the Emperor ordered Marshal Ney to summon the town to surrender, but the Russian General Wassiltschikoff refused to deliver up the town": Count de Langeron, *Mémoires*, p. 438. See also Fain, *Manuscript of 1814*, Chapter X—marches and counter-marches against Vitry, Saint-Dizier and Doulevent, March 21–28. LAON—The battle for Laon took place on March 9 and 10, 1814. It was only on the thirteenth that Napoleon set out for Rheims; see *Mémoires of Marmont*, Vol. VI, p. 208—for criticism of the Emperor's ordering of troops—and pp. 214ff. Colonel Fabvier, in *Journal of the Operations of the VI Corps* (Marmont's), upholds the criticisms of his corps commander and complains of too much artillery.

DULAULOY (General)—Fr. Dulauloy was, in fact, originally from Laon, where he was born December 9, 1764.

MARMONT—Acccording to his *Mémoires*, Vol. VI, p. 210, Marmont took up his position in the Chivi Marsh before establishing himself at Corbeny, from where, on March 10 at 2 A.M., he sent a report to the Emperor (quoted by J. Thiry in *The Fall of Napoleon*, Vol. I, p. 314). The defection of Marmont and of Augereau was stigmatized in the Proclamation of June 1, 1815, countersigned by Bertrand, acting as Major General: "Soldiers, we have not been defeated. Two men from our own ranks have betrayed their honors, their country, and their benefactor." See the *Mémoires of Napoleon*, Vol. IV, p. 363, or his *General Correspondence*, Vol. XXXI, p. 241, for the changes in the Emperor's attitude on the subject of the "betrayal" of Marmont and the "defection" of Murat, to use the title used by Rappetti, and for what he says concerning them during his conversations on the Island of Elba with Lord Ebrington. Consult Amédée Pichot, *Chronicle of Events 1814–15*, p. 325. The Countess de Boigne, *Mémoires*, Vol. I, p. 341, recounts the self-defense of the Duke of Ragusa: "When Napoleon said, '*All for France!*' I served with enthusiasm; when he said, '*France and I*', I served with zeal; when he said, '*I and France*', I served obediently; but when he said, '*I without France*', I felt called upon to leave him."

POZZO DI BORGO, CHARLES-ANDRÉ (Count)—This man was Deputy for Corsica to the Legislative Assembly, President of the Corsican Council in 1794; a member of the Péraldi clan, he became an enemy of the Bonapartes. In 1803 Pozzo entered the service of the Russians. "He was a man of talent, an intriguer who knew France well," Napoleon told O'Meara; *Nap. in Exile*, Vol. I, p. 268. "Emperor Alexander was not of the opinion that the capital should be attacked," wrote Queen Hortense in her *Mémoires*, Vol. II, p. 266; she does not, however, attribute this decision to Pozzo's intervention. Méneval, *Mémoires*, Vol. II, pp. 329 and 331 confirms the remark quoted here as having been made by the Grand Duke Constantine, but he attributes the decision to Pozzo personally. The same note is to be found in Chateaubriand's *Memoirs beyond the Tomb*, Vol. II, p. 487.

CAULAINCOURT AND ANTWERP—In principle, Napoleon had given *carte blanche* to his representative at the Congress of Châtillon, but in actual fact he frustrated every initiative. See *Mémoires* of Caulaincourt, Vol. II, p. 15, note, and p. 26. See also in O'Meara, *Nap. in Exile*, Vol. I, p. 455, a letter by the Duke of Vicenza, and another by him, written January 21, 1820, to the editor of the *Constitutionnel* (mentioned by Las Cases, *Memorial*, Vol. VII, p. 66, and note). Maret, by order, had told Caulaincourt on March 19 to cede neither Antwerp nor Mainz—which was what the Emperor had himself written to his father-in-law, the Austrian Emperor; see Bignon, *Hist. France*, Vol. III, p. 334, and the *General Correspondence*, No. 21, 344. Bignon cleared Caulaincourt of the charge of clumsiness, which is made here. Koch and Schoelle, *Short Hist. Peace Treaties*, Vol. X, p. 413, mention a letter from Maret to Caulaincourt, dated March 19, which was intercepted by the allies and which advised Caulaincourt not to make "any commitments." Under such conditions, negotiations were fore-doomed. In his counter proposal of March 15, Caulaincourt stipulated for reserves for the Principality of Neufchâtel (in favor of General Berthier), for Lucca (in favor of Elisa), and for Bénévent (in favor of Talleyrand)—see Fain, *Manuscript of 1814*, p. 317, Articles 7, 8, 9—for which the Emperor blames him here.

TREATY OF FONTAINEBLEAU—Napoleon had already said in front of Las Cases (*Memorial*, Vol. III, p. 411): "I could have reserved for myself what I wanted . . . the humor of the moment made me decide on Elba." But he fails to say that his real aim would have been to have taken refuge in Corsica. Compare this with Montholon, *Tales of the Captivity*, Vol. I, p. 269. "Had I wanted to negotiate sensibly," he repeated in August 1816 (Las Cases, Vol. V., p. 354), "I could have obtained the Kingdom of Italy, Tuscany, or Corsica."

January 26

DIVORCE AND REMARRIAGE—In a letter to Stadion, Metternich (*Mémoires*, Vol. II, pp. 140-44) records the suggestion of the re-marriage of Napoleon with one of the Grand Duchesses: "Sustained inquiries and contacts with certain persons in touch with the Empress obtained for me certain very confidential information." This shows what very crude details may lie hidden behind such careful diplomatic phrases.

MME. DUCHÂTEL, MARIE-ANTOINETTE-ADÈLE PAPI—Born at Aire (Landes), July 4, 1782; died in Paris, May 20, 1860. She married in 1802 a man thirty years her senior. Appointed to the Court, June 30, 1804, she had the honor of a liaison with the Emperor. Both Queen Hortense (*Mémoires*, Vol. I, p. 202) and Mme. de Rémusat (*Mémoires*, Vol. II, p. 87) have left portraits of her, which F. Masson used later in *Napoleon and Women*, Chapter XI.

PRINCE DE M—This initial would seem to stand for the Hereditary Prince of Mecklenburg-Schwerin (1788–1819). Since 1803 he had been the widowed husband of Helena Pavlona, Russian Grand Duchess, which would have put him in close touch with the Czar. He was present at the Meeting at Erfurt; see Bausset, *Mémoires*, Vol. I, p. 330.

COMPARISONS AND VARIANTS ON THE STORY OF THE DIVORCE—Henri Welschinger, in *Napoleon's Divorce*, bases his account on that given by Thiers, who follows the very lively version given by Bausset,

Prefect of the Palace (*Mémoires*, Vol. I, p. 370), who would appear to have dramatized the whole episode. There are striking divergences between Bertrand's version and that of Mme. de Rémusat: *Mémoires*, Vol. II, pp. 50 and 58, or Vol. III, p. 283.

WALEWSKA, MARIE (Countess)—Marie Leczinska was born in Warsaw in 1789. In 1814 she was the widow of Count Walewski. Remarried in Paris in April 1816 to General Count d'Ornano, she first met Napoleon at Bronie, January 1, 1809. From this meeting dated her affair with the Emperor. She had one son by the Emperor, Florian-Alexander-Joseph, who was born at Walewice, Poland, on May 4, 1810, and who is mentioned in the Imperial Will. Upon his return from the Russian campaign, Napoleon, passing through Lowicz on December 11, 1812, wanted to make a detour to visit the Château of Walewice, but Caulaincourt dissuaded him.

January 27

BENJAMIN CONSTANT—The pamphlet the Emperor was reading on January 27, 1821, was *Memoirs of the Hundred Days in the Form of Letters*, which appeared in Paris in 1820. The peasants are mentioned on pp. 76 and 86, and in Part II, Letter V, p. 55f. can be found "Napoleon's views on the peerage." Constant was born October 25, 1767, at Lausanne. His mother was Henriette Chardieu, descendant of an old French family which had taken refuge in the Vaud on account of their religious principles. See Constant's *Autobiography*. For a time Constant was a Gentleman of the Bedchamber to the Duke of Brunswick: "I waste ten hours a day at Court, and they loathe me because they know that I am a democrat." The first meeting between Mme. de Staël and Constant was on September 19, 1794; see Paul Léon, *Constant*, ed. Rieder, Chapter VI. Constant spoke before the Tribunate during the sitting of the 15th Nivôse, Year VIII (January 5, 1800). See *Parliamentary Archives*, Vol. I, p. 30.

DUVEYRIER—A Tribune, and friend of General Leclerc. He spoke before the Tribunate at the séances of the 11th and 13th Nivôse, Year VIII (*Parliamentary Archives*, Vol. I, pp. 10f. and 17), when Camille Desmoulins was mentioned. See also F. Masson, *Napoleon and His Family*, Vol. I, p. 305.

BENJAMIN CONSTANT AND NAPOLEON'S RETURN FROM ELBA—The famous anti-Bonapartist article by Benjamin Constant appeared in the *Journal des Débats*, March 19, on the very eve of the Emperor's return to the Tuileries, which was just sheer bad luck! Constant wanted to flee at the approach of the Emperor. See Paul Léon, *Constant*, p. 79, who makes an excellent analysis of Constant's state of mind and political position at that moment: "Big news! Bonaparte returns. The collapse is appalling. I am in peril of my life. But let's chance it. If we have to die, let us die well!" See *Journal Intime*, published by D. Melegari, in 1895, p. 149 and Chateaubriand's *Memoirs beyond the Tomb*, ed. Levaillant, Vol. II, p. 565.

BARING AND HOLMES—These two banking houses, affiliated with London, were the financial agents of the colony at Longwood. In the Grand Maréchal's accounts, as in those of the Emperor, letters of exchange are frequently found drawn on the firm of Baring. William Holmes, a friend of O'Meara, negotiated the promissory notes that Bertrand drew on Laffitte and on Prince Eugène.

IBBETSON, DENZIL—English Commissioner at St. Helena. He joined the British Army Commissariat in 1801, took part in the Peninsular War, arrived at St. Helena on board the *Northumberland*, and remained there until June 1823. He was one of the two officers who were at St. Helena throughout the Captivity. After the departure of Balcombe, he was put in charge of the provisioning of Longwood. He made several sketches of Napoleon on board the *Northumberland*, and a drawing of the Emperor on his deathbed. See Arnold Chaplin, *A St. Helena's Who's Who.*

ARNOTT, DR. ARCHIBALD—Born 1771; died 1855. Educated at Edinburgh. A surgeon attached to the 20th Infantry Regiment in 1799, he took part in the campaigns of this regiment, especially at the battle of Maida and in the Walcheren Expedition. He followed the regiment to St. Helena in 1819. It was not until April 1, 1821, that he was called to the bedside of the Emperor, who asked him a lot of questions (see, below, his April conversations), gave him a snuffbox engraved with the initial N, and allotted him six hundred livres. In 1822, Dr. Arnott published an *Account of the Last Illness of Napoleon*, in which may be noted considerable divergences from his medical reports, preserved among the *Lowe Papers* in the British Museum. For some time, Hudson Lowe had been trying to place an English doctor in attendance upon his prisoner and he had already mentioned this to Montholon (*Tales of the Captivity*, Vol. II, p. 479). It is hardly necessary to add that all the pompous speeches credited to Napoleon by Dr. Antommarchi were complete inventions, intended to hide his own deficiencies.

January 29

VACCA, ANDREA BERLINGHIERE—A famous Italian surgeon (1772–1826). Professor at the Pisa School of Medicine. Locatelli had held the post of First Medical Officer at the Court of Prince Eugène, Viceroy of Italy.

GUSTAVE IV—He reigned from 1792 until his deposition in 1809. He was the son of Gustave III, who was supposed to be impotent. It seems that his father, who badly wanted an heir, had had the idea of having his wife sleep with one of his chamberlains. "And it was thanks to that, that the stupid ass who resigned the throne a few years back, came into the world." Napoleon, who appeared to credit this backstairs gossip when talking to O'Meara (*Nap. in Exile*, Vol. II, p. 61), ceases to treat it seriously in front of the grave Count Bertrand. On the subject of the birth of Gustave III, and the doubts to which it gave rise, consult A. Geffroy, *Gustav III*, 1867, Vol. II, p. 55. The Duke of Sudermania, uncle of the deposed sovereign, mounted the throne as Charles XIII. He was succeeded by Bernadotte, Prince Royal of Sweden. The son of Gustave IV, born in 1799, bore the title of Prince of Vasa and served in Austria.

MME. DILLON—On account of the remarriage of Arthur Dillon—le "grand" Dillon—some confusion has arisen between the two mesdames Dillon. The first, who was Thérèse-Lucy de Rothe, gave birth to a daughter, Henriette Lucy Dillon, who later became Marquise de la Tour du Pin Gouvernet and wrote the *Diary of a Woman of Fifty*. The second, Laure Girardin de Montgérald, "Josephine's cousin german," was the mother of Fanny Dillon, later Countess Bertrand. In the aforementioned *Diary*, p. 3, the writer defends her mother's memory: "The Prince de Guémené, nephew of the notorious Cardinal de Rohan, appeared, therefore, in the eyes of the world, as my mother's lover. But I do not believe this to have been true." Nevertheless, a few pages farther on, she adds ingenuously: "We went to Spa. M. de Guémené joined us there, I have never been able to understand why."

January 31

ANTOMMARCHI UNWANTED AT LONGWOOD—The letter written by Antommarchi requesting his release and announcing his departure, bears the date January 31. Montholon, in *Tales of the Captivity*, Vol. II, p. 481, quotes the reply dictated to him by the Emperor: "During the fifteen months that you have been here you have never given His Majesty cause to have any confidence in your moral character. You can be of no assistance to him in his illness. And your remaining here for several more months would be pointless."

The tactless moments of Antommarchi were innumerable. So much so indeed, that Marchand had been obliged to take him aside and tell him that, when speaking of Count Montholon or of the Grand Maréchal, he must not call them "Montholon" or "Bertrand." "The Emperor may call them that, but you must not permit yourself to take such a liberty." The book, whose completion is here invoked, was a sequel to Mascagni's work on Anatomy. Antommarchi boasted of having been a disciple of Mascagni. As with everything else, he used this as a means for speculation and fraud.

NOTES TO CHAPTER TWO—FEBRUARY 1821

February 1

LIVINGSTONE, DR. MATTHEW—This doctor, associated with the East India Company, landed at St. Helena in 1815 and died there on October 10, 1821. He was called in to attend both the Montholon and Bertrand families. He jibed at giving Mme. de Montholon a medical certificate that would have made it easier for her to return to Europe. There were constant bickerings between him and his German colleague Verling. The latter didn't spare Dr. Livingstone in his *Journal*, a translation of which was published in May 1921–April 1922 under the title *Carnet de la sabretache*.

February 6

LADY LOWE—On December 31, 1815, the Governor of St. Helena, Sir Hudson Lowe, who was forty-six, married the widow of Lieutenant Colonel William Johnston. Lady Lowe had two children by her first marriage: Charlotte, who was married in March 1820 to Count Alexander de Balmain, the Russian Commissioner, who landed on the island on June 17, 1816; and a second daughter called Susan. The pleasant manner and fine presence of Lady Lowe made her popular with everyone, even with "the Longwood people." Her husband served as such a foil to her that there was no one who didn't subscribe to the reply made by the surgeon William Warden when Napoleon asked: "And what do you think of the Governor's face?" "To tell the truth," Warden answered, "I greatly prefer that of Lady Lowe."

THE NEW HOUSE—This residence was situated one hundred and fifty meters north of the old building that was overlooked by the barn and the flagstaff. The Emperor would never consent to occupy it, because the iron railings that enclosed it gave him the feeling "of being inside a cage." See Forsyth, *Hist. Captivity*, Vol. III, p. 268, and Ernest d'Hauterive, *St. Helena*, published by Calmann, 1933, pp. 112ff.

February 7

ADMIRAL LAMBERT—Rear Admiral Robert Lambert (1772–1836), who succeeded Admiral Plampin in the command of the St. Helena naval station. Lambert retained his post from July 14, 1820 to September 11, 1821. Having reached St. Helena on board the *Vigo*, he tried in vain to be received by Napoleon. He was destined never to see the Emperor except after his death, when he lay in state.

February 8

BERNARDIN DE SAINT-PIERRE—Some confusion crept into the Emperor's analysis of Bernardin's novel *Paul and Virginia*. The black slave Domingo was the servant of Marguerite, who was the neighbor of Mme. de la Tour and not her attendant. The "hermit" is the narrator of the recital which, in book II of the novel, extols the benefits of solitude. Napoleon often reread *Paul and Virginia*. Gourgaud, who points out this fact (*Journal*, May 10, 1817), remarks that "to read such things in our present circumstances is far too harrowing to the soul." Aimé Martin, editor of the complete works of Bernardin (12 vols., 1818–20), published a Notice on the life of Bernardin, whose widow—daughter of the printer Didot—he had married. The Emperor never forgave Bernardin for taking advantage of his generosity upon his return from the Army of Italy. See Las Cases, *Memorial*, Vol. II, pp. 173ff.

LAPLACE AND BERNARDIN—Gourgaud reports in his *Journal*, May 10, 1817: "Saint-Pierre claims, quite erroneously, that Laplace did him much harm in the opinion of the Emperor." After reading Bertrand, it is obvious that "quite erroneously" should be changed to "quite correctly." Las Cases, *Memorial*, Vol. II, p. 174, records this conversation: "Do you understand differential calculus, Monsieur Bernardin?" the First Consul inquired. (The author had complained of being maltreated by the learned professors who reproached him for his ignorance of scientific matters.)—— "Well then, go and learn it."

February 9

THE EGYPTIAN COMMISSION—Concerning the composition of the first Egyptian Institute, see the study by J.-E. Goby, taken from the *Bull. of the Egypt. Institute*, Vol. XIX session 1946–47, which gives some useful information such as lists of members, full titles of each of the scientists, etc. In the *Memoirs of the Egypt. Institute*, published in Year VIII, *in fine* is a map of the reconnaissance of the Valley of the Lakes, or Wâdi en Natrûn, and of the "waterless river," made during Pluviôse of Year VII by General Andreossy.

VIVANT-DENON—Born 1747; died 1825. He became a member of the Institute of Egyptology, in the department devoted to literature and the arts, on August 22, 1798. He had had an extraordinary career as a traveler, scientist, and artist (engraver). He was later to be made Director of the Medal Section of the Mint, and Director of the Napoleon Museum. His official letterhead, on which he had all his titles listed, has since become famous. See Pierre Lelièvre, *Vivant-Denon, director of Beaux-Arts under Napoleon*, 1942, and a very lively criticism of his directorship in Chaptal, *Souvenirs*, pp. 272f. See also Vox (*Six Hundred Letters about Work*, p. 432), who, in regard to the municipal administration of Paris, had admired both the man and the artist.

VISCONTI, E. Q.—Born 1745; died 1818. A famous Roman archeologist; in 1799 appointed administrator of the Museum of Antiquities in the Louvre. *Notice on the Two Zodiacs of Dendera*, written in Paris May 8, 1801, was published in Milan, 1830, by Dr. G. Labus.

February 11
VERSES BY VOLTAIRE—

> *To look again on Paris I may no more pretend.*
> *Behold! towards the grave I am ready to descend.*

"These lines, which Voltaire put in the mouth of Lusignan, were quoted by Napoleon in the voice of a man who had lost all hope, and in such a way as to convey the same feelings to all those about him"; according to Ali, *Souvenirs*, p. 260. The Emperor frequently accompanied them with the exclamation, "Ah, poor me!" also noted by his valet, Marchand.

THE EGYPTIAN CAMPAIGN—General Ch. F. J. Dugua (1744–1802) was acting commander in chief of the Kléber Division on July 3, 1798, and of the Cairo garrison on February 9, 1799. He returned to France in March 1800: see *Notice concerning Dugua*, Caën, 1802.

GENERAL JEAN-LOUIS-EBENEZER REYNIER (1771–1844)—Born at Lausanne. He was attached to the Army of the East from March 26, 1798, except for a brief mission to Lyons. He was present at the Battle of the Pyramids, took part in the Syrian Expedition, and captured the

Fort of El-Arisch, February 9, 1799. He helped to quell the Cairo Revolt. He opposed General Menou, who had him arrested at Alexandria and sent back to France in 1801. He was returned to active service and in 1805–06 he commanded the Army of Naples (see the note on Maida, below).

THE LETTER TO THE GRAND VIZIER—This letter, dated August 18, 1799 and written from Cairo, appears in *General Correspondence*, No. 4367, and in *Correspondance inédite*, published by Panckoucke, 1819, Vol. II, p. 445.

February 12

MAIDA—The battle here was fought in 1806. Besides the detailed report of General Reynier, see the thesis of J. Rambaud, *Naples under Joseph Bonaparte*, Vol. I, pp. 63–80, and *Memoirs of King Joseph*, Vol. II, pp. 378ff. Neither Ralfe (*Naval Chronology*, Vol. I, p. 254), who quotes from two reports by Sidney Smith to Admiral Collingwood, both written on board the *Pompey*, nor E. Gachot (*The Third Campaign in Italy*, Part II, Chapter V) makes any reference to the very unusual feat of arms described here by Bertrand. Neither does General Compère in the *Moniteur*, 1806, p. 1132.

February 13

MURAT'S LANDING AT NAPLES—"It was a fool's undertaking," Napoleon said to O'Meara: *Nap. in Exile*, Vol. II, p. 99. For interesting details, see: Bausset, *Mémoires*, Vol. IV, pp. 33ff., who gives as reference the *Giornale delle Due Sicilie* of October 15, 1815, and who prints the text of the proclamation "to the good people of Naples," that was found on the person of the ex-King of Naples at the time of his arrest at Pizzo; also Méneval, *Mémoires*, Vol. III, p. 491, and General Bélliard, *Mémoires*, Vol. I, pp. 242ff.

February 14

VICTORIES AND CONQUESTS—EGYPT—General François-Etienne Damas (1764–1828), chief of staff of the Kléber Division, was accused by General Menou of having maneuvered badly at Canope on March 21, 1801. The narrator in *Victories and Conquests*, Vol. XIII, pp. 247f., passed a very severe judgment upon General Menou, calling him a "renegade." Bignon, *Hist. France*, Vol. I, p. 32 reported that Masséna having asked what kind of man General Kléber was, the First Consul said: "Picture to yourself a very tall man, with an imposing head, the most handsome warrior you have ever seen. . . . He was a good tactician despite his Austrian training, but lazy, excessively arrogant, sarcastic, and sardonic . . . because in this manner his laziness and personal vanity obtained satisfaction. He allows himself to be pushed to the extreme limit. It is true that his pride then comes to his assistance and he remembers his capabilities and occasionally does some very fine things." Bignon himself added: "Those who knew Kléber, found this a very true likeness of him." General Jean-Antoine Soulier (1766–1835) took part in the capture of El-Arisch and was made prisoner at Canope in March 1801. For Napoleon's observations and comments on the landing of Abercromby, see *General Correspondence*, Vol. XXX, Chapter XIV.

February 15

OLD UNCLE LUCIEN—Born 1715; died October 16, 1791. He was the young Bonaparte's paternal grand-uncle. He has occupied only an episodic place in Napoleonic biographies, yet from the Emperor's conversations with Bertrand, it appears that he exercised a considerable influence over Napoleon. Considered the head of the family after the death of Charles Bonaparte, Uncle Lucien became on August 16, 1785, the children's guardian. This official act has been quoted by Coston, *Biog. of the Early Years*, Vol. II, p. 50. Archdeacon Lucien was: "a venerable parson, greatly respected and possessing a genuine moral ascendancy in the region. He advised the inhabitants and was the arbiter of their disputes": Coston, ibid, Vol. I, p. 14. His spritely nature, his peasant wisdom and his faithfulness to the barter system, left great and profound marks on the immature mind of Bonaparte. His death placed the family in possession of an inheritance that helped to make certain Napoleon's election to the post of second lieutenant colonel in the regiment of Ajaccio volunteers, and set the seal on his future fortunes. See F. Masson, *The Unknown Napoleon*, in *At St. Helena*, Vol. I, p. 49.

February 19

MARCHAND, LOUIS—A son of the King of Rome's cradle-rocker, he entered the service of the Imperial House at the age of nineteen, in 1811. In 1814 he was chosen by Bertrand to take the place of first valet to the Emperor, formerly held by a certain Constant who had fled after the Abdication at Fontainebleau. Having followed the Emperor to Elba, this faithful servant was not without a certain degree of education. A conscientious "Sunday" painter, he was more of a landscape artist than a portraitist. Several of his carefully executed views of Longwood have been preserved. The *Album* of Livingstone's *Carnet de la sabretache*, 1921, centenary ed., reproduced one from the Girardin Collection, of which the Marmottan Library at Boulogne possessed a similar one; E. d'Hauterive also reproduced one in his *Saint Helena*, pp. 104f. A view of Longwood, drawn by Marchand and given by him to Tristan de Montholon, was destroyed by fire in Brussels. It seems that it had been one that the Emperor had admired. "On my walks," Marchand said, "I always had a notebook and pencil with me . . . My box of water-colors . . . was to be of great use to me. I was far from expecting any success for my painting, and even less that it would be shown to the Emperor": see *Mémoires inédits*.

HUNT—A Radical Deputy and supporter of Parliamentary reform. He fomented the Manchester rioters. As a result of this outburst, he was arrested, brought into court, and defended by Pearson. See *Journal des Débats*, August 22 and September 3, 1819.

THE IMPERIAL NOBILITY—In the Smorgoni sleigh, Napoleon explained in detail to Caulaincourt (*Mémoires*, Vol. II, p. 330) his aims in founding a new nobility and a new aristocracy. "The aristocracy," he repeated to Las Cases (*Memorial*, Vol. V, p. 36), "is the true and sole support of a monarchy." "The new nobility," observed Pasquier (*Mémoires*, Vol. I, p. 346), "was not slow in taking root in the country. It had even less difficulty in obtaining recognition abroad, where it could appear surrounded by all the prestige of military glory."

MEN OF THE MANÈGE—The Society of the Manège was an extension of the Jacobin Club that had been reformed under the Directory. It held its meetings first of all in the Manège or riding school of the Tuileries, and later in the disaffected church of St. Thomas Aquinas—alias "the Temple of Peace." The club was closed on August 14, 1799. This police measure was carried out by Fouché at the instigation of Sieyès. See Fouché's *Mémoires*, Madelin ed., p. 84. See also Barante, *Hist. Directory*, Vol. II, pp. 463ff.

February 20

AENEID AND ILIAD—The same parallel, though somewhat more developed, is to be found in the various fragments published by Marchand at the end of *Summary of the Wars of Julius Caesar*, 1836, pp. 228ff.

February 21

CARNOT'S CORRESPONDENCE—This correspondence with the Emperor during the Hundred Days was published in 1819 by Regnault Warin. It appears with its counterpart, the Emperor's letters to Carnot, in *Collection of Authentic Pieces Concerning the Captive of St. Helena*, Vol. V, pp. 445–521.

LAFAYETTE'S LETTER—See note below on Napoleon's will. The relationship of Lafayette and Napoleon was restricted to a couple of interviews on October 3 and 4, 1800, when the Treaty with the United States was signed at Morfontaine, in the house of Joseph Bonaparte. The gesture of defiance contained in the letter written to Lafayette by the First Consul on May 20, 1802 (quoted by E. Charavay, in *Lafayette*, p. 386), put an end to their relationship. In revenge, Lafayette preserved the most cordial relations with both Lucien and Joseph Bonaparte.

THE LETTER FROM BERNADOTTE—The correspondence of the Swedish Crown Prince with Napoleon during 1810–14, published by Bail in 1819, does not contain the letter mentioned here, which was dated May 11, 1812, but it may be found in the *Memoirs of Charles XIV*, and it is repudiated in Napoleon's *Memoirs*, Vol. IV, pp. 294f., as being a false document. In return there is also a false letter in *Memorial* (Las Cases, Vol. V, p. 207), but this time it is from Napoleon to Bernadotte. Las Cases dates it August 8, 1811. Lord Rosebery in *The Last Phase*, p. 14, exposed this fraud.

BATHURST, LORD HENRY—One of the leading members of the English Tory party. In 1809 he was made Secretary of State for the Colonies. He was an irreconcilable enemy of Napoleonic France. It was he who recommended Hudson Lowe for the position of Governor of St. Helena. Therefore, it was to him that the prisoner of Longwood owed most of his sufferings.

ARNAULT AND DENON—In anticipation of the departure of General Bertrand from St. Helena, Napoleon had dictated to Montholon (*Tales of the Captivity*, Vol. II, p. 481), on January 30, 1821, a letter in which he appointed either Arnault or Denon to replace the Grand Maréchal. Arnault, who had been presented to Bonaparte by General Leclerc, had followed Napoleon to Egypt and then to Italy. A brother-in-law of Regnault de Saint-Jean d'Angely, under the Empire he had become General Secretary to the Ministry of Public Education. He was the author not only of *Marius at Minturno* but, luckily, also of the *Souvenirs of a Sexagenarian*. He and Denon were mentioned in Napoleon's will. See the previous note on Denon.

CURRICULUM VITAE OF NAPOLEON—The childhood and youthful memories of Bonaparte were little known at the period in which Bertrand noted them down, whereas today they are common knowledge, thanks to the works of Coston, F. Masson, Chuquet, etc.

MARBEUF, LOUIS-CHARLES-RENÉ (Count, then Marquis of)—Born 1712; died 1786. He was the first King's Commissioner in Corsica. On the part he played in the organization of Corsica, see *Review of Napoleonic Studies*, November–December 1923. The protection he granted to "the sons of Charles" has caused it to be thought, though without any proof, that Letizia had formerly been his mistress.

THE SCHOOL OF AUTUN—At Autun, where Monseigneur de Marbeuf, nephew of the "Governor," lived, Napoleon entered the school on January 1, 1779, and left it on April 21: see Garros, *Itinerary*, p. 21. His stay at Autun lasted, therefore, exactly three months and twenty days: see Marcaggi, *Genesis of Napoleon*, p. 69. The tradition of his having stayed with the Champeaux at Thoisy is here confirmed.

THE MILITARY ACADEMY OF BRIENNE—Napoleon entered the Brienne Military Academy on May 15 or 16, 1779: see Schuermans, and Garros, *Itinerary*. Concerning regulations of the military school of Brienne, see F. Masson, *The Unknown Napoleon*, Vol. I, pp. 53ff.; page 87 lists Bonaparte's classmates. Napoleon left Brienne on October 30, 1784. He passed through Arcis-sur-Aube again, at the time of the fighting on May 20 and 21, 1814. See Fain, *Manuscript of 1814*, pp. 207ff.

THE MILITARY SCHOOL OF PARIS—The date of Napoleon's entry here was the thirtieth of October according to Masson, the seventeenth according to Madelin in *Bonaparte's Youth*, p. 43. On the subject of the school regulations, see Masson, *The Unknown Nap.*, Vol. I, pp. 87ff. Coston (*Biog. of the Early Years*, Vol. II, p. 51) gives a list of the fifty-eight cadets who were promoted on September 1, 1785, to the rank of second lieutenant. Bonaparte was forty-second on the list, although F. Masson states that his placement was not known.

THE LIEUR DE VILLE-SUR-ARCE (1768–1820)—His name does not figure among those of Napoleon's traveling companions as quoted by Masson in *The Unknown Nap.*, Vol. I, p. 87. There were two brothers of this name; for information about them see the note by Chuquet, *Napoleon's Youth*, Vol. I, p. 396.

DES MAZIS—Two brothers. Alexander, like Le Lieur, left with Bonaparte to join the Regiment de la Fère, on September 3; see Garros, *Itinerary*. He later became administrator of the personal property of the Crown. The other brother, Gabriel, became Director of the State Lottery. According to Coston, Alexander was fifty-sixth on the promotion list of the Paris Military School. Concerning the careers of the brothers, see Chuquet, *Napoleon's Youth*, Vol. I, p. 423, who also gives an account of the future General Sorbier in Vol. I, p. 469, of Malet on p. 467, of General Mabille on p. 471, and of Picot de Peccaduc (p. 422), a Breton who immigrated to Austria under the name of Hertzogenberg and later became Director of the Vienna Ritter-Akademie. For information concerning him and Le Picard de Phelippeaux, Bonaparte's opponent at the Siege of Acre, see F. Masson, *The Unknown Nap.*, Vol. I, pp. 112 and 114.

RULHIÈRE, CHRISEUIL-OMER-FRANÇOIS DE—Born 1764; died 1802. After having been a Commissioner for the Directory at Zante and at Corfou, he changed over to a prefectorial career and held a post first at Falaise, and then in the Roer. See Chuquet, *Napoleon's Youth*, Vol. I, p. 446.

DU TEIL DE BEAUMONT, JEAN-PIERRE—Colonel in command of the Regiment de la Fère in 1777, before taking over command of the Artillery School at Auxonne. He was an officer of the *ancien régime*, whose hatred of revolutionary ideas was to cost him his life. While he was Inspector General of Artillery, attached to the Army of the Alps in 1793, he was arrested at Grenoble and shot at Lyons, February 27, 1794.

ROSSI, ANTOINE-FRANÇOIS—Commanded by *interim*, the 23rd Military Division at Bastia and was promoted to the rank of lieutenant general, July 12, 1792. In 1789 he was only the camp marshal. M. de Narbonne, Minister for War, authorized him to appoint Bonaparte to the rank of adjutant in the Battalion of Corsican Volunteers, February 22, 1791. See Chuquet, *Napoleon's Youth*, Vol. II, p. 243. Rossi issued the certificate for this promotion. See F. Masson, *The Unknown Nap.*, Vol. II, p. 345.

August 10, 1792—It was in consequence of the uprising of April 1792 at Ajaccio that Bonaparte set out for Paris, where he arrived on May 28. On this subject, see *Justificatory Memorandum*, published by Nasica, and F. Masson, *The Unknown Nap.*, Vol. II, pp. 357ff. On Napoleon's arrival in Paris, see J.-B. Marcaggi, *Genesis of Nap.*, 1902, Chapters V and VI.

THE TRUGUET EXPEDITION—Reaching Ajaccio in mid-November 1792 (see Nasica, *Justificatory Memorandum*, p. 308) this naval squadron, under the command of Rear Admiral Truguet, was a source of considerable trouble. The report, quoted by Chuquet, *Napoleon's Youth*, Vol. III, p. 264, deals solely with the hanging of the two National Guards. See also Marcaggi, *Genesis of Nap.*, Chapter VII.

VILLANTROYS—In 1793 he commanded the detachment of artillery intrusted with the defense of Bastia. See his report of March 1, quoted by Chuquet, Vol. III, p. 275. Paoli had been ordered to appear at the bar of the Convention on April 2.

LACOMBE-SAINT-MICHEL, JEAN-PIERRE—Artillery general and member of the National Convention 1751–1812. He was sent on a mission to Corsica on February 5, 1793, with Saliceti and Delcher. See *Mémoires* of Lucien Bonaparte, Vol. I, pp. 55ff., as well as Chuquet, *Napoleon's Youth*, Vol. III, p. 284.

DUJARD, JEAN-LAMBERT-MARCHAL—Artillery general, born on September 17, 1739, at Lunéville. He commanded the artillery of the Army of Italy, and was made an acting brigadier general and artillery chief of staff under Bonaparte. He was assassinated while on his way to Nice in July 1796.

BRUNET, GASPARD-JEAN-BAPTISTE—Born June 4, 1734. He was condemned to death on November 14, 1793, for having disregarded the orders of Barras and Fréron, and was guillotined the day after his trial.

THE AVIGNON PAMPHLET—Doubtless this is the first version of what subsequently became *Le Souper de Beaucaire*, of which two editions were printed. The first, sixteen pages in length, was published by

Sabin Tournai, printer of the *Courrier of Avignon*, with the following sub-title: "Conversation between a soldier from Carteaux's Army, a man from Marseilles, a man from Nîmes, and a manufacturer from Montpellier, upon the events that took place in the former County of Avignon, prior to the arrival of the Men from Marseilles." The second one consisted of some twenty pages and was printed without the sub-title by Marc Aurel. The chronology of Napoleon's movements after July 1793 has remained confused and subject to discussion. See L. Garros, *Itinerary*, pp. 60–62. The recollections of the Emperor are here in agreement with the theories advanced by Captain Olivier Le Moine (in *Captain Bonaparte at Avignon*, 1899) despite the fact that Masson (in *The Unknown Nap.*, Vol. II, p. 477, note 1) considered the itinerary, Avignon–Lyons–Auxonne–Paris, to be "improbable." According to Garros, Schuermans had made a mistake in advancing the theory that Bonaparte had served under General de Vaubois (1748–1839) at Lyons. In this context Bertrand upholds Schuermans.

CARTEAUX, JEAN-FRANÇOIS—Born at Gouhenans on January 31, 1751; died in Paris on April 12, 1813. Commander in chief of the forces engaged with the Rebels from the South (the Federalists). He served against Toulon and was made commander in chief to the Army of Italy on October 23, 1793, replacing Brunet. "From having been an indifferent sign-painter in Paris, he had attained generalship as devoid of ability as of years of service and . . . through the machinations of the clubs": Chaptal, *Souvenirs*, p. 190.

SOJOURN AT AUXONNE WITH LOUIS—On this subject, see Marcaggi, *Genesis of Nap.*, Chapter II, p. 239. Lombard had formerly taught Napoleon mathematics and, according to Coston, *Biog. of the Early Years*, Vol. I, p. 122, he had remarked of his pupil: "this young man will go far."

February 22

JULIE CLARY—A sister to Désirée. Born at Marseilles on December 26, 1771. She married Joseph Bonaparte, future King of Naples and of Spain, at Cuges in the Bouches-du-Rhône on August 1, 1794. She died at Florence, April 7, 1845.

February 23

POWERS OF CONCENTRATION—Roederer (*Diary*, p. 95) had also remarked that "what characterised Bonaparte's mind, was the power and duration of his concentration. He was able to spend eighteen hours in succession at work, on the same work, or on different types of work. I never saw him mentally tired," etc. At the end of Bertrand's remark there are several lines that are quite illegible, or which have at least been impossible to decipher: see the Introduction and the facsimile reproduction of this passage.

February 24

LODI—At St. Helena, the Emperor frequently discussed the importance of the Battle of Lodi. In his career, the date of May 10, 1796, and the name of this battle had marked the point of departure. It was the "control tower" of his ambition. "I felt the world flying past beneath my feet," he remarked. The interview between Melzi and Bonaparte took place at Melegnago on May 13, 1796 (25th Floréal of the Year IV). In his *Memorie*, published in Milan in 1865, Melzi referred to this incident (Vol. I, p. 144). It was also on May 13 that General Bonaparte received the letter from the Directory; he replied the following day (see *General Correspondence*, no. 421), telling Carnot: "I think that one *bad* general is needed, rather than two *good* ones."

PERALDI, MARIO, AND POZZO—Both men were leaders of Corsican clans which were opposed to the Bonapartes, and both of them influenced Paoli against the "Family." See Marcaggi, *Genesis of Nap.*, pp. 271ff.: *la révolution en Corse*. Mario Peraldi even went so far as to denounce Bonaparte after the troubles in Ajaccio in April 1792, which forced Napoleon to go to Paris in May to justify himself: see Coston, *Biog. of the Early Years*, Vol. I, p. 212.

February 25

ARRIGHI DE CASANOVA—The family had originally come from Corte, where the future Duke of Padua was born on March 8, 1778, son of Hyacinthe Arrighi, a Deputy to the Legislative Body, and a cousin by marriage of Napoleon.

COLONNA D'ISTRIA—Consecrated Bishop of Nice on June 11, 1802 (22 Thermidor of the Year X).

THE ELECTION OF BERNADOTTE—There were numerous people who were mixed up in the candidacy and subsequent election of Bernadotte to the Swedish Throne besides Count Fersen. On the subject of his meetings with Napoleon see Emile Dard, *Among the Entourage of the Emperor*, p. 76, and Ch. Schefer, *Bernadotte*, p. 16. Among them were Signeul, Swedish Consul General in Paris; Fournier, a former vice-consul at Gottenburg; and finally Desaugiers, a minor official, whom Vandal (in *Nap. and Alexander II*, p. 461) qualified as "a humble Legation secretary," acting as Chargé d'affaires, but concerning whom Bignon (in *Hist. France*, Vol. II, p. 298) wrote: "The French Minister gave no instructions or any orders to Desaugiers; he was considered to be non-existant. This was wrong. It is part of the nature of any agent, of no matter how lowly a degree, to wish to give to himself and to the position he occupies a certain importance." His activities made the Duke of Cadore request his recall, July 26, 1810. In the overtures made by Bernadotte at Dresden through the intermediary of Signeul, in May 1812, there was no mention of Finland but "he only hoped that Norway would be conceded to him": see Vandal, ibid., Vol. III, p. 440.

THE SPANISH BUSINESS—At St. Helena, Napoleon used the same language to Bertrand that he had previously used in the Smorgoni sleigh to Caulaincourt (*Mémoires*, Vol. II, p. 234). "No doubt," he said, "it would have been better to have finished the war in Spain before throwing ourselves into the Russian expedition." The perpetual question of "war on two fronts." The same tone recurs when Napoleon speaks of the military incapacity of Joseph, as noted by General Bélliard: "Joseph thinks he is a great general. He is convinced that he possesses an inborn knowledge of the science of war and that he can lead an army as well as I." The same writer (*Mémoires*, Vol. I, pp. 177f.) recorded the remark made by the Emperor at the time of the capitulation of Paris: "Well, I see that everyone has lost his head. Joseph is a c—— and Feltre either a blackguard or a traitor."

CASTLEREAGH, LORD—Robert Stewart, Marquess of Londonderry, was born in Ireland in 1769; he committed suicide in 1822. He was the moving spirit in the coalition governments after 1811, at which date he entered the Government. After the Fall of Napoleon, he became Ambassador to the Allied Powers at the Congress of Vienna. After the prosecution of the Queen of England [see previous note on this subject], it was rumored that he had resigned. See *Journal des Débats*, November 19 and 20, 1820.

THE CASE OF THE QUEEN'S NECKLACE—In the mind of Napoleon there was a close connection between the case of the Queen's Necklace and Moreau's Trial; so close indeed that in his mental processes the one would *automatically* invoke the other. Yet the two cases had nothing in common except for the unfortunate publicity given to their proceedings. Concerning the case of the Queen's Necklace, in which Cardinal de Rohan, Countess de Lamotte, Caliostro, and Mlle. d'Oliva were implicated, see the *Mémoires de Beugnot*, Vol. I., Chapters I and II; the account by Mercier de St.-Léger in *Souvenirs and Mémoires*, a monthly publication, for July–December 1898; and Funck-Brentano, *Affair of the Necklace*. Regarding the Trial of Moreau, compare what the Emperor had said about it to Las Cases (*Memorial*, Vol. III, p. 426): "Statesmen have made comparisons between my mistake and that of Louis XVI over the case of the Queen's Necklace, which he had placed in the hands of Parliament instead of allowing a commission to sit on the matter . . ." The truth is that Napoleon was reproaching himself for having, once at least, resembled that *che coliogne*—his good uncle Lucien!

February 26

LIVERPOOL, LORD—Son of a former Sea Lord, he became Prime Minister in 1812. It was he who persecuted Queen Caroline. The Queen's lawsuit almost caused the fall of the English Cabinet.

ENGLISH COTTON GOODS—On the question of the English Cotton Industry, see Bertrand de Jouvenal, *Napoleon and Planned Economy*, 1942, Vol. I, p. 260, the report of Camille Percier.

THE THIRTEENTH VENDÉMIAIRE—The account of this day's events which was dictated by Napoleon at St. Helena, appeared in 1822, in *Collection of Authentic Pieces*, Vol. IV. See also *General Correspondence*, Vol. XXIX, pp. 48f. There the account is much less direct than here. At that time Murat was a squadron leader in the 21st Light Cavalry Regiment. Bonaparte had placed his artillery in position at the top of the Pont de la Concorde, at the tops of the rue Royale and the rue de Rohan, and at the top of the Dauphine blind alley—situated between the rue St.-Honoré and the rue de Rivoli—and also at the Pont Tournant.

ELIOTT, GILBERT (later Lord Minto)—This General had been made Viceroy of Corsica, and while there he had become friendly with Pozzo di Borgo, whom he was to meet again in Vienna and with Edward Dillon, who commanded the Irish Regiment that occupied the island. See *Mémoires of Mme. Boigne*, Vol. I, p. 192.

BIRTHPLACE—The house in which Napoleon was born was sacked, but not burned down, by partisans in the pay of Paoli. See Claims for Loss and Damage, set up the 13th Prairial of the Year VI (July 1789) and quoted by Marcaggi, *Genesis of Nap.*, p. 433. The house was rebuilt by Meuron, who in 1791 had occupied the post of Architect to the King, in Corsica: see C. Bosc, *Ephémérides ajacciennes*, p. 143. Like Bonaparte, Meuron was a member of the Club of Friends of the Constitution. Napoleon was mistaken when he said that he touched at Ajaccio in September. The visit took place upon his return from Egypt between October 2–6, 1799. See *Mémoires* of Lavalette, Vol. I, p. 337. "See here, Montholon," the Emperor said to the General one day, holding up a piece of his Sèvres dinner service on which were painted views of Ajaccio, "that's my house. I am convinced that that ship beside the frigate [*Muiron*] belonged to my nurse. She was among the first to come to meet me. The town had been in the hands of some hotheads who were much disconcerted at my arrival . . . Nevertheless, everyone wanted to see this wonderful Napoleon. The entire population of Ajaccio had turned out to line the banks, and the garrison . . . had formed a guard of honor up to my house": Marchand, *Souvenirs inédits*.

February 28

GRENVILLE, WILLIAM—Son of the Chancellor of the Exchequer, it was he who had been responsible for the revolt of the American colonies. In 1790 he was made Foreign Secretary. He returned to power in 1806.

NOTES TO CHAPTER THREE—March 1821

March 1

THE ARMY OF THE RESERVE—In April 1800, Bonaparte left to take command of the Army of the Reserve, which was destined for operations in Italy. On the third of the same month, General Berthier had the title of Commander in chief conferred upon him, but he commanded the Army "under the eyes of the First Consul." See *Biography of Contemporaries.*

THE FIRST CONSUL'S CLOTHES—The costume mentioned here is that in which Napoleon posed for his portrait by Ingres. See the picture in the Liège Museum, reproduced in *Napoleon*, published by the Editions nationales as a color supplement, Vol. I, p. 220a.

LORD WHITWORTH—English Ambassador at Paris in 1802–03 (see Laquiante, *A Winter in Paris under the Consulate*). According to the letters of Reichardt, *passim.* "He was always superbly dressed, even at the Consular court": D'Abrantès. Arabella Diana, a daughter of Sir Charles Cope and widow of the third Duke of Dorset, who died in 1797, married Lord Whitworth in 1801. For information concerning her, see *Diary of Lady Malcolm*, p. 109. The *Argus* of December 12, 1802, reported the presentation of Lord Whitworth to the First Consul. On the subject of the escapade that set the First Consul and the Ambassador at loggerheads, at the time of the breaking up of the Peace of Amiens, see Las Cases, *Memorial*, Vol. IV, pp. 190ff.; Miot de Melito, *Mémoires*, Vol. II, pp. 81 and 91; and O'Meara, *Nap. in Exile*, Vol. I, p. 463, and Vol. II, p. 117.

March 4

SIEGE OF TOULON—An account of this siege is found in *Victories and Conquests*, Vol. II, pp. 155ff. The 13th Vendémiaire is described in Vol. IV, pp. 334ff., in which version there is a slight contradiction of the foregoing judgment pronounced on Barras. The 18th Fructidor is told in such a way as not to throw into relief the importance of the Speeches to the Army that were to decide the day. Compare with Las Cases, *Memorial*, Vol. IV, p. 181.

DUMOURIEZ—Roederer, *Diary*, Vol. III, p. 274, has traced a very lively portrait of this general; and General Bélliard, *Mémoires*, Vol. I, pp. 67ff., has analyzed the Campaign of Valmy in which he, the writer, figured as an adjutant attached to the Army General Staff. Napoleon repeated in Gourgaud's presence (see *Journal*, December 16, 1816) the praise that he began to express here on the subject of Dumouriez. "His campaign in Champagne was very fine and very audacious. He was the only man produced by the nobility." In front of Montholon (*Tales of Captivity*, Vol. I, p. 434) he expressed himself in a similar fashion.

March 5

THE EGYPTIAN CAMPAIGN—JAFFA—See *Victories and Conquests*, Vol. IX, pp. 356ff. General Dominique-Martin Dupuy (1767–98) was appointed Governor General of Cairo on July 22, 1798. An account of his death is to be found in the *General Correspondence*, Vol. XXIX, p. 499.

PLAGUE-STRICKEN MEN OF JAFFA—This incident has caused much ink to flow—possibly more ink than blood. See, for instance, the account in Warden, *Collection of Authentic Documents*, Vol. II, pp. 244ff.; that in O'Meara, *Nap. in Exile*, Vol. I, pp. 305ff.; and the version of Amédée Pichot, *Chronicle of Events 1814–15*, which gives the account of Napoleon's conversation at Elba with Lord Ebrington. Finally, see a dissertation in *Victories and Conquests*, Vol. X, pp. 309–14, from which it transpires that: 1) Bonaparte was of the opinion that opium should have been administered to those stricken with the plague, while Desgenettes was opposed to it, 2) the Chief Apothecary to the Army of Egypt, a man named Royer, procured this drug, and 3) the stormy session at the Cairo Institute was on the subject of the plague, and not on the opportunities for poisoning hopeless cases. Nevertheless, in reply to Lord Ebrington's question "as to whether it was true to say, as Robert Wilson had claimed, that he Bonaparte, would have had the sick men poisoned." Napoleon would have replied: "there is a certain amount of truth in that." In Bertrand's account the Emperor has retouched the first version and established the one he wished posterity to retain. "Your scurrilous writers," he was to remark to Dr.

Arnott, "have accused me of having had my soldiers poisoned, whereas I had given my own horses for their transportation. The apothecary (Royer) . . . was a poor fellow who had been kicked out of the Army for having made use of the drugs to his own advantage (. . .). There were some sick men still in hospital and I left my aide-de-camp Lavalette with them until their death took place on the following day: they had been considered unfit to be moved": Marchand, *Souvenirs inédits*. See the account by Lavalette in his *Mémoires*, Vol. I., p. 324, which confirms this.

WILSON, SIR ROBERT—This English colonel's report on the Syrian Expedition contained the very definite accusation in question. His attitude was that of an enemy trying to discredit his adversary. The attitude of Desgenettes is less easy to understand. It should not be forgotten that this was the same Wilson who had the grace to help Lavalette escape.

DESGENETTES, RENÉ-NICOLAS-DUFRICHE (Baron)—Born 1762; died 1837. He was the author of *Medical Hist. of the Army of the East*. Both the 1802 and 1830 editions of this book remain strangely obscure on a subject which Desgenettes was best qualified to clarify. He tried throughout to prove that he had played a leading part, if it is indeed true that he told the Commanding General that his job was "to save the sick men and not to finish them off." As for the plague, he denied the assertion here put forward by the Emperor and said that: "knowing how strongly the power of a name may wrongly influence the human mind, I refused to mention the word plague": ibid, p. 51. But there is one truth for the troops and one for the commander in chief.

LARREY, DOMINIQUE (Baron)—Born 1768; died at Lyons in 1842. The "good Larrey" was appointed at the age of twenty-six to be Surgeon in chief to the Army of Italy, later to the Army of the East. His most prolific interpreter is Paul Triaire, whose biography of him appeared in 1902.

BERTHOLLET, CLAUDE-LOUIS—Born in Savoy in 1748; died 1822. He was a doctor and medical attendant to the Duke of Orleans before he became a chemist. He figured among the oldest of the intimates of the First Consul, who while at Malmaison had taken pleasure in the society of men of science. "Those whom I saw there most frequently," wrote Queen Hortense in her *Mémoires*, Vol. I, p. 83, "were Monge, Berthollet, Fourcroy, Volney, Laplace, Lagrange, Prony."

MONGE, GASPARD—Born at Beaune in 1746; died 1818. One of the founders of the Polytechnic School, he was president of the Cairo Institute and one of the first batch of Senators; he became Count de Péluse in 1799. He had an attack of apoplexy during the reading of the 29th Dispatch that announced the disasters in Russia. According to Arago, in his eulogy of May 11, 1846, he then showed himself "more assiduous in his attendance upon the General who had been betrayed by fortune, than he had been regarding the victor of Marengo (. . .). At the Elysée Palace and at Malmaison, then all but deserted, the great geometrist was received morning and evening."

March 8

THE SPANISH CAMPAIGN—An account of this campaign is in *Victories and Conquests*, Vol. XVIII.

FERDINAND VII—The Emperor refers here to the letter that Ferdinand wrote to him on November 18, 1807. See G. de Grandmaison, *Spain and Napoleon*, p. 108. Napoleon subsequently denied having received any such letter. "The circumstances were such that had I declared myself to be on the side of the legitimate authority of the father [Charles IV], and against his son's usurpation of the throne, it would have amounted to a declaration against the wishes of the nation and would have brought down on France the hatred of the Spaniards": Caulaincourt, *Mémoires*, Vol. II, p. 246.

ESCOÏQUIZ, DON JUAN DE—Born 1762; died 1822. He was Archdeacon of Toledo and former tutor to the Prince of the Asturias. A "man of petty intrigues," Napoleon remarked of him to Caulaincourt: *Mémoires*, Vol. II, p. 249. In *The Revolution in Spain*, 2nd ed., 1816, pp. 267ff., the Abbé de Pradt gives a transcription of the talks that took place between Escoïquiz and Napoleon at the Château de Marracq near Bayonne, in May 1808. Escoïquiz later wrote a memorandum justifying his actions, which was published in May 1823. Don Pedro de Toledo, third son of the Duke of Infantado (1771-1841), was an intimate friend of Ferdinand. "The persistence of the illusions of these men, especially of M. Escoïquiz and of l'Infantado, was really tiresome," judged the Abbé de Pradt, who agreed for once with the Emperor.

GODOY, DON MANUEL—"Prince of Peace." Born at Badajoz in 1767; died in Paris in 1851. A favorite of the Spanish royal couple, in 1801 he signed the treaty of Badajoz with the French Republic. "The Favorite, as much to keep his place as to protect himself from the vengeance of the son—in the event of the father's death—proposed to me, in the name of Charles IV, that we should undertake the conquest of Portugal together, reserving for himself the kingdom of the Algarves as an asylum": Napoleon to Las Cases, Memorial, Vol. IV, pp. 239f.

March 9

THE AUSTRIAN CAMPAIGN: ECKMÜHL—At Eckmühl, Davout renewed on April 22, 1809, his exploit of Auerstadt. He withstood the forces of Archduke Charles alone, until Napoleon and Masséna could come up from Landshut, which however, did not prevent the Emperor from remarking one day that: "Davout is a man on whom I may confer honor, but he will never know how to wear it": Mme. de Rémusat, Mémoires, Vol. II, p. 370. The Five Days Campaign is described in Victories and Conquests, Vol. XIX, p. 121. After the Battle of Raab, June 14, 1809, Napoleon wrote to Prince Eugène: "your victory is a grandchild of Marengo." See Bignon, Hist. France, Vol. II, p. 205.

GORREQUER, MAJOR GIDEON—Born 1777; died suddenly in 1841. He was aide-de-camp and military secretary to Sir Hudson Lowe. He had campaigned in Sicily and in the Ionian Islands where he had become friendly with Lowe. He reached St. Helena at the same time as the Governor, April 14, 1816. He remained five years with his chief, whose entire confidence he enjoyed. He was an active, watchful, and devoted secretary and—in consequence—was suspect to the French at Longwood.

March 10

LOUISIANA—This territory was transferred to the United States under the Consulate, for the sum of eighty million francs. When his brothers Lucien and Joseph reproached him with this transaction Napoleon explained the motives governing his action. See Mémoires of Lucien Bonaparte, Vol. II, Chapter VIII.

LA ROCHEFOUCAULT-LIANCOURT (Duke of)—Author of Travels in the United States of America, in 8 volumes, published in 1800. Abbé Pradt's book on the American colonies dated from 1820. With an acute sense of the future, Napoleon foresaw here the development and ultra-rapid expansion of the North American continent, which quickly rendered most books on the subject out of date. Concerning the "visionary" qualities of Napoleon, this whole passage is worth considering.

March 13

PIERRON—At Longwood he filled the rôle of taster, between the major-domo Cipriani and the cook Lepage. After the death of Cipriani on February 26, 1818, he took his place as major-domo. He had a special gift for making confectionary.

DARLING, ANDREW—Born 1784; died 1841. A St. Helena upholsterer and decorator. At the time of the Emperor's death, it was he who looked after all the funeral arrangements. He left a manuscript on this subject, which, according to the Lockwood guides, was published in 1851 in the *St. Helena Advocate*, a periodical that is unobtainable even in England. See Arnold Chaplin, *A St. Helena's Who's Who*.

March 14

MARBOT—Colonel, later general Baron Marbot is best known for his *Mémoires*, published in three volumes in 1891. His critical observations written to refute the General of Engineers, Joseph Rogniat—whom Napoleon himself had also refuted—caused his name to be entered in the Imperial Will: according to Article 31 of Paragraph II, Napoleon left him the sum of one hundred thousand francs to encourage him to "continue to write to defend the honor of the French Army and to confound all calumniators and apostates."

MEMOIRS OF MLLE. LENORMAND—This collection of anecdotes was published in two volumes by Berville and Barrière, chez Baudouin, and appeared in 1820. Mme. du Chât(eau)-Ren(aud) is mentioned in Vol. I, pp. 220, 479, and 566. The Vicomte de B(eauharnais), ibid, p. 419. It would seem that Napoleon had not bothered to read to the end of the note on the subject of Beauharnais's death sentence; the name of Mme. Tallien is also mentioned, on pp. 392ff., and in a note on p. 405.

TALLIEN, TÉRÉSIA CABARRUS—Called Our Lady of Thermidor because of the number of victims she saved from the knife; a result of the passion her beauty inspired in Tallien. Mme. de Rémusat confirms the fact in her *Mémoires*, Vol. I, p. 149, that upon his return from

Egypt Bonaparte "demanded that his wife break off relations with Madame Tallien and all her Directory society." The same note is to be found in Montholon, *Tales of the Captivity*, Vol. II, p. 20, and in Constant, *Mémoires*, Vol. III, p. 79.

JOSEPHINE AND THE DEATH OF THE DUKE OF ENGHIEN—"The supposed scene in which Josephine on her knees implored Napoleon to spare the Duke of Enghien . . . is one of those melodramatic accounts by means of which our legend-makers of today invent authentic history. On the evening of March 19, Josephine was unaware that the Duke of Enghien was to be tried; she merely knew that he had been arrested": Chateaubriand, *Memoirs beyond the Tomb*, Levaillant edition, Vol. II, p. 163—it is apparent from this that Chateaubriand was well informed.

CHARLES, LOUIS HIPPOLYTE—Born at Roman, in the Drôme, July 5, 1772; a son of François Charles and Madeleine Machon. He was their ninth child. On August 12, 1791, he joined as a volunteer the 3rd Company of the 2nd Battalion of the Drôme National Guard. He was nicknamed "Wide-awake" because of his quickness of mind. He obtained his substitution leave on January 10, 1793. After being a battalion adjutant of the garrisons of Marseilles and of Avignon, he later became acting commandant of the Marseilles garrison and was seconded adjutant to the Military Commander of the Marseilles Garrison, called Leclerc, whom he accompanied to Paris on April 19, 1796. On the twenty-seventh of the same month he was detailed to join the Army of the Interior. The following May third he was attached to the Army of Italy as an Adjutant to Adjutant General Leclerc. He rejoined his post on June 24, traveling with Josephine Bonaparte. On September 15, the Commander in chief of the Army of Italy mentioned him in his report to the Directory as having behaved perfectly. See the *Moniteur*, September 26, 1796.

Gazetted a captain on the active list attached to the 1st Regiment of Hussars, June 21, 1797, he was ordered on November 30, 1797, to go to Paris where he would receive another appointment. Berthier confirmed this order on December 22. Charles reached Paris on January 8, 1798, and handed in his resignation to the Minister of War the following March 17. Thanks to Josephine, whose favors he had enjoyed since 1796, he became the partner of an Army contractor named Bodin. While Bonaparte was in Egypt, Charles was seen everywhere in the company of Josephine, who had just bought Malmaison. After Bonaparte's return from Egypt, there was a violent scene between Napoleon and his wife, and the rupture between the two lovers appears to have been complete.

After having bought and then resold the estate near l'Isle-Adam, Charles retired in 1820 into the Drôme at Génissieux, where he died, unmarried, on March 9, 1837. Chinard, who executed the busts of Napoleon and Josephine, also did one of Charles. (Information contributed by Louis Hastier.)

MLLE. DESPIAUX—A famous Parisian modiste. Josephine was one of her best customers.

LA RAUCOURT, MARIE-ANTOINETTE SAUCEROTTE—An actress of the Comédie Française. Born March 3, 1756; died January 15, 1815. Her funeral caused a slight demonstration at the Church of St.-Roch. Her notorious lesbian tendencies fully justified the hostility of the clergy. Upon the relationship of this tragedienne with Josephine, see *Memoirs of Mlle. Georges*, quoted by Méneval in *The Empress Josephine*, p. 36; and Jean de Reuilly, *La Raucourt and Her Friends*, 1909, p. 204.

CHÂTEAU DE MARRACQ—The property of a well-known Bordeaux Jew, M. Margfroy. Napoleon stayed at Marracq, near Bayonne, from April 17 to July 20, 1808.

MME. GAZZANI, CARLOTTA—A Genoese who was appointed reader to Josephine after the coronation at Milan, and Lady of the Palace after the divorce. On the subject of her liaison with the Emperor, see F. Masson, *Napoleon and Women*, p. 117.

MLLE. GUILLEBAULT—The story of her affair with the Emperor was frequently described by him at St. Helena, in the presence of Las Cases (*Memorial*, Vol. IV, p. 354), Montholon (*Tales of the Captivity*, Vol. I, p. 306) and Gourgaud (*Diary*, June 16, 1816). All of which goes to prove that Josephine, according to the expression of Méneval, was not always "white as snow." F. Masson in *Napoleon and Women*, p. 115, reproduces Mlle. Guillebault's letter of dismissal.

PÈRE PATRAULT—He belonged to the Order of Minimes. A former Professor of Mathematics at Brienne, he abandoned the frock after the Revolution and subsequently became destitute. It is therefore not surprising to find him involved in a matrimonial affair.

EMMERY, JEAN-MARIE-JOSEPH—Born at Dunkirk, January 16, 1754; died there, February 11, 1825. Merchant and banker, he was a member of the Legislative body until 1815.

March 15-16

HODSON, CHARLES ROBERT GEORGE—A major in the St. Helena Regiment and a judge advocate who remained at St. Helena throughout the Captivity. Because of his great height, Napoleon nicknamed him Hercules. Bertrand is here mistaken as to his rank.

THE RESEMBLANCE WITH THE KING OF ROME—This anecdote, which contains a "malicious" insinuation on the part of Mme. Bertrand, would appear to confirm the fact that little Napoléone-Joséphine de Montholon, born at Longwood, June 18, 1818, may have been the Emperor's child. For information concerning her, see Paul Duvivier "The Emperor's Last Goddaughter," in *Rev. of the University of Brussels*, 1909.

BUTTINI—This doctor from Geneva had formerly been called in as a consultant by Pauline Borghèse. See Fleuriot de Langle, *La Paolina*, ed. in-4, p. 204.

THE LETTER FROM BERTRAND TO LORD LIVERPOOL—This letter had already been written on September 2, 1820, but Hudson Lowe had returned it to the sender. Bertrand forwarded the letter through Buonavita, who was repatriated on March 17, 1821; sending it with a postscript, dated March 13, which stated that he was taking "advantage of the return of the Abbé Buonavita, to have it reach you."

GUIZOT—This must be the political brochure *Representative Government* published by Guizot in 1816. The distinction drawn between the *interests* and the *theories* of the Revolution is subtle and remarkable. This passage forms a sort of synthesis of the entire Napoleonic doctrine on matters appertaining to government. As heir to the Revolution, Napoleon had consolidated its institutions, while appearing to destroy its dogma. A king of the people and a Republican emperor, he was monarchist without being reactionary.

The reference to the "brochure sent from here," that is, from St.

Helena, refers—so it is thought by Fleuriot de Langle—to a *factum* which had appeared at Ridgeway's in London in 1820, entitled "The Bourbons in 1815, by Count . . ."

March 19

ILLNESS—Marchand, too, noted this attack, in his *Souvenirs inédits*: "On March 19, the Emperor again had a recurrence of the fever. It attacked him, as he himself said, like a snake. The doctor was sent for, but by misfortune once again he was not at home"—which in no way prevented this charlatan from later issuing a bulletin. On March 24 the Emperor sent Antommarchi packing. "You can go chase yourself and stuff it up." This referred to the emetic he had been ordered. On March 27 Montholon noted that "The Emperor persists in refusing to accept Antommarchi's care." The diagnosis and prescriptions of Dr. Arnott given the day before deserve to be noted by all those who believe that the Emperor did not die of cancer of the liver but of a suppurating gastric ulcer.

March 27

RELIGIOUS BELIEFS OF NAPOLEON—This astounding declaration of faith demolishes with a single stroke the thesis of all those pious conformists who have held forth upon this subject. For example, the ineffable Chevalier de Beauterne, or the candid Antoine Guillois. Vaguely deist in the manner of Jean-Jacques Rousseau, Napoleon believed neither in the divine existence of Christ or in the distributative justice of a rewarding God. "With the onset of age, Napoleon grew more hostile towards Christianity": Lord Rosebery, *The Last Phase*, p. 214. Here he rejects the consolations of the life after death. Never before had the barren scepticism of Napoleonic thought appeared in a more crude and hopeless light. He was not delirious. The observers around him noted a lessening of the fever. O. Aubry (*St. Helena*, Vol. II, note to p. 225) has assumed that to please the incredulous Bertrand, Napoleon pretended to hold no beliefs. But this is proved wrong by the avowals made to Gourgaud and quoted by Lord Rosebery, "Were I forced to profess a religion, I would worship the sun . . . the real God of the Earth." "I might believe in a religion had one existed since the beginning of the world." In contrast to this, he said to Montholon, (*Tales of the Captivity*, Vol. I, p. 354), "I felt the need to believe; therefore I believed"; and to Las Cases (*Memorial*, Vol. IV, p. 160), "The discontent of man is such that he needs the vagueness and sense of wonder that religion affords him." To sum up and reconcile all these contrasts, it is necessary always to distinguish between Napoleon's attitude towards religious *policy* and religious *doctrine*. Bertrand's testimony is categorical: the martyr of Longwood had absolutely no worries about the life after death. He had made a clean sweep of such things. A pagan would have retained the comfort of a belief in the laws of fate and of the presence of invisible beings. But not in this case. At his bedside, "the august idols who bent over the couch of the sage or hero of antiquity, were totally lacking": Maximilian Vox.

March 30

READE, SIR THOMAS—Born 1785; died 1849. He was a lieutenant colonel when he arrived at St. Helena on April 14, 1815, with Sir Hudson Lowe, who attached him to his staff as a deputy-adjutant-general. Very strict in his own orders, he considered Hudson Lowe to be too soft! He had occasion to see the Emperor on April 17, May 27, and October 4, 1816. He left the island on July 12, 1821.

NOTES TO CHAPTER FOUR—APRIL 1821

April 3

DEIANIRA—A mythological recollection of the tunic which before his death, Nessus had given to Deianira, wife of Hercules. Betrayed by her husband, Deianira in turn gave the fatal tunic to him, causing Hercules to die in the cruelest torment.

April 9

ANTOMMARCHI—"The conduct of Antommarchi" (says Forsyth, *Hist. Captivity*, Vol. III, p. 285 of the French translation) "was even more strange. He made no attempt to disguise his opinion as to the precarious state of the Emperor's health; nonetheless, he asked to be allowed to return to Europe. On April 9 he went to Plantation House," where the Governor lived, etc. There was nothing ambiguous about that. Bertrand explained that Dr. Antommarchi had been kicked out by Napoleon. That was all there was to it. Yet the expelled doctor noted imperturbably in his misleading *Diario*, on April 9, 1821: "The patient is in a restless and sullen mood . . . He is in a state of extreme prostration!"

PERCY, P. FRANÇOIS (Baron)—Born 1754; died 1825. A military surgeon, appointed inspector general of the health services under the Empire. He has left a delightful *Journal of His Campaigns*, which was published in 1904.

NAGLE, MICHEL—Born 1795; died 1841. A lieutenant attached to the 53rd Regiment quartered at St. Helena. His wife, née Emma Valentine, was the daughter of a Portsmouth clergyman.

SAINT-DENIS, LOUIS-ETIENNE (called Ali)—Born at Versailles on September 22, 1788. A protégé of the Duke of Vicenza, he entered the service of the Imperial Household in May 1806, and joined the Emperor at Elba. He accompanied him to St. Helena, where he sorted out Napoleon's dictations, and was promoted to the rank of "librarian." In his *Souvenirs*, published in 1926, the Mameluke Ali left one of the most vivid portrayals that we possess of the last years of the Captivity.

April 10

BAVAROISE—A kind of molded cream usually served as a sweet.

April 13

On this day, the Emperor locked himself in his room with Montholon (*Tales of the Captivity*, Vol. II, p. 508) not only to dictate a letter to the Prince Regent of England, but to dictate for "two hours without stopping" certain clauses in his will. He repeats here, with reference to the English ruling classes, what he had previously written to Marshal Davout on the eve of the Battle of Essling, when speaking of the Austrian princes: "Those people are as vile in adversity as they are arrogant and haughty at the least flicker of prosperity."

THE LIFE OF MARLBOROUGH—This book, *The Life of John Churchill, Duke of Marlborough*, by Coxe, bearing the Imperial coat of arms, had been sent to St. Helena by R. Spencer: see Forsyth, *Hist. Captivity*, Vol. III, p. 287. The gift of this work to the library of the 20th Regiment was an opportunity for Hudson Lowe to behave with supreme caddishness, which even Forsyth, who is indulgent towards the Governer, deplored, and for Antommarchi, censured by Marchand, the occasion for a shocking outburst.

LADY HOLLAND—Née Elisabeth Vassall. She was married in July 1797 to Henry Richard Fox, third Lord Holland, who left some diplomatic memoirs, which were published by his son. In gratitude for the innumerable attentions for which the prisoner of St. Helena was indebted to Lady Holland, Napoleon mentioned her in his will (see below). She died on November 16, 1845.

April 14

OAKLEY, R. C.—He was a lieutenant with the effective force of the 20th of the Line. See Arnold Chaplin, *A St. Helena's Who's Who*.

April 15

BROOKE, THOMAS HENRY—Born 1774; died 1849. He was secretary and member of the St. Helena Council, of which he was the most influential and active representative. A nephew of Colonel Robert

Brooke, a former Governor of the island, he became interim Governor after the departure of Sir Hudson Lowe. He had an audience with Napoleon on January 7, 1816. In 1808 he had published a history of St. Helena, of which a second edition appeared in 1824. See Arnold Chaplin, *A St. Helena's Who's Who.*

THE FORTY HOURS OF PRAYER—This service consisted of a relay of prayers passing from one parish to another or from one group to another without interruption and lasting, in theory, for forty hours. The length of this service has been shortened by the Church, although the name of the ceremony has been retained.

"THE EMPEROR . . . HAD WRITTEN A GREAT DEAL"—It is well known that Napoleon wrote his will entirely by hand, as well as the codicil of April 16.

"Some marks of ink on the sheet bore witness to the fact that the Emperor had done a great deal of writing," noted Marchand, who added a little further on, this picturesque detail: "The Emperor was sitting up in bed, in one hand he held a piece of cardboard, while he wrote with the other, without leaning on anything. Beside the bed stood Count Montholon, holding an inkwell." A first will, made out earlier, had been intrusted to Bertrand on August 19, 1819, as has been proved by a manuscript certificate of authentication written in pencil and signed with an N, which has been preserved among the papers of Count Bertrand. Marchand was told to ask the Grand Maréchal for this document. "The Emperor read it through, then tore it in half and told me to put it in the fire," says Marchand. But Montholon, *Tales of the Captivity,* Vol. II, p. 504, nevertheless, gives a hint of it, according to a penciled note "found among the Emperor's papers."

April 17

THE ROOM WITH THE CLOCK—The room had been given this name on account of a clock there which had been a present from Mme. de Montholon; the face was surmounted by a rose and supported on either side by two small genii. This relic is at present in the collection of Prince Napoleon.

CARACCIOLI, DOMINIQUE (Marquess)—Born 1715; died 1789. He was Ambassador of the King of Naples to England and afterwards to France, where he became friendly with the Encyclopedists; he was later appointed Viceroy of Sicily.

April 18

THE "NYMPH"—A nickname given by the people at Longwood to a certain Miss Robinson, a farmer's daughter who lived on the slopes of Prosperous Valley, also known as the Valley of the Nymph. On July 26, 1817, when paying her farewell visit to the Emperor, she presented her husband Captain Edwards, who returned to England with her on board the *Dora*. It is learned here that he came back to St. Helena alone, in 1821.

April 19

TOULONGEON, ÉMMANUEL (Viscount of)—Born 1748; died 1812. Deputy for the Nièves to the Legislative Body. The four volumes of his *History of France* appeared between 1801 and 1810. Marchand mentions a reading of the Campaigns of Hannibal on April 19, but does not refer to this work by Toulongeon.

April 21

GUILLAUME, FRÉDÉRIC-FRANÇOIS (called de Vaudoncourt)—Born 1772; died 1845. This general and military writer was the author of *Hist. of the Ital. Campaign, 1813-14*; also *Hist. of Prince Eugène*; and *The Russian Campaign*.

April 22

THE WILL: RELIGION—In contrast with the avowal previously made to Bertrand on March 27, this paragraph reflects the official thought and attitude of the Emperor on religious matters. This time he appears as a conformist, submissive to the rites of the Church out of respect for custom, preoccupied with family traditions, and logically inclined to attune the dignity of his death to the doctrines which he had professed as head of the Government.

BURIAL—SHORTT, THOMAS—Born 1788; died 1843. He was the chief military doctor on the island. He had arrived at St. Helena in December 1820. He wrote the official report of the autopsy on the body of the Emperor.

THE FOUNTAIN—Known as Torbett's Fountain from the name of the man who owned the land on which it was situated. This fountain was near the cottage of Dr. Kay.

CHARLES BONAPARTE—Died at Montpellier on February 24, 1785. His body was at first interred in the Chapel of the Communauté de l'Observance. In 1803 it was transferred to St.-Leu, from where the Prince of Condé had it removed on October 19, 1819, to the vaults of the Church of St.-Leu-Taverny.

ESTABLISHED FACTS—The part referring to the Duke of Enghien is to be found in the commentary to Article 8, Part I, of the will. After which it is pointless to try and establish a distinction between "trial" and "execution" as O. Aubry has sought to do: *St. Helena*, Vol. II, p. 228. In this context the Emperor has stated expressly that he had the Duke "executed" and under similar conditions "would do it again." It is known that this *addendum* was appended as the result of reading an English newspaper in which the assassination of the Duke had been attributed to Savary and Caulaincourt. The *Manuscript of St. Helena*, which is here categorically disowned, has been attributed to a great variety of people. All the mémoire writers of Longwood have discussed its authorship. The names of Mme. de Staël, Benjamin Constant, Lullin de Chateauvieux, etc., have been put forward. The state of the question has been well summed up by Louis Villat in his *Manual of 1936, Clio* collection, pp. xiv–xv.

GOURVILLE—Before becoming Collector of Taxes, Gourville had started life as a manservant in the household of the Abbé de la Rochefoucauld. By quoting this example, the Emperor, who had just raised his manservant Marchand to the rank of an employer, sought to prove that *fidelity pays*. Constant Wairy, who had abandoned his master at Fontainebleau, was an example of the exact opposite; in article 17 of the Instructions to the executors (Montholon, *Tales of the Captivity*, Vol. II, p. 534), the Emperor called him a "rogue." On the subject of this deserter, see *Mémoires of Caulaincourt*, Vol. II, p. 357, and the note by J. Hanoteau which tells people to beware of Constant as a writer of mémoires. The "Mameluke" Roustan had been guilty of the same vile and cowardly conduct when he abandoned his master: see Ali, *Souvenirs*, p. 59.

COURSOT—The butler Coursot had been a manservant in the household of Madame Mère. In the bequests to his servants it can be seen that the hierarchical mind of the Emperor had visualized a kind of helping hand extended to Marchand by Bertrand or Montholon, and by Marchand in turn to Ali.

TURENNE, HENRY-AMÉDÉE-MERCURE (Count of)—He had replaced Rémusat as Master of the Robes and had cared for the Emperor at the time of the attempted poisoning of Napoleon at Fontainebleau. See Caulaincourt's *Mémoires*, Vol. III, p. 366. See Part B of the will: "Inventory of the effects I have left in the care of Count de Turenne."

INDIVIDUAL BEQUESTS—BIGNON, LOUIS-PIERRE-EDOUARD (Baron) —Born 1771; died 1841. He was a diplomat who fulfilled the wishes of the Emperor by writing the *History of France*, to which we have referred. MARBOT—See previous note. CLAUZEL (Bernard Count)—Born 1772; died 1842. He had sailed for the United States in November 1815, in flight from the consequences of being condemned to death on September 11. Amnestied on April 26, 1820, he had only just returned to France. LEFEBVRE, DESNOUETTES—A cavalry general (1773-1822), condemned to death by default on May 11, 1816; he had also sought refuge in the United States. REAL, PIERRE-FRANÇOIS (Count)—Appointed Prefect of Police during the Hundred Days; consequently upon the return of the Bourbons he was sent into exile. He was one of the French émigrés in the Low Countries, and later went to the United States, and returned to France in 1818. DROUOT, ANTOINE—Known as the *sage de la Grande* (Armée), he was banished on July 24, 1815. He was later court-martialed and acquitted. GENERAL CAMBRONNE—Called upon to appear before a court-martial in 1816, he was also acquitted. CORBINEAU, JEAN-BAPTISTE JUVÉNAL—A cavalry general (1776-1848). He was the man who, at the time of the Retreat from Russia, had found the ford at Studienka, which saved the French. "They are a family of brave men," said Napoleon, "I did not do enough for him. He will feel embarrassed because he is without means." See Caulaincourt's *Mémoires*, Vol. III, pp. 389f. In *General Correspondence* under No. 21, p. 559, see the letter of praise dated April 13, 1814, and bearing the Emperor's signature. LETORT, L. MICHEL—Cavalry general. Born August 28, 1773; killed at Gilly, June 15, 1815, while leading a charge against the Prussian rear-guard on the Chaussée de Charleroi. DEJEAN (1749-1824)—A former aide-de-camp to Napoleon and a general of a division in the Engineers, he refused to vote for the downfall of the Emperor on April 3, 1814. RAPP—Aide-de-camp to the First Consul, appointed June 15, 1800. LE MAROIS (1776-1836)—Aide-de-camp from November 5, 1795 to 1814. LOBAU, MOUTON (Count of)— Appointed aide-de-camp, March 6, 1805. DUROSNEL (1771-1849)— Appointed aide-de-camp, April 1809. DUROC, MARIE DE LAS NIEVES DE HERVAS—Widow of Michel Duroc, Grand Marshal of the Palace, killed May 23, 1813. She subsequently married General Baron Fabvier.

BESSIÈRES—Killed on May 1, 1813; left an only son, Napoleon, Duke of Istria.

LALLEMAND—The two Lallemand brothers, François-Antoine, who was a cavalry general, and Henry-Dominique, an artillery general, were both condemned to death by default on August 20 and 21, 1816. They left France and settled in Texas, where they founded a colony known as the Champ d'Asile (Field of Sanctuary).

GILLY—Second valet de chambre to Napoleon at Elba. See Pons de l'Hérault, *The Island of Elba*, pp. 192f.

BALCOMBE, WILLIAM—Born 1779; died 1829. He was the accredited purveyor of supplies to Longwood, and a partner of W. Fowler and J. Cole. On October 18, 1815, Napoleon stayed in the small house called The Briars, which was next to the cottage of the Balcombes. Betsy Balcombe, Mme. L.-E. Abell, left *Souvenirs*, which were translated into French by Aimé Le Gras in 1898. As the result of quarrels with Sir Hudson Lowe, the Balcombe family left the island on March 18, 1818.

O'MEARA, BARRY EDWARD—Born in County Cork in 1782; died in 1836. A doctor on board the *Bellerophon*, he was attached to the service of the Emperor until July 25, 1818; he left the island on August 2 of that same year. In 1822 his *Voice of St. Helena* was published, which he declared in his will to be "a truthful book, in which is recorded an account of the treatment inflicted by Sir Hudson Lowe and his subordinates on that great man, Napoleon."

STOKOE, JOHN—Born 1775; died 1852. A doctor on board the Conqueror, he visited Napoleon five times between January 17 and 21, 1819, for consultations, which earned him the disapprobation of Hudson Lowe. Called upon to appear before a court-martial, on August 30, he was subsequently stricken from the Naval Register.

LAVALETTE, MARIE-JOSEPH CHAMANS (Count of)—Postmaster general in 1814, a post of which he was relieved by the Bourbons. During the Hundred Days he returned to his post. He was later condemned to death, but escaped from prison thanks to the devotion of his wife Emilie-Louise de Beauharnais, who went insane and died at Paris on June 18, 1855. His *Mémoires* were published in 1831.

LAFFITTE, JACQUES—The banker with whom Napoleon had deposited his money. "Monsieur Laffitte, in 1815 at the time of my departure from Paris, I left in your possession a sum which amounted to nearly six million francs . . ." See the letter written from Longwood on April 25, 1821, which was attached to the will.

THE EMPRESS—A part of the Treasury had followed the Empress first to Blois and then to Orleans. On April 8, 1814, the Provisional Government sent a representative of the Treasury to Orleans to recover the State funds. Reaching Orleans on the tenth, the Treasury representative, Dudon, came up against the opposition of La Bouillerie. On the twelfth, Lt. Colonel Janin, who commanded the Empress's escort, saddled up and had the loot returned to Paris. On the subject of this episode, see the *Mémoires* of *Caulaincourt*, Vol. III, pp. 319-23; F. Masson, *L'Affaire Maubreuil*, pp. 107 and 121, and Las Cases, *Memorial*, Vol. IV, pp. 135ff. In 1815 Napoleon refused to receive Roullet de la Bouillerie, Treasurer General to the Crown. The inquiry held to investigate the disappearance of the funds was fruitless. "It was necessary to resign oneself to knowing nothing": Peyrusse, *Memorial*, p. 309.

PRIVATE ESTATE—Compare this with Part III of the Will, wherein a detailed account of the resources of the private estate had been drawn up.

LUCIEN'S FAMILY—The Emperor alludes here to the marriages made by the daughters and step-daughters of his brother. First Charlotte, who had married, December 27, 1815, Prince Marie Gabrielli; then Anne Jouberthon, daughter of Alexandrine Bonaparte by her first marriage, who was married in Rome, April 5, 1818, to Prince Alphonse Hercolani; and finally Christine, who married Arved de Posse, a Swede, on March 28, 1818.

ORNANO—Count d'Ornano in April 1816 married Countess Marie Walewska by whom he had a son, Rodolphe-Auguste, born June 9, 1817. See Count d'Ornano, *Marie Walewska*, p. 252, who remarks that this remarriage was not mentioned in the conversations at St. Helena. Concerning the career of this illegitimate son of Napoleon, born May 4, 1810 at Walewice, see the biography by Philippe Poirson.

LÉON—Through his liaison with Eléanore Denuelle de la Plaigne (1787-1868), who had been reader to Caroline Murat, Napoleon had one son, Charles, called Count Léon, who was born in Paris on December, 6, 1806, and died at Pontoise on April 15, 1881. On the lamentable life of this waif, see Lenôtre, *Outline of an Epic*, pp. 253-69, and *Review of Napoleonic Studies*, May–June, 1926.

THE HOUSE IN THE RUE DE LA VICTOIRE—For information concerning this house, which has since disappeared, consult G. Bord and L. Bigard, *The House in the rue Chantereine*; and the *Review of Napoleonic Studies*, 1926, Vol. II, pp. 145-62, ill.

LADY HOLLAND—On the subject of this bequest see the letter of May 15, 1821, from Sir Hudson Lowe to Lady Holland (printed in *Diplomatic Reminiscences of Lord Holland*, 1851, pp. 149ff.), which explains the relationship of the Holland family with Napoleon. The snuffbox was reproduced in F. Masson's *St. Helena*, ed. in-4, ill.

CORRESPONDENCE WITH THE SOVEREIGNS: JOSEPH—At St. Helena Napoleon was very worried about these letters. A first volume of them was published by Prince Napoleon in 1939 (Plon edition) with an important preface by J. Hanoteau, who unraveled the past history of these documents and cleared up almost all the doubtful points.

LIBELS—This referred to a book published by ex-King Louis, in London in 1820, entitled *Historical Documents and Reflections on the Government of Holland*. After reading his brother's effort, the Emperor was unable to prevent himself from saying in pained accents: "Oh! Louis, you too." See Ali, *Souvenirs*, p. 246.

DUCIS, JEAN-FRANÇOIS—Born at Versailles in 1733; died in 1816. He was a tragic poet who, in 1778, succeeded to Voltaire's chair in the French Academy. He was elected to the Conservative Senate, the 3rd Nivôse of the Year VIII (December 24, 1800), but refused the post. See the *Moniteur* for the Year VII, pp. 384 and 388.

LAFAYETTE—On the subject of the relations of Lafayette with Joseph Bonaparte, see the *Mémoires* of Méneval, Vol. III, p. 541. The letter alleged to have been written by Lafayette to Bonaparte at the time of the Consulate in perpetuity—May 20, 1802—has been reproduced as an authentic document by Etienne Charavay in his monumental biography, published in 1898, p. 386.

VARIOUS BEQUESTS—HUBERT, the valet de chambre, had followed the Emperor to Elba: Pons, *The Island of Elba*, p. 192. LAVIGNE, the groom had accompanied Bonaparte to Egypt. CAESAR, the coachman, an old drunkard, had in spite of himself, saved the Emperor at the time of the attempt on his life by the infernal machine: see Las Cases, *Memorial*, Vol. I, p. 459. The Lieutenant of Police in question has been named by Pons, ibid., p. 79, who attributes the favor this insignificant person enjoyed to his having been a Corsican. COSTA, a native of Bastellica is mentioned in the Article 27, Part II, of the will. ZENON VANTINI had formerly been a page of Elisa Bonaparte's of whom the Emperor had also been fond: see Pons, ibid., p. 78.—In preference to Taillade, Captain of the *Inconstant* whom Pons considered to be not very devoted to the Emperor, we think that Napoleon meant to refer to Lieutenant Commander Chautard, who had succeeded Taillade: see Pons, pp. 360f. SECOND LIEUTENANT SARRI had been promoted to the St.-Cyr Military Academy: see Pons, p. 349. MUIRON was mentioned in the fourth codicil of April 24. "THE ASSASSIN OF WELLINGTON" was the noncommissioned officer Cantillon. This bequest aroused the ire of the English.

April 24

DIALOGUES WITH ARNOTT—Among the Bertrand papers are to be found two versions of these conversations; one shorter than the other. We have blended the variations in the present edition or completed one text from the other. These dialogues are typical of the Emperor's mania for asking questions.

CORRESPONDENCE WITH THE SOVEREIGNS—See note above on page 303.

THE FAMILY OF LUCIEN BONAPARTE—The descendants of Lucien later produced a cardinal. His grandson, Lucien son of Charles, (born in Rome, November 15, 1828; died there, November 19, 1895) became a cardinal priest on March 13, 1868, in the name of Sainte Pudenzia and later of *San Lorenzo in Lucina* . . .

THE FESCH COLLECTION—This famous collection of pictures, the value of which had been overestimated, was sold in 1843. The catalogue was made by George.

WATTEVILLE—Of Swiss extraction, this family had had a Landamman, Charles-Emmanuel de Watteville, father of young Albert de

Watteville, who had been aide-de-camp to the Emperor. See *Memoirs of Queen Hortense*, Vol. III, p. 100.

LUCIEN—The author of *Charlemagne or the Church Delivered*, he attempted to fulfill his brother's wishes by writing, for example, *The Truth Concerning the Hundred Days*. As for his *Mémoires*, published in Th. Jung in three volumes in 1822, the extremely hostile tone frequently adopted in them towards Napoleon leads one to suspect that the Emperor had deluded himself in calling upon Lucien not to confine himself solely to the writing of poetry, or perhaps it would be wiser to say, versification. Lucien's files contained a goodly supply of historical documents. See the summary list of these papers, published in *Alexandrine Bonaparte, Princess de Canino*, Annex II, by Fleuriot de Langle.

THE CIVIL LIST—On this subject consult the article by Alphonse Gautier, *State of the Civil List*, 1882, and *Memoirs of Mme. de Rémusat*, Vol. II, p. 327.

April 25

DENON—"Denon and D'Albe have in their possession a great many maps which belong to me": Article 14 of the Instructions to the testamentary executors. For this work Denon had received 10–12,000 francs a month over a period of several years.

BACLER D'ALBE (General Baron)—Born 1761; died 1824. An ordnance survey officer from 1801 onwards; among other things he established the big map of Italy. In memory of his campaigns he left a collection of lithographs, which were published by Englemann. Concerning him, see Fain, *Mémoires*, 1908, p. 39.

WARD—Ensign John Ward was attached to the 66th Regiment. He did not leave St. Helena quite as early as Bertrand says, since he was present at the funeral and helped Dr. Burton to make the death mask. Also, he and Major Hudson were the only English officers to have been present at the burial of Napoleon; they later assisted at the exhumation of the Emperor's body in 1840. Ward died in 1878.

CROCKATT, WILLIAM—Born at Edinburgh in 1789; died in 1879. Duty officer at Longwood from April 15 to May 7, 1821. His great height renders him easily recognizable in the picture by Steuben, which depicts the Emperor on his death bed, surrounded by his companions.

LUYTENS, ENGLEBERT—Born 1784; died 1830. A captain of the 20th Regiment. Made orderly officer to the Governor, February 10, 1820, he resigned from this post April 15, 1821, as a result of the blame laid on him by Major Jackson for having accepted from Dr. Arnott the *Life of Marlborough* that had been presented to the regiment by the Emperor. He was replaced by Captain William Crockatt.

April 26

OFFICIAL REPORT ON THE WILLS—The text of the official report has been quoted by Montholon, in *Tales of the Captivity*, Vol. II. p. 540. "Today, April 27, 1821, at nine o'clock in the evening, we, Count Bertrand, Grand Marshal of the Emperor Napoleon, in execution of his orders had brought to us the various wills, codicils, and instructions which had been intrusted to M. Marchand; amounting in all to nine letters or separate packets . . . three of them with a red tape, the six others with green tape, etc. . . ."

ANTOMMARCHI AND MADAME BERTRAND—The remarks made about them by the dying Emperor whether they please or offend nevertheless prove conclusively that the dying man was unable to raise himself to the sublime heights of Christian forgiveness. To have sought to edify us in this respect would have been to deceive us. Bertrand deserves our thanks for once again having been truthful and sincere.

April 26 in the evening

ADVICE TO HIS SON—These remarks are of a much more practical character than the exhortations—on the whole very fine—which Montholon took down from dictation on April 17; see the Introduction. In the course of ten days, his illness had made such strides that in his solicitude Napoleon had to restrict himself, when speaking to his son, to the most important thing, which was to deflect from that beloved mind all the perils of a distorted education.

MÉNEVAL, CLAUDE-FRANÇOIS (Baron of)—Born in Paris in 1778; died there in 1850. Member in charge of all petitions addressed to the Conseil d'Etat. Confidential secretary or acting cabinet minister between 1802 and 1813; a post which had been filled by Bourrienne until

1802. His three-volume *Mémoires* were published by his grandson in 1890. Méneval followed the King of Rome to Vienna.

FAIN, AGATHON-JEAN-FRANÇOIS (Baron)—Born in Paris in 1778; Died there in 1857. He succeeded Méneval as private secretary in 1813, a post in which he had deputized for Méneval since 1806. His historical work, *Manuscript of 1812, 1813 and 1814* may be recommended for vividness and truthfulness.

ARNAULT—See previous note, page 275.

THE EMPEROR'S HEART—When the autopsy was performed, the heart of Napoleon was inclosed in a silver vessel in accordance with his wishes, but Sir Hudson Lowe refused to allow this relic to be removed from the place of burial.

REGNAULT DE ST.-JEAN-D'ANGELY, ÉTIENNE—President of the Council of State, Division for the Interior. Sent into exile by the Bourbons from 1815 to 1819. He died in 1820.

DARU, PIERRE (Count)—His cousin Stendhal wrote of Daru that "the Emperor had had the pleasure of meeting him." Fain called him "the cleverest of our military administrators." In the words of Maret, he possessed "two kinds of merit rarely met together. He was a distinguished man of letters and the most untiring worker of modern bureaucracy." In addition to these professional capabilities, he also possessed courage: see Bausset, *Mémoires*, Vol. II, p. 138.

HAUTERIVE (d')—This former father of the Order of the Oratorians was a Councillor of State and a very experienced diplomat, who brought to his duties "a kind of spiritual innocence, which constantly enabled him to see the good side of things": Pasquier, *Mémoires*, Vol. I, p. 348. A friend of Fouché, he was at the same time Talleyrand's right-hand man, as a principal in the French Foreign Office.

BOURRIENNE, FAUVELET DE—An old comrade of Bonaparte, he was secretary to the First Consul until 1802. Then as French chargé d'affaires at Hamburg, this corrupt individual indulged in some shady business which ended by bringing down upon him the anger of the Emperor. His *Mémoires*, edited by Villemarest, are as unreliable as they are interesting. See in *Mémoires of Queen Hortense*, Vol. I, p. 105, the Queen's personal comments on this subject.

April 29

THE QUESTIONING OF PIERRON—The existence of this interrogation *in extremis* is attested to by Ali, in his *Souvenirs*, p. 275. Marchand, however, passes over this scene, where the piercing multiplicity of the questions asked is so suggestive of the way in which the Emperor's mind worked.

DEAFNESS—Bertrand's extreme attention to detail in his diary serves him and serves us as well, by preserving this small detail that no one else at Longwood has noted.

"The little piece of china." In their mémoires, several of Napoleon's contemporaries have mentioned the bladder difficulty which Napoleon experienced at various periods in his life. He would lean his forehead against a tree or wall, and standing there would wait patiently.

"SO GREAT A CHANGE"—Devoid of declamation, moving by its very soberness, this passage avenges all the blown-up speeches in Plutarchian style that the arch-impostor Antommarchi credited to the dying Emperor.

NOTES TO CHAPTER FIVE—MAY 1821

May 1

MME. BERTRAND'S VISIT TO THE EMPEROR—Less laconic than the Grand Maréchal, Marchand, in his *Souvenirs inédits* noted: "On the first of May, at eleven o'clock, Countess Bertrand was shown to the Emperor's bedside. After telling her to sit down and after having asked her how she was, the Emperor said: 'Well, Madame, you too have been ill. But now you are better. Your illness is known whereas mine is not, and therefore I am dying. How are your children? You should have brought Hortense to see me . . . etc.' The Countess then took her leave so as to avoid tiring the Emperor. It was then that she gave way to her feelings. . . . I went with her as far as the garden and there, sobbing, she said to me: 'What a change has taken place in the Emperor since last I saw him! The sharpness of his features and that long beard struck me most poignantly.' "

THE LAST SACRAMENTS—On the subject of the Emperor's communion, Montholon has weakly avoided the issue. Ali and Marchand agree in what they say about the intervention of Abbé Vignali, called to the bedside of the Emperor. But Marchand adds the further detail that the Abbé, "dressed in civilian clothes, held under his coat something which he strove to hide and at which I made no attempt to guess, feeling sure that he had just carried out some religious rite." It is possible that the last part of the sentence, in Bertrand's version, was an outline of the official picture which it was considered decent to leave to posterity. According to the testimony of Marchand, Vignali said that the condition of the Emperor's stomach did not allow him to administer communion. What do the orthodox think of such a defeat as this?

May 3

THE ENEMA—This is a scene whose realism would seem to have been inspired by the verve of Molière, and enhanced by Shakespeare. A half-amusing, half-macabre engraving bit with acid.

May 6

THE AUTOPSY: MARRYAT—Captain Frederick Marryat (1791–1848), Captain of the *Beaver* and one of the three naval officers who examined the body of the Emperor. At the request of Hudson Lowe, on May 6, 1821, he made a sketch of Napoleon on his deathbed, as well as a water-color of the funeral procession. This has been reproduced in F. Masson's *St. Helena*, ill. ed. in-4, Vol. II, p. 229.

MITCHELL, CHARLES—Born 1783; died 1856. During 1820–21 he was doctor on board the *Vigo*, the flagship of the naval station at St. Helena. He was called in for a consultation on the Emperor, May 3, 1821, but was not admitted to see the patient.

BURTON, FRANCIS—Born 1784; died 1828. He was the doctor of the 66th Regiment, which reached St. Helena on March 31, 1821. An important letter from him is to be found among the *Lowe Papers*, Vol. XX, p. 214, in which he reveals that Antommarchi refused to sign the official report on the autopsy.

RUTLEDGE, GEORGE HENRY—Born 1789; died 1833. He was an assistant doctor attached to the 20th of the Line. He had come to St. Helena in 1819. Sir Thomas Reade ordered him to mount guard over the corpse until it had been placed in the coffin. He has left a critical account of the story of Antommarchi and a report of the autopsy.

HENRY, WALTER—Born 1791; died 1860. He was assistant doctor to the 55th Regiment. He arrived at St. Helena on July 5, 1817. He has given his impressions of St. Helena in the second volume of a book of memoirs entitled *Events of My Military Life*.

HARRISON, CHARLES (Captain-Major)—He reached the island in October 1815 as a captain in the 53rd Regiment. He transferred to the 20th of the Line after the departure of the 53rd from St. Helena on March 29, 1821. He was one of the two British officers to remain at their post throughout the entire period of Napoleon's captivity.

THE MAKING OF THE DEATH MASK—See Appendix II of this book for the letters in which Dr. Francis Burton lays before M. and Mme. Bertrand his claim to having been the author of the death mask.

Nothing is better suited to fill in the gaps in Bertrand's scanty story —written as it is in the style of an inventory—than the florid prose of Chateaubriand, author of *Memoirs beyond the Tomb:* "Booted and spurred, dressed in the uniform of a colonel of the Guards, with the Cross of the Legion of Honor on his breast, Napoleon was laid on his iron bedstead. On this face which in life had never shown surprise, the soul, in retiring, had left a sublime stupefaction. Carpenters and cabinetmakers sealed and nailed Bonaparte into a quadruple coffin of mahogany, lead, again mahogany, and finally tin. It was as though they feared that he could never be sufficiently imprisoned. The cloak that the former victor had worn at the immense funerals of Marengo hung like a pall over the coffin."

May 11

THE LYSTER AFFAIR—The matter here concerns the challenge to a duel between Bertrand and Thomas Lyster, then Coastal Inspector of St. Helena, who had become, on July 16, 1818, the English orderly officer attached to Napoleon, replacing Captain Blakeney who had resigned. Napoleon had taken offence at this change, the more so as he suspected Lyster of having formerly belonged to the Corsican Rangers, which had been under the command of Hudson Lowe in Sicily. As the result of a letter of reproach, Lyster had tried to provoke the Grand Maréchal to a duel.

May 12

"They say that the body of the Emperor will not remain there for long." It stayed on St. Helena only nineteen years and five months, in the peace of the green Valley of the Geranium, where, like a vignette of the romantic period, weeping willows spread their leafy foliage, and the spring silently sheds its tears.

APPENDIX I: NOTE ON THE TRANSCRIPTION OF BERTRAND'S DIARY

The Grand Maréchal, who invariably refers to himself in the third person, has employed the same method when reporting the conversations, observations, or remarks of the Emperor at St. Helena. He uses what may be described as a round-about form of the indirect style. It is the method of Tacitus; in preference to that of Titus-Livius, who reported his heroes' speeches as they were supposed to have been spoken.

However, there is nothing more difficult to handle successfully than the indirect style. Sentences quickly become involved in relative clauses which, in the long run, may give rise to regrettable ambiguities, to the point of rendering the discourse unintelligible. On the other hand, everything becomes clear if, without modifying in any way the meaning of the author, the text· is transposed into the direct style, like the following example taken from Méneval (Mémoires, Vol. III, p. 521), who wrote:

"The most remarkable thing the Emperor said to me was that upon his return from Elba, it was not Louis XVIII whom he had dethroned, but the Duke of Orleans; that he had been annoyed by it, because this was the only Frenchman of his family . . . etc."

In place of this one should read: "Upon returning from the Island of Elba, it was not Louis XVIII whom I dethroned, but the Duke of Orleans. I was much annoyed by it, because this was the only Frenchman of his family . . . etc." It is very legitimate to substitute the I for the third person singular from the moment the identity of the person speaking is quite obvious and beyond any possible doubt.

Add to this the fact that Bertrand intruded himself as rarely as possible—and then only once or twice in the course of a conversation. He never mingled his *I* with the Imperial words he was taking down. Through a slip of the pen, he occasionally substituted, in the course of a long phrase, the *I* of the Emperor for the *he* with which he had begun the sentence. We crave indulgence of the shades of the Grand Maréchal for having, in the interests of clearness and readability, smoothed out these slight incongruities and adopted a uniform mode of transcription.

The Grand Maréchal, that faithful old veteran for whom there was only one Emperor in the world, used and abused this title without taking into account the absurdity of certain anachronisms which resulted; for example, when speaking of the childhood of his hero, or the 18th Brumaire, or the Italian Campaigns. It therefore seemed permissible, without committing lèse-imperialism, to prefer the name Bonaparte or Napoleon to the title of Emperor in such cases.

APPENDIX II: THE EMPEROR'S DEATH MASK

THREE LETTERS FROM DR. FRANCIS BURTON
AND A REPLY FROM THE GRAND MARÉCHAL

The originals of the letters by Dr. Burton were written in English. Since they were not available, the publishers give here a translation of Fleuriot de Langle's French versions.

In a little book which appeared in 1909 (*At St. Helena*, Series I), F. Masson published, under "The Case of Dr. Antommarchi," the documents of the lawsuit from which it had transpired that Antommarchi was not responsible for the death mask of the emperor, but instead the English surgeon Francis Burton. Masson quotes, among other things, the booklet written by Dr. Gravel, a cousin of Dr. Burton's, who had pleaded the falsity of the claims advanced by Dr. Antommarchi. Masson agrees with Dr. Gravel that it was definitely the surgeon of the 66th Regiment of St. Helena, and not the pseudo-doctor Antommarchi, to whom "France and Europe are indebted for the invaluable mask" which has preserved for us the image of Napoleon I.

In support of Masson's thesis and to reinforce his arguments, we reproduce here copies of three letters found among Bertrand's personal papers and addressed by Dr. Burton to Count and Countess Bertrand. All three of these letters expressly claim for Burton the authorship of the mask and aim at preventing any discussion on this subject.

TO MADAME LA COMTESSE BERTRAND

> *Jamestown, St. Helena*
> *May 22, 1821*

Madame,
As definite arrangements had been made for the embarkation of the 66th Regiment and as this prevented me from having the honor of

your company on the same ship to Europe, I am very distressed about the buste[1] of Napoleon, which I succeeded in making with a great deal of trouble.

You will excuse, I hope, Madame, the liberty that I am taking in writing you a letter upon this subject, springing as it does from a wish to be as little trouble as possible in a moment when you are so busy; yet desiring to put before you a statement of the facts in a clearer way than I have reason to believe that anyone else has done so far.

My first intention had been to take a copy from the original, so that I would have been in a position to leave it with you; but in view of the very poor quality of the plaster of Paris, Dr. Antommarchi and I agreed that it would be very risky to try this before coming to England; but as you yourself and others informed me that your landing in England had not been assured, I wish to have the mask in my possession; at the same time, I solemnly promise on my honor that you will receive one of the best (copies) that can be executed in London, where it will remain or will be sent to you, in any part of the world that you indicate.

Everyone agrees, Madame, that this is all that can be expected of me, seeing that it would have been impossible to make the mask without my help. It is said that M. Antommarchi intends taking it to Italy. With reference to any claim that he may have in this matter, you, Madame, Count Montholon, Dr. Rutledge, M. Payne, the portrait painter, and several others who were in the room, know that he himself refused to attempt the job. As he said that he was unable to succeed in doing it. Feeling that I could succeed in doing it, he lent me his assistance. Nevertheless, with the greatest pleasure I shall let him have a mask (a copy), but I positively protest against his having the original.

He will certainly agree with me that it would be a great injustice if he had the honor and the ownership of my work (. . .). I also beg to inform you that I am in possession of the back of the head, without which the mask would be imperfect in that part which marks so strongly the character of a great man.

In examining this situation of things, I think, Madame, that you will not refuse to send me the mask; and allow me to repeat in most solemn fashion the promise that I made you above; that you—you and Dr. Antommarchi—shall have the best masks that can be made in London.

I have the honor, etc.

Francis Burton, M.D. Surgeon 66th Regiment
(P.C.C. Cte Bertrand.)

[1]Throughout the letter, Burton uses the word buste in the sense of mask.

The four pages of this formal claim having remained unanswered, Francis Burton repeated it again in the following note.

Dr. Burton not having been favored with a reply to his letter of May 22 beseeches one through the medium of the bearer of this note; the imminence of embarkation allows only a very short interval for settling the object of his claim.

Jamestown. Wednesday (May 23)

The next day Dr. Burton sent a third letter renewing his claim, but this time he addressed it to Count Bertrand.

St. Helena. Jamestown, May 24, 1821

Monsieur, I have twice had the honor of forwarding to Countess Bertrand a letter concerning the mask of Napoleon sequestered by some one of Longwood, and as she has not deigned to reply to any of my letters, which distresses me greatly, I am taking the liberty of turning to you, the legal representative of your wife, and of asking you to refer to my letter of the twenty-second addressed to the countess, the letter where I claimed, as my personal property, a mask for which I, and I alone, furnished the materials, and which I modeled myself with your consent. At the same time, allow me to reiterate my formal pledge to give you, as soon as I have arrived in London, one of the best copies that can be made from it, nay even, if you so wish, the original itself, from which I shall have first taken a copy for myself. I am not able, I think, to make you a fairer proposition.

If however my request is not done justice, I see myself constrained to notify you in plain language that in case the mask should not be delivered to me this very day, I shall have immediate recourse to all legal means in use in this island, which will permit putting the object under seals, until our difference is settled. If the island does not afford me these means, the same ship that carries you to England will also carry my claim to the English authorities, as well as to the customs agents, with the complete account of our difference—and those not only in England, but in France, where I do not doubt that the case will be thoroughly examined and the grounds duly investigated.

With all regrets for having expressed myself so categorically, I have the honor, etc.

Francis Burton to maréchal comte Bertrand—Longwood

For reasons that remain unknown the Grand Maréchal preferred not to answer this letter himself. Or at least he collaborated with General Montholon, who wrote the following reply, possibly in his capacity as chief testamentary executor.

Sir,

In accordance with the wishes of the Emperor Napoleon, General Montholon and I requested Monsieur Antommarchi, his surgeon in ordinary, to make[2] a plaster cast of the Emperor's head for his family. A request for the necessary materials was addressed to the Governor.[3]

Never, Sir, did you set forth to me any claim to this mask being your property. Nor did you obtain my consent in this matter. I had not the honor then to know you either personally or by name, although I now assume you to have been one of the health officers who were present at the post mortem examination of the Emperor's body.

You assisted Monsieur Antommarchi, and I witnessed with gratitude the trouble which you took. The copy of the mask which you claim as your property should the original be refused to you, it had been our intention to request the family of the Emperor to present to you. But had I given you the permission—which I did not do—to make a plaster cast of the Emperor's head, had I especially authorized you to retain the original or even a copy, you could still claim legally only the rights accorded to any artist who makes a portrait head or bust, and who is under the obligation of surrendering it to the person who has commissioned it. And in England, I imagine, it is the same as in other European countries, where an artist who tries to retain a copy of a portrait or bust without the consent of the person who commissioned it would be subject to legal action.

I cannot therefore, Sir, admit that you have any kind of right to the ownership of the original cast, nor even to that of one of the copies. But I shall always be ready to testify to the readiness with which you assisted Monsieur Antommarchi in the operation which had been intrusted to him, and I have no doubts but what the Emperor's family will show its gratitude by presenting you with one of the finest[4] examples of the Emperor's death mask.

[2]To have made has been crossed out here.

[3]Through the legal channels. It should not be forgotten that these materials were found to be unsuitable for the making of the mask.

[4]Here first has been struck out; also in accordance with your wish.

After this dismissal of Burton's case in which, truth to tell, the Grand Maréchal would seem to have systematically reversed the positions, the very complex affair of the mask was to find its epilogue in London—an epilogue entirely contrary to the hopes of Dr. Burton.

Immediately upon arriving in London, the Grand Maréchal hastened to place the relic—matrix or plaster cast—in a safe place, as is shown by the following note attached to a packing case that he deposited with Monsieur X (the name is left blank).

This packing case contains a plaster cast of the head of the Emperor Napoleon, made from a mask executed at Longwood by Dr. Antommarchi. Count Bertrand has placed this cast in the care of X——, so that in the event of the original being lost or damaged on the way from London to Rome, copies can be made from it. The plaster cast in the packing case may not be disposed of except upon an order from Count Bertrand and in agreement with intentions that Madame, mother of the Emperor, will transmit to him. London, September 1, 1821.

(signed) *Count Bertrand*

At the same time the Grand Maréchal deposited in this packing case piles of documents—among them possibly the manuscript of his diary—specifying that no one was to dispose of them without express orders from him.

After the death of the Grand Maréchal, the copy of the mask referred to here passed into the care of his daughter Madame Thayer, who left it in her will to Prince Victor Napoleon; the Marquis de Gontaut-Biron being intrusted with delivering the bequest.

Even after the refutations contained in the Grand Maréchal's reply, the claims of Dr. Burton remain very strong, especially when it is remembered that he had in his possession the back of the matrix. Does this remarkable piece of evidence still exist somewhere in England? And if so, where is the seeker or enthusiast who will put us in the way of recovering it? Important as it is to the phrenologists, this discovery is indispensable to the final settlement of a dispute that has hung fire since 1821.